BARRON'S

MACRO-ECONOMICS

THE
EASY
WAY

George E. Kroon, Ph.D. (Economics)
Professor of Marketing
Fordham University

BARRON'S

About the Author: George E. Kroon, Ph.D. in economics (from UCLA), has taught economics and marketing courses at Fordham University, New York University, Fashion Institute of Technology, Rutgers, and Pace University. He also has served as an economics and marketing consultant to major corporations.

All inquiries should be addressed to:
Barron's Educational Series, Inc.
250 Wireless Boulevard
Hauppauge, New York 11788
www.barronseduc.com

ISBN-13: 978-0-7641-3237-7
ISBN-10: 0-7641-3237-7

Library of Congress Catalog Card No.: 2006022987

Library of Congress Cataloging-in-Publication Data
George E. Kroon Ph.D.
    Macroeconomics the easy way / George E. Kroon.
        p. cm.
    Includes index.
    ISBN-13: 978-0-7641-3237-7
    ISBN-10: 0-7641-3237-7
    1. Macroeconomics 2. Microeconomics—Problems,
exercises, etc. I. Title.

HB172.5K76 2007
339—dc22   2006022987

PRINTED IN THE UNITED STATES OF AMERICA
9 8 7 6 5 4 3 2 1

CONTENTS

About This Book

This book is meant primarily for students who seek an easy-to-understand introduction to the field of macroeconomics. To that end, it defines and explains all of the fundamental terms and concepts that one must master in order to gain a firm grasp of macroeconomics. Mathematical equations and diagrams are necessarily a part of any economics textbook; however, in the interest of ensuring that the concepts in this book are accessible to students with no prior background in economics, these have been kept to a minimum.

In my experience, repetition helps learning; therefore, this book intentionally provides multiple reviews of the same concepts. It is also my experience that students learn in different ways. Some students prefer textual descriptions, while others prefer visual learning. To appeal to different modes of learning, this book presents macroeconomic principles in four ways. There are:

1. traditional supply and demand diagrams (because they summarize the simplified models economists use and are a major part of the economist's toolbox);

2. conceptual flow diagrams at the beginning of each chapter to demonstrate how the concepts in that chapter fit together;

3. repeated summaries of key points as the text moves along; and

4. shorthand descriptions to map a complex series of changes in the economy. This shorthand goes as follows: demand → supply → equilibrium → disturbance → new equilibrium → who gains/who loses → political/policy implications. (Most economics professors use the same type of shorthand in their classes.)

Most chapters in this book are followed by review questions, which are meant to reinforce the concepts discussed in these chapters. You should attempt the questions and look over the accompanying answer explanations after you read a chapter in order solidify important concepts in your mind.

Economics is never light reading; however, by being accessible to students with no background in the discipline, this book will hopefully allow you to understand the complexity of the macroeconomic concepts that influence the national economy on a daily basis.

George E. Kroon, Ph.D.

PART ONE

INTRODUCTION TO ECONOMICS

CHAPTER 1

THE ECONOMICS FRAMEWORK

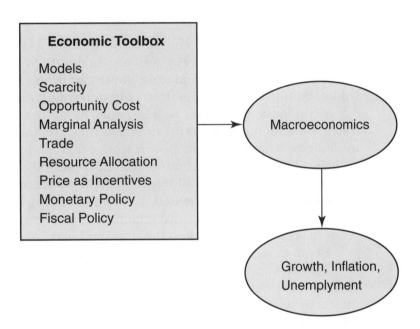

Economic Toolbox

Models
Scarcity
Opportunity Cost
Marginal Analysis
Trade
Resource Allocation
Price as Incentives
Monetary Policy
Fiscal Policy

Macroeconomics

Growth, Inflation, Unemplyment

This first chapter begins with an examination of the economist's toolbox, the main analytical tools and concepts that economists use. We then point to the main concerns of macroeconomics—growth, inflation, and employment. The two policy tools of monetary and fiscal policy help the economy stabilize and grow.

Economists look at the world differently. They have a different vantage point and use a different set of tools to understand and predict economic behavior. As a social science, economics is interested in explaining how individuals, companies, and nations respond to economic changes. **Economics is a social science** because it is concerned with human and institutional behavior. The focus is on how our behavior changes as events change around us. Economics uses analytical structures common to many sciences; it suggests theories and constructs models to explain relationships. If the facts don't support the theories, they are discarded or revised.

To view the world as economists do, you have to get into their shoes and mindset. You will also need to become familiar with the most common tools and concepts they use. This initial chapter will give you an overview that will help you do just that.

The goal of economic analysis is to be able to understand the very complex world of prices, regulations, taxes, exchange rates, inflation, unemployment, and growth. Not only do economists need to understand these economic relationships, but they must also be able to predict the effects that changes will have on the behavior of individuals, firms and countries. In this sense economics is a behavioral science.

THE ECONOMIST'S TOOLBOX

The **economist's toolbox** is a set of concepts and ways of looking at the world. It includes the way that economists frame or approach their analysis. The toolbox comes with its special jargon. Without understanding this jargon, you can neither fully understand the basics of economics nor make sense of the business section of the daily newspaper.

Economists limit the complexities involved to understand the basic workings of the economy. We set up and use models to predict behavior. The process isolates the most obvious and most important things much as a physician initially looks at four or five key indicators to determine your health.

Economists use a positive framework to approach their analysis. A **positive statement** attempts to describe events as they are and how they are related and to describe what exists and how it works. This framework leads to statements such as "If the government raises taxes, people will consume less" and "If event X happens, then event Y will result." The importance of a positive framework is that it can be tested and verified. It is like a working hypothesis.

More important, a positive statement is one that can be proven false. If it is, economists have to go back to the drawing board.

Economists are not the only ones who continually have to revise their theories. Theories and models continually change in both the physical and social sciences. For the entire twentieth century physicians believed that peptic ulcers were caused by stress and nerves until it was discovered that they are caused by bacteria. This finding earned two Australian doctors the Nobel Prize in medicine.

The economic analyses presented in this book are almost universally agreed on by economists. They are fundamental concepts, and they do not change very often. After you have mastered the fundamentals, we will present the major disagreements among economists in later chapters because economists certainly disagree. These disagreements and arguments among economists are usually about the strength of a particular effect, not about its direction. Economists do not disagree that consumers consume less when taxes go up. How much consumers reduce their consumption is a much more complex issue and gives wide room for debate.

Economists guard against using a normative statement such as "Lowering taxes is the best way to stimulate consumption." Normative statements cannot be proven correct or incorrect. A **normative statement** involves a judgment of good or bad and is concerned with how the world should be, not how the world is. Economics has been called the "dismal science" because of statements like "If there is less food than needed, people will die until there is just the right amount of food to feed the population." To some this is a cold and impersonal approach, but to most economists it is an attempt to explain what will happen, not whether what happens is good or bad.

Economists use a special toolbox complete with its own jargon and unique set of concepts. This chapter introduces you to some major tools and concepts in this toolbox. The final section covers the major issues and concerns that comprise macroeconomics. Later chapters will give you practice in using the tools and analyzing the consequences. We will then discuss the importance and use of models in economics.

As you become familiar with this toolbox and how it is used, you will begin to think like an economist.

SCARCITY

Everyone operates under scarcity. **Scarcity** means that there are not enough goods, services, time, or money compared to what individuals want. There is not enough to go around. Individuals want more time, and more spending power, companies want larger budgets, and nations want to grow faster, defend themselves, and take better care of their citizens—all at the same time.

Because everyone operates under scarcity, economists pay special attention to the trade-offs people make. Examples of some trade-offs that we may have to make are "Which child of three goes to college" and "If I take a second job, I will have to give up that time with my family." On a national level, if we produce more weapons for national defense, we will have fewer resources for improving health care. Note we are already using an "If X then Y" framework.

In other words, scarcity means that we make decisions under some limits or constraints. For example, there are only 24 hours in a day. These constraints can take various forms: a family budget, a limited amount of time, or a limited amount of a natural resource such as oil.

Trade-offs are a fundamental part of the framework that economists use to understand the economy. Often this kind of thinking bothers beginning students. Economists point out that reducing the price of gasoline will increase pollution because it will encourage the use of gasoline, so the trade-off is cheaper vacations by car for more pollution. But we are getting ahead of ourselves.

Scarcity also means that individuals are forced to trade between spending time at home or at work because they are limited to 24 hours a day. Countries also must choose how to use their limited resources; spending more resources on war leaves fewer funds available for education. Economics provides an analytical framework that can evaluate the costs and benefits of these trade-offs.

Scarcity does not depend on how many resources you have. Developing economies and rich, industrialized economies all have scarcity problems. They all have to determine how to allocate resources and what trade-offs they will make.

RESOURCE ALLOCATION

How much of our national resources are devoted to education, to health care, to building highways, and to government services? The answer to this question represents a particular resource allocation—how the available resources are divided among different uses. On a company level, how much of a company's budget is spent on research and development? How much of an individual's time is spent learning new skills or networking?

How a country's resources are allocated is a central issue in macroeconomics in two important ways. The first is how the available resources are currently divided. If more of a country's resources are devoted to producing oil, less will be available for education. We look at how the pie is divided in the current period. If we as a nation want to work more hours, we will have to give up some leisure hours.

Macroeconomics is also vitally concerned about the allocation of resources over time. Investing in some areas of the economy will lead to more future growth, resulting in a larger pie for our children. Some current allocations of resources can slow down the future growth of the economy. During wars many countries take resources from infrastructure maintenance (roads, highways, and public works) to fund the war effort. These are not easy choices, and the allocation decisions are politically charged because they affect so many. The choices we make today in terms of what to produce also affect how much we can produce in the future.

These two resource allocation aspects are summarized as follows.

The **current consumption trade-off** is between producing more of one good and less of another. Scarcity means that a country has to choose between the production of military goods and the production of civilian goods. The resulting choice represents a current allocation of resources.

The **future growth trade-off** is between current consumption and investment for the future. If we chose to consume more today and invest less, that will mean a slower growth path for the economy. Scarcity means that countries have to decide between allocating resources to current consumption and investment. The more goods and resources devoted to current consumption, the more limited future growth will be.

Individuals face the same problem in their decisions to save or consume their monthly incomes. The scarcity comes in the fact that the current month's income is limited. Saving more today will help future consumption. Consuming more now and saving less will mean less is available in the future to help out in retirement.

OPPORTUNITY COST

Related to scarcity is the notion that in order to do one thing you have to give up something else. Individuals have to give up time with their family and probably some sleep time to take on a second job. To stay within their budgets, companies have to give up something if they want to buy a new computer system. Nations face similar constraints: they cannot produce more health care without cutting back on some other item. The cost or value of what they give up in exchange is a core principle of economics. The **opportunity cost** of something is the value of what you give up to get it.

Opportunity cost, in different words, is the highest valued opportunity foregone. Economists spend a lot of time figuring out what something costs. What does it cost you to go to lunch? The opportunity cost of going to lunch is the highest valued use of your time for that lunch. A chief executive officer (CEO) pays much more for a $20 lunch than a young teenager who buys the same lunch, because they each give up an hour's salary. They forego or give up an hour's wage to spend time eating lunch.

The explicit or monetary cost is the lunch bill. To predict behavior accurately, you have to consider opportunity cost as well. Lowering the money cost of lunch will attract more lower-wage customers because they have a lower opportunity cost. If you make $400 an hour as an attorney, reducing the cost of lunch from $20 to $14 will not be as strong an incentive for you to eat more of these lunches as it will be for a secretary who earns $8 an hour.

I owned an older Mercedes and was shopping around for a good price to restore it. I went into a repair shop that clearly understood opportunity cost. I asked the owner how much it would cost to restore my 1961 Mercedes. The owner thought about it and quickly said $6,000. I asked him how he had arrived at that number so quickly and he told me. I was expecting a list of labor, parts, and so on, but he didn't give me one. He said, "It will take me about 3 months to do it, and in that time I can earn $100 a day repairing banged-up taxi doors in the space it would take up. That's how I got $6,000." His quick calculation, a clear example of opportunity cost, was 20 days open each month times $100 a day = $2,000 a month times 3 months = $6,000.

Companies also use opportunity cost, though they don't necessarily call it that. In the late 1970s the Internal Revenue Service (IRS) had a fixed penalty rate of about 7 percent for late payment of corporate quarterly income taxes. When inflation was rampant in the early 1980s, the prime interest rate rose above 18 percent. Many corporations delayed paying their quarterly income tax, essentially taking a loan from the IRS at 7 percent instead of a loan at a rate of 18 percent or higher if the company couldn't qualify for a prime rate loan. The IRS subsequently stopped using a fixed-rate penalty.

Cities also tax some property on the basis of opportunity cost. Vacant lots in many cities used to be taxed at very low rates because the land was unused. A major change in the approach to taxing urban land came about when cities decided to tax based on "the highest valued use" of the property, using the opportunity cost of the land to increase tax revenues and to discourage people from holding land vacant.

STOCKS AND FLOWS

An important economic distinction is the one between stocks and flows. Many pieces of the macroeconomic puzzle are flows: income, consumption, investment. They are flows because they represent an amount per week or year or some other time period. If you earn $100 a week and spend $90 a week, that leaves $10 per week for other things. All of these are flows because they are measured per time period.

If you are ill 3 days and earn only $70 that week, you can maintain your $90 weekly consumption if you take $20 out of your savings. Your savings is a stock; that is, it is not dependent on time. If you have $200 saved and now draw down that savings by $20, your savings will be $180, and it will remain at that level until you add to it or subtract from it. It is a stock. Think of it as what some people keep in the cookie jar.

Savings (a stock) represent an amount that can be used for emergencies. Saving rates (a flow) contribute funds to the savings of individuals. An automated saving plan deducts some of your income and puts it into your savings. This is not nitpicking—savings are a stock and saving is a flow.

For the first time in many years, the U.S. national saving rate was negative in 2005. This means that as a nation we spent more than we earned, increasing our level of personal debt as a nation. On the other hand, countries like Switzerland and Japan have long traditions of high national saving rates.

Saving per year is an important indicator of how much of today's resources are being set aside for tomorrow. A low saving rate corresponds to a high consumption rate (out of fixed current income). All these measurements are flows. We will see later on that running a government budget deficit (a flow) increases the national debt (a stock).

ECONOMIC INCENTIVES CHANGE BEHAVIOR

Price changes and profitability prospects shift resources from one part of the economy to another, changing the allocation of resources. Individuals will buy fewer cigarettes if cigarette prices rise. Companies will enter new lines of business based on a higher expected profit, and they will leave areas with declining profit prospects. Countries continually shift the mix of items they trade because of profit or price changes. One year a country may be a net exporter of beef (exporting more beef than it imports) and the next year it may be a net importer of beef (importing more beef than it exports). It is exactly this change in behavior in response to price, cost, and profit changes that gets the attention of economists. In this sense prices and profits act as signals to participants, resulting in a new allocation of resources. We will see a practical example in the next chapter.

MARGINAL ANALYSIS IS IMPORTANT

Economists use marginal analysis to explain behavior. Marginal cost is the additional or extra cost of doing something. Marginal actions are incremental actions. For example, if you have to go to another part of the city, should you take a cab or walk? Economists frame this discussion by asking, "Is the extra cost of going by taxi worth the additional benefit?" or "Is the additional cost of a slice of apple pie worth the additional benefit after a full meal?"

For a producer, the marginal cost of adding a feature to a cell phone is how much the total cost of the cell phone is increased. If the feature contributes more additional revenue than it costs, the producer will add that feature.

If you are working late on a presentation, the marginal question is, "Is an additional hour of preparation (marginal benefit) worth the sacrifice of an additional hour of sleep (marginal cost)?"

In all these cases it is the additional or marginal benefit compared to the marginal cost of the action that provides a sound basis for the decision. We do not need to know the total cost or the total benefit to be able to make sound decisions.

A COUNTRY'S STANDARD OF LIVING DEPENDS ON ITS ABILITY TO PRODUCE GOODS AND SERVICES

All the goods and services produced by a nation represent its total output per year. The common measure of national well-being is total output per capita—the nation's output divided by the nation's population. The more goods and services available per capita, the higher the standard of living. Sometimes we use the real market value of these goods and services on a per-capita basis [gross domestic product (GDP) per capita] to measure the standard of living.

As we saw earlier, the more current resources devoted to future production, the higher the future standard of living (with the same population).

ECONOMICS AND POLITICS ARE INTERRELATED

Politics and economics are interrelated, and some controls are inevitable. Changes in economic policy have political results, and most political decisions have economic consequences. A trade-off that any society faces is between efficiency and equity. **Efficiency** means getting the most out of the available resources. **Equity** means that the benefits or costs of these resources are distributed fairly among society's members. Economists are most often concerned with efficiency, and politicians with equity.

The free market system cannot be avoided nor can government actions in the market. If the government fixes the price of an item, the market will adjust around that fixed price. Think of a fixed price as a finger poking a balloon. The balloon reshapes itself around the finger, much as the economy adjusts around the fixed price.

Many free market or laissez faire (literally, "to leave alone") results are neither nice nor acceptable—selling human beings or killing competitors to remove them, to make an obvious point. This may be straightforward economic analysis, but it is lousy politics. There are many examples of excellent politics and bad economics. I hope you have been uncomfortable with this paragraph. Most of it is based on normative judgments, which usually lead to very heated debates.

The market system does not guarantee that everyone has enough food or that people born with disabilities can purchase adequate health care. Many public policies such as welfare, unemployment, and the tax system try to improve the distribution of goods and services. Economic analysis can figure out that policy A delivers more benefits than policy B and leave the decision on which one to pursue up to the politicians.

Changes in economic variables influence politics, and vice versa. Computer jobs migrate overseas because the pool of highly skilled overseas workers is willing to work for lower wages than workers in the United States. U.S. computer workers are harmed, and some are let go. Losing these jobs has prompted a political debate on what to do about it and how to protect American computer industry workers. The most common policy alternatives are either to try to keep the jobs here or to retrain workers for other positions.

Each of these policies has economic implications. If regulations are passed to protect U.S. computer employees' jobs, producers and consumers of computer services will have to pay more. To retrain these workers means that the resources have to come from some other activity such as medical care. Economists are often asked to compare the benefits and costs of these two measures.

When analyzing the effect of policy decisions, we have to look at the indirect effects that work through incentives, as well as the direct effects. For example, Mexico wanted to keep the price of corn tortillas low because it is a staple food. They artificially kept the price of corn low, and corn tortillas prices remained low—the direct effect was achieved. Unfortunately, the prices facing corn farmers were so low that so many of them left corn production that the Mexican government had to import corn. The low price helped the corn tortilla consumer initially, but the incentives for many farmers to continue producing corn disappeared.

Governments often intervene to change the market outcome. A government may intervene to slow down very rapid inflation, to lower the unemployment rate, or to encourage production in the event of a recession. These three concepts are the main pillars of macroeconomics. They will occupy the entire book.

MACROECONOMICS

Macroeconomics is the study of the economy as a whole. It is the study of how all individuals, companies, government, the private sector, and financial markets interact to determine our standard of living, growth, employment, inflation, and many other things.

Microeconomics focuses on individual consumers and firms, the two major decision-making units. Macroeconomics shifts the focus to the larger units of the national and global economies and their interaction.

One of the major national concerns, very visible in the current Chinese economy, is the trade-off between rapid growth and pollution. Restraining industrial development by imposing environmental controls on new plants and factories will slow the pace of economic growth. The United States faces a similar problem with environmental restrictions.

TRADE CAN MAKE EVERYONE BETTER OFF

Trade between two individuals or two countries can make them both better off. Specializing in what you can do best and selling these products or services allows you to buy a greater variety of goods and services than you could produce by yourself.

Watch what happens when students are given a promotional package of items at the beginning of the school year. Included are cosmetics, combs, and other toiletries. As soon as the students get the gift packages, they sit down and exchange with one another. "I'll give you this comb for your toothpaste," and so on. After all of the trading is done, each person has, in their view, a better combination than what they were initially given.

The same holds true for someone who specializes in financial accounting and spends the money received from that job on fresh bread and groceries. An accountant can buy consume other goods and services by specializing in accounting and using the money received to purchase other consumable goods.

The major macroeconomic concerns are

1. how to increase growth

2. how to reduce inflation

3. how to reduce unemployment

4. how to increase investment

5. why some countries grow faster than others.

ECONOMIC MODELS

Economists set up simple models to understand behavior and to predict what will happen when something changes. The overall approach is a scientific one needed to bring some order to a very complicated process. The economic world is as complex as the human body, so in order to predict the effects of medicine, both sciences rely on simplified models to predict results.

We know from the beginning that the model cannot include everything. The goal is to set up simple models that can be proven correct with existing data and discarded or changed if proven to be incomplete or inadequate.

BASIC ANALYTICAL PROCESS FOLLOWED IN THIS BOOK

The process we will follow is to master the basic concepts, incorporate them into economic models, change the basics and examine the changes they produce, and finally examine the impacts on the system. From this kind of process we can easily predict that an increase in the tax on gasoline will result in a higher price for gasoline, and less gasoline consumed, and among the impacts, an increased incentive over time for car manufacturers to produce engines with more miles per gallon.

TABLE 1.1 BASIC PROCESS

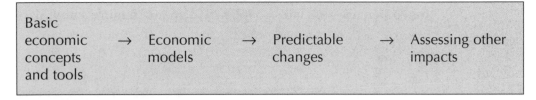

| Basic economic concepts and tools | → | Economic models | → | Predictable changes | → | Assessing other impacts |

When you can easily use the macroeconomic tools presented here, you will be able to work this chain of reasoning forward and backward. An example of working the process backward is if a certain impact is desired, such as decreasing unemployment, what changes are necessary to deliver the desired results.

If X then Y is a framework based on simple models of how the world works. We want to know what will be the consequences of our actions. If I get a masters in business administration (MBA), what additional salary can I expect? Firms want to know what productivity increases they can expect if they invest $1 million in a new computer system. Frequent use of this type of analysis will quickly get the reader to a comfortable level in this very basic economist's way of looking at the world.

Table 1.2 illustrates "If X then Y" in brief. You should read the last row of the table this way: *A decrease in taxes will influence aggregate demand so that consumption, gross national product (GNP), and inflation increase. The decrease in taxes will lower unemployment and lead to an increase in wages.*

TABLE 1.2 IF X THEN Y

Change introduced	→	Economic models	→	New outcome or result	→	Other impacts
Decrease in taxes	→	Aggregate demand	→	Consumption, GNP, and inflation increase	→	Lower unemployment, increase in wages

A CHALLENGE

The purpose of this book is to quickly get you to a point where you can use the basic tools of economics to analyze the macroeconomy, national and international economic forces and policies, and how they affect all of us. This will allow you to use the economist's toolbox to examine the world through economists' eyes.

Economics is based on a few fundamental concepts that are applied many times and in different circumstances. Careful understanding of the simplifying assumptions made in the models in the early chapters will serve you well later on when the models are expanded to incorporate factors like the global economy.

If you spend your time carefully studying the early chapters—mastering the fundamentals—the later chapters will go much more smoothly.

REVIEW QUESTIONS

Add the word or words that correctly complete each of the following statements.

1. A _____ statement attempts to describe events as they are and how they are related.

2. _____ statements cannot be proven correct or incorrect.

3. The _____ trade-off is between producing more of one good today at the cost of less of another good.

4. The choice between current consumption and investment for the future is called the _____ growth trade-off.

5. The _____ cost of something is the value of what you give up to get it.

6. An amount per week, or year or some other time period is a _____ concept.

7. If you have $750 in a savings account, this is a _____ concept.

8. If I increase my saving rate to 15 percent of my income, this will add to my _____ of savings.

9. _____ is the study of the economy as a whole.

10. _____ is the study of individual markets like the computer market.

Circle the letter of the item that correctly completes each of the following statements.

1. An example of a positive statement is:
    a. An increase in taxes is a bad thing.
    b. If the costs increase, people will buy less.
    c. You should save at least 10 percent of your income.
    d. The more it costs, the better a bottle of wine.

2. Which of the following is a normative statement?
    a. The best way to save is by buying a savings bond.
    b. When prices rise, people want to buy less.
    c. To save more from the same income, you have to consume less.
    d. Taking on another job will mean less leisure time available.

3. An example of the current consumption trade-off is
   a. producing more corn and less wheat.
   b. producing more wheat and less corn.
   c. saving more now to afford a better car.
   d. giving up some sleep to finish a project on time.

4. The future growth trade-off for a gardener is to
   a. leave part of the garden unplanted this year to get better results next year.
   b. plant more tomatoes and less basil.
   c. plant more flowers and fewer vegetables.
   d. use more fertilizer this year.

5. The opportunity cost of taking a long lunch
   a. is the cost of the lunch.
   b. depends on the weather.
   c. will decrease when my wages increase.
   d. will increase when my wage increases.

6. The opportunity cost of something is
   a. how many dollars it costs.
   b. how many real dollars it costs.
   c. the value of what you have to give up to get it.
   d. how much of your income it costs.

7. The amount of income you earn each month is an example of
   a. a flow.
   b. the opportunity cost of eating a restaurant lunch.
   c. a current consumption trade-off.
   d. a stock.

8. Your dollar savings that you keep hidden in a shoe box represent
   a. a stock because savings are not dependent on time.
   b. a flow because you accumulated them over the last year.
   c. a real savings.
   d. a real asset.

9. The extra cost of having your presentation professionally printed is
   a. an example of a nominal cost.
   b. an example of a marginal cost.
   c. an example of a marginal benefit.
   d. an example of opportunity cost.

10. The major macroeconomic concerns are
    a. unemployment, inflation, and real growth.
    b. unemployment, a fair distribution of income, and real growth.
    c. an equitable distribution of income, real growth, and reducing government spending.
    d. reducing inflation and pollution and stimulating real growth.

ANSWERS TO FILL-IN QUESTIONS

1. positive

2. Normative

3. current consumption

4. future

5. opportunity

6. flow

7. stock

8. stock

9. Macroeconomics

10. Microeconomics

ANSWERS TO MULTIPLE-CHOICE QUESTIONS

1. **b.** This can be proven, and there is no right or wrong judgment involved.

2. **a.** This cannot be proven and is a value judgment.

3. **d.** The trade-off occurs at the present time.

4. **a.** The trade-off is from this year to next year.

5. **d.** Opportunity cost is what you have to give up, in this case the value of the time required for the long lunch.

6. **c.** This is the definition of opportunity cost.

7. **a.** It is the income per month, therefore a flow.

8. **a.** Savings are a stock such as a savings account.

9. **b.** It is an additional cost because your presentation was already completed.

10. **a.** This is the definition. In addition, pollution and income distribution are not major areas.

CHAPTER 2

THE ECONOMIC PROBLEM: SCARCITY AND CHOICE

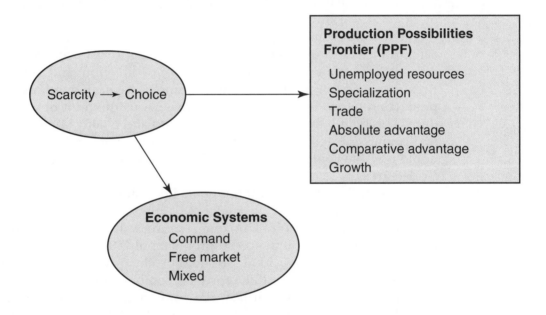

This second chapter takes us to our first model, the production possibilities frontier (PPF). From this simple model, we will develop examples and analyses of unemployed resources, specialization, trade, and growth. We will end the chapter with a discussion of different ways that economic systems are organized.

There is never enough time to spend with friends and not enough money to buy all the things we want. Economists refer to this as the problem of scarcity. Scarcity is based on what we would like to have compared with what we actually have or can afford.

This is also true for countries. As a nation, we would like to be able to provide health insurance for all, free education, a strong national defense, and lower or no taxes—all at the same time. We laugh at this absurdity because we know that we cannot afford to do everything we want as individuals or as a country.

SCARCITY

Scarcity means we cannot have everything we want and have to choose among different things.

Economists use several models to help clarify the discussion of scarcity and the choices and priorities we have to make. These models help us understand the core economic concepts of trade and the gains from trade. We will see how the choices we make change with changes in prices, costs, and the available opportunities. We will look at individuals first and then generalize to nations.

How many hours a day we spend sleeping or working is an example of the scarcity problem that individuals face. The more time we sleep, the less time is available for other activities. We are constrained and forced to figure out how we spend the 24 hours we have each day. This constraint is beyond our individual control. The individual's choice is how to allocate that time between sleeping and, say, working. To sleep an hour more means that we have to give up an hour of work or some other activity. We can also spend 24 hours sleeping with no work or 24 hours working with no sleep.

The simplest model showing this choice for a nation is one in which society can produce only two goods, food and oil. In Figure 2.1 each axis represents the amount of output produced—food in one direction and oil in the other. Because we cannot produce an infinite amount of each good, we introduce the **production possibilities frontier**, which shows us the limit of what we can produce. This limit is determined by the amount and quality of our human and natural resources, capital goods, and existing technology and managerial skills. All of the possible combinations of food and oil we can produce are shown as the shaded area.

As we will see throughout this book, lines often represent boundaries in the diagrams we use. The PPF in Figure 2.1 represents the maximum that we can currently produce using all of our resources. If we were to use all of our resources to produce oil, we could produce only 200 million barrels per year. If we chose to produce only food, we could produce 100 million tons of food each year. All the points on the PPF represent combinations of food and oil that are producible or obtainable. In fact, the combinations on the line represent the most that could be produced. Points inside the PPF represent combinations of oil and food production that are all obtainable, whereas points outside the PPF are unobtainable given our current resources.

Suppose that we are at point **A** on the diagram, a point that represents 50 food and 30 oil. We are not fully utilizing all our resources, some are idle because we are below capacity or below the maximum we could produce if we were fully utilizing our resources. From **A** we can increase our output of food by moving vertically up to the line at **B**, where we can produce 80 food and still maintain our production of 30 oil. Notice that we have maintained our production of oil while increasing our production of food.

While we are holding oil production constant, what we cannot do is continue to produce more food beyond **B**. We run into the limit or maximum on the PPF.

At point **D** on the frontier, to produce more than 65 million tons of food a year, we will have to give up some oil. For example, if we want to produce 80 tons of food each year, we would have to give up 40 oil, ending up with the combination at **B**. This 40 oil given up represents the opportunity cost of producing 15 more food.

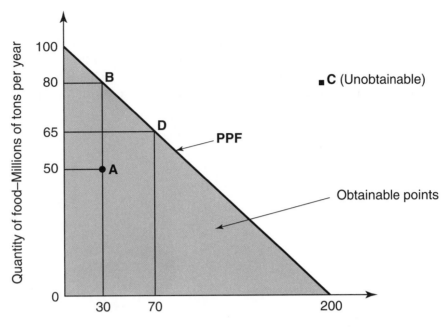

FIGURE 2.1. Production possibilities frontier.

Describes the production choices an economy faces.

In other words, moving upward **on** the PPF as we increase food production, we have to give up 2 million barrels of oil for each additional 1 million tons of food. This is the slope of the PPF, 1 million tons of food for each 2 million barrels of oil, and is the opportunity cost of producing an additional ton of food.

To summarize so far, points such as **A**, inside the PPF are obtainable, and points like **C** outside the PPF are not possible given our current resources. Moving up and down **on** the PPF shows the trade-off or opportunity cost society has to accept to increase the production of one good.

SPECIALIZATION AND THE GAINS FROM TRADE

The PPF illustrates the trade-off an individual person or country can make in producing different goods. Moving along it, one has to give up some of one good to get more of another good, and vice versa. To show the gains from trade we will show how a decision to specialize and trade with each other makes Bill and Mary **both** better off.

If Bill is producing as much water and food as he can, he will be producing on his PPF. He can consume all of the points on the boundary. If he wants to consume more food, he has to move along his PPF and sacrifice some water. We introduce Mary, who also can produce food and water, and if they exchange goods, we will see that Bill can end up consuming a combination that is greater than what he can produce by himself.

Let's see how this works. In Bill's case in Figure 2.2, using all his resources, she can produce 50 food and 50 water. He has the **absolute advantage** in producing water because he can produce more food if he dedicates all his efforts on water. He decides to completely specialize and produce no food and 100 water. He then exchanges 50 water for 60 food that Mary has produced, ending up with 50 water and 60 food, a combination that he could not have produced by himself.

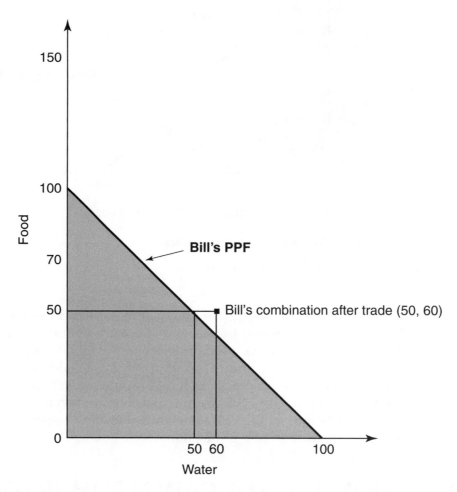

FIGURE 2.2. **Production possibilities for Bill.**

Trading allows Bill to consume a combination outside his production possibilities frontier.

In Figure 2.3 Mary has the absolute advantage in producing food because she can produce more food than Bill can if she dedicates all her efforts toward food. She can produce 150 food while Bill can only produce 100 food. To gain from the trade, Mary produces 90 food and 20 water using all her resources. She then exchanges 60 food for 50 water that Bill has produced, ending up with 30 food and 70 water, a combination that she could not have produced by herself.

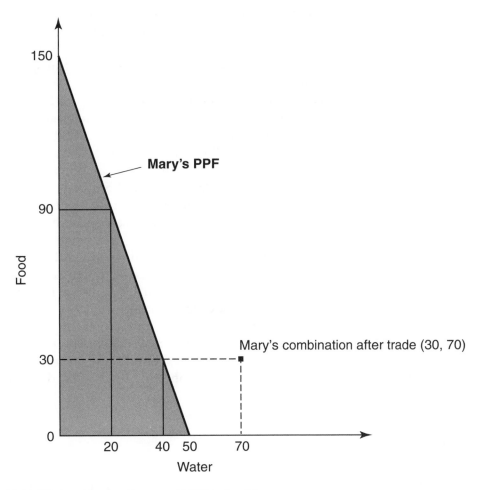

FIGURE 2.3. Production possibilities for Mary.

With trade Mary can consume a combination outside her PPF.

Table 2.1 shows the production and exchange between Bill and Mary.

TABLE 2.1 SPECIALIZATION AND TRADE

	Bill	
	Water	**Food**
Produces	100	0
Trades	−50	**+60**
Ends up with	50	60
	Mary	
	Food	**Water**
Produces	90	20
Trades	**−60**	+50
Ends up with	30	70

The gains from trade for Bill result when he specializes in producing water. By specializing and trading, he ends up with 50 water and 60 food. If he did not trade, Bill could produce only 50 water and 50 food, the point on his PPF. By trading he has gained 10 additional units of food. You can see this in Figure 2.2 as the horizontal line at 50 food.

Mary similarly specializes and trades, ending up with a combination of 30 food and 70 water. If she did not specialize and trade, Mary could produce and consume only 40 units of water, a gain from trade of 30 units of water. This is shown in the horizontal line at 30 food in Figure 2.3.

By trading, Mary and Bill can consume a combination of food and water that is outside their individual PPFs. They will **both** be better off trading. When we extend this concept from two individuals to two countries, we can see that by trading with another country *both* countries can consume more than they can produce alone.

This is a core concept in economics: Individuals and countries can trade to be better off. The **gains from trade** are that each party can consume a basket of goods that is larger than what they could produce alone. If we measure national well-being by the amount of goods and services available for consumption, then by trading we will be better off.

The PPF is a simple but powerful concept to explain the advantages of trade for individuals and nations. A third very important macroeconomic concern is economic growth. How does the economy grow? What determines how fast a country can grow?

ECONOMIC GROWTH

Productive capacity changes over time. A common assumption made is that next year the economy will be able to produce more because of technological advancements. We can show this by an outward shift of the PPF when there is an advance in technology. In Figure 2.4, we have assumed for simplicity that the change in technology affects both goods equally, so that the shift is seen as in parallel shift in the PPF.

The effects of adopting this new technology are that we can now produce 125 million tons of food per year if we devote all of our resources to food production and that we can produce 250 million barrels of oil per year by producing just oil.

Note that point **Z**, which formerly was not obtainable with the PPF_1, is now possible because the frontier has expanded with the better technology. This same expansion in productive capacity could occur with an increase in capital goods, more highly skilled labor, or an influx of immigrants.

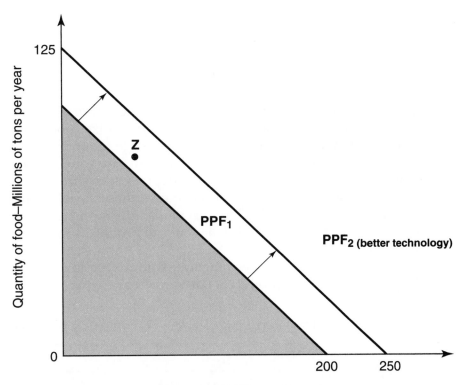

FIGURE 2.4. **Production possibilities frontier.**

A change in technology enables more of both goods to be produced.

SUMMARY OF THE PPF

A summary of the PPF and what we have learned in this oversimplified example follows.

    1. **Scarcity:** What we produce and consume is limited or constrained and is not in our control; we can produce less but not more than our constraints.

    2. **Allocation of resources:** Each country has a choice of the combination of goods to produce. **Opportunity cost:** When we are utilizing all of our resources, we can produce more of one good only by giving up another.

    3. Some countries have an **absolute advantage** in the production of some items.

    4. **Unemployment and inefficiency:** If countries underutilize their resources, they will produce and consume less than is possible.

    5. **Gains from trade:** We can consume and produce more by trading with other producers.

    6. **Economic growth:** When we improve our technology or human resources and their management, we can produce more.

CHOICE AND OPPORTUNITY COST

Absolute and Comparative Advantage

Absolute advantage means that you can produce more of one item than another country if you devote all of your resources to that good's production. In the example above, Bill had the absolute advantage in producing water.

Table 2.2 illustrates the **comparative advantage** for Bill and for Mary. The table shows the most each can produce if they specialize completely in the item listed. The producer who can produce food most cheaply in terms of what they have to give up is Mary. She has the comparative advantage in the production of food because it costs her only 0.33 water to produce 1 food. It costs Bill 1 water to produce 1 food.

As you see, Bill has the comparative advantage in the production of water. It costs him 1 food to produce a water, whereas it costs Mary 3 foods.

TABLE 2.2 TRADE AND COMPARATIVE ADVANTAGE

	Food	Water
Bill	100	100
Mary	150	50
Bill's opportunity cost to produce 1 unit	100/100 = 1 water	**100/100 = 1 food**
Mary's opportunity cost to produce 1 unit	**50 water/150 food = 0.33 water**	150 water/50 food = 3 food

When we are on the boundary of the PPF, we can measure what we have to give up in oil production to gain a ton of food. Economists call this opportunity cost. Remember that opportunity cost is what you have to give up in order to get something.

We have used a simplified PPF and represented it as a straight line. In the real world, there is usually increasing opportunity cost, which we will show by a PPF that is convex—curved.

The following example refers to a farmer with a limited number of acres that he can devote to producing either soybeans or wheat. The acres can be used to produce either good.

If the farmer devotes all of his acreage to the production of soybeans, he can produce 80 soy each year, and if all the acreage is in wheat, he can produce 100 wheat. Starting at 80 soy and 0 wheat, the intersection of the PPF and the soy axis, the more wheat the farmer chooses to produce, the more it costs him in soy that he has to give up. Segment **A** is much smaller than segment **B**. Note that in each case the increase in wheat is 10 units.

Why does this happen? Not all acreage is equally suited to producing each crop. To produce the first wheat, the farmer takes the worst acre for soy out of soy production and loses very little. As more and more wheat is produced and you are getting to **B** in the diagram, higher yielding acres of soy have to be given up to get the same increase of 10 units of wheat.

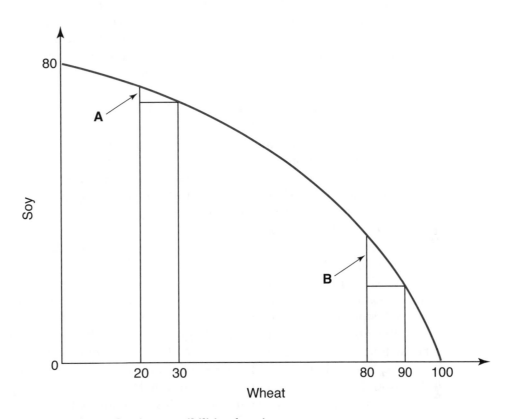

FIGURE 2.5. Production possibilities frontier.

This graph shows the increasing opportunity cost to produce more wheat. **(B > A)**

ECONOMIC SYSTEMS

Different economic systems deal with the problems of scarcity in different ways. Every economy solves three basic questions in one way or another.

1. What is produced?

2. How is it produced?

3. Who gets it?

Remember we are interested in the positive framework (how is it produced), not in the normative question (is that a good way or a bad way?).

Command Economy

In a command economy, the basic economic questions above are answered by the leaders, whether the military or the central government. Planned economies like the former Soviet Union, and to some extent China today, exercise strong central control over economic activities. The central authority sets output targets, income levels, and prices. The usual scenarios also include 5-year plans or more elaborate and complex programs like the Great Leap Forward. These should not be confused with some noncommand economy programs that attach a slogan to a much milder and less controlled effort.

Free Market or Laissez Faire Economy

The major decisions in these economies are made by the market interactions of many individuals, households, firms, or companies. The defining characteristic is that the outcomes are *market-determined* and not dictated or proscribed by any authority. Laissez faire means essentially "Let them (the market) do it," meaning that the market should be left alone without government involvement and all of the basic questions will be resolved.

A laissez faire system works through **markets** where buyers and sellers get together to exchange goods. Markets can be for exchanging goods, commodities, services, or money, among the most prominent examples. The markets can have locations such as retail stores or can be electronic meeting places to buy and sell stock or goods on eBay. There is a wide variety of markets.

Because the U.S. economy is largely based on the market system, the market system will be the continuing topic of exploration throughout this book.

What is unique to market systems is that participants and players take their directions from prices and profits, which signal which are promising areas to enter and which areas should be abandoned. This direction of the laissez faire economy by prices and profits works on both consumers and producers. You cannot make a profit on an item unless someone else wants to buy it. However, others will also see that you are making a profit and want to supply goods to that market. Prices and profits are major coordinating systems across and between markets.

Consumer sovereignty is a concept that is at the core of a market system: If enough consumers want something produced, suppliers will supply these goods. The sovereignty comes from the consumers' ability to "rule" or determine what goods and services are produced. Goods and services that are produced are determined by what consumers want without a central plan or authority.

Individuals are free to choose how much they work, how much they spend or save for a rainy day, and how many vacations to take. The total of all these individual decisions in a market economy determines what is produced, who consumes it, how it is produced, and how it is distributed.

Mixed Systems

Between command economies at one extreme and laissez faire or capitalist economies on the other are mixed systems that have some command elements and some laissez faire elements. All real-world systems are some sort of mixture. A "pure" command or "pure" laissez faire economic system does not exist. In every economy in the world, there is a role for government.

In the U.S. economy, consumers control roughly 70 percent of the economy. More accurately, with a little macro jargon, consumer spending has been very close to 70 percent of the total spending in the US economy, whereas government spending has amounted to about 19 percent. This underestimates the role of the government, but we are getting ahead of ourselves. It is an underestimate because of the added role that government plays in regulating the economy.

However, one of the major items in any economy is the continual political and economic battle between laissez faire and government involvement. If left completely alone, the market will fall down in certain areas. A centrally planned economy fails to do other things felt to be desirable. The result for most countries is a mixture.

Free market systems are often plagued with unemployment and inflation, they do not always produce what people want at the lowest cost, and they can result in a distribution of income and rewards that may not be viewed as fair.

ECONOMIC SIGNALS ONCE AGAIN

Prices

Changes in prices and profits direct resources. A rapid increase in the price of oil that is sustained over time will create incentives for building automobile and other gasoline engines that will economize on gasoline. At the same time high oil prices will create incentives for the development of non-gasoline-burning engines and other ways of heating homes and producing energy such as solar or wind power. The recent development of hybrid cars, ethanol, and biofuels is a result of increasing global prices for oil and gasoline.

A change in prices in one market affects many other markets. To economize on something is to use it sparingly. When gasoline prices increase rapidly because of a temporary disruption in supply, people use their cars less, combine trips to economize on gas, and use public transportation more.

What causes prices and profits to increase and decrease is as important a part of economics as how people, industries, and countries respond to these changes.

Prices and profits are incentives to change behavior. High profits act as magnets that attract new producers, and declining profits act to discourage existing companies and potential entrants. Potential entrants watch profits very closely. A student of mine making a lot of money in a new business came to me and very seriously asked my advice: "How can I disguise the fact that I am making lots of money? Practically anybody can do this business and I am really scared that lots of other people will come into the business and my profits will be ruined." His high rate of profits was attracting potential entrants, some shifting from their current, less profitable businesses. There was no meaningful advice I could give him that I thought would work. In short, I could not help him. On the other side of the coin, a company losing sales and customers because they are producing something that customers do not want is in real trouble in a market system.

Sometimes we become preoccupied with a particular market or economic change and fail to follow the analysis through to see the effects on other markets and other participants in the economy. Careful students of economics pay attention to what changes "off the diagram" as well as how the new equilibrium is reached in the market we are examining. Policies based only on the results in the directly affected market are incomplete.

REVIEW QUESTIONS

Add the word or words that correctly complete each of the following statements.

1. The production possibilities frontier (PPF) shows us the _____ of what we can produce.

2. The PPF divides the production possibilities into obtainable combinations and _____ combinations.

3. Better technology will shift the PPF _____.

4. A significant famine will shift the PPF _____.

5. Bill has the _____ advantage in producing water if he can produce more water than Susan can.

6. The gains from trade are that each party can _____ a basket of goods that is larger than what they could produce by themselves.

7. In a command economy, the _____ decide the basic economic questions such as how much of what is produced.

8. In a _____ system, the major decisions are made by the market interactions of many individuals, households, and firms.

9. Consumer sovereignty is a concept that is at the core of a _____ system.

10. Rapidly declining profits are a signal for firms to _____ that line of business.

Circle the letter of the item that correctly completes each of the following statements.

1. A point inside the production possibilities frontier represents
   a. an impossible production combination.
   b. unemployed resources.
   c. a combination of two goods that cannot be consumed.
   d. a combination of two goods that cannot be produced.

2. Moving along the PPF curve
   a. shows an increasing demand for one good.
   b. shows all the combinations that are unobtainable.
   c. shows the opportunity cost of producing more of one good.
   d. shows the increase in the production of one good holding production of the other constant.

3. The development of a major technological innovation like the microchip resulted in
   a. shifting the PPF outward.
   b. shifting the PPF inward.
   c. no change in the PPF.
   d. a movement along the existing PPF.

4. Growth in the economy can be shown with the PPF
   a. by an inward shift.
   b. by an outward shift.
   c. by a movement up the PPF
   d. by a movement down the PPF

5. If Don has the absolute advantage in producing water, he
   a. can produce more water than Jane can if he dedicates all his efforts to water.
   b. has to give up less water for food than Jane does.
   c. has to give up more water for food than Jane does.
   d. also has the comparative advantage in water production.

6. The gains from trade are that each party can
   a. earn more money for their products.
   b. produce more of both goods.
   c. learn from each other.
   d. consume a basket of goods larger than they could produce alone.

7. In a command economy, the basic economic problems are solved by
   a. the leaders, whether the military or the central government.
   b. the marketplace.
   c. the trading partners.
   d. the consumers.

8. The major economic decisions in free market economies are determined by
   a. the government.
   b. the biggest businesses.
   c. the market interactions of many individuals, household, or firms.
   d. the trading partners.

9. Consumer sovereignty means that
   a. producers will survive producing what they want to produce.
   b. consumers have little say in the economy.
   c. if enough consumers want something produced, suppliers will supply these goods.
   d. The sovereign government represents the consumers in the economy.

10. A rapid increase in the price of oil that is sustained over time
   a. will always mean that more oil is consumed.
   b. will stimulate the development of higher mile-per-gallon cars.
   c. will always mean that less oil is consumed.
   d. will discourage more oil exploration.

ANSWERS TO FILL-IN QUESTIONS

1. limit
2. unobtainable
3. outward
4. inward
5. absolute
6. consume
7. leaders
8. free market
9. market
10. leave

ANSWERS TO MULTIPLE-CHOICE QUESTIONS

1. **b.** Because the economy is not producing all it can, there are unemployed or idle resources.

2. **c.** The only way to increase production of one good is to give up some of the other, and this trade shows the opportunity cost.

3. **a.** Better technology allows us to produce more of both goods.

4. **b.** Better technology or labor allows us to produce more of both goods.

5. **a.** This is the definition.

6. **d.** Specialization and trade allow both sides to be better off.

7. **a.** Commander, dictator, or czar—not the marketplace

8. **c.** The free market.

9. **c.** If there is enough consumer demand, producers will produce it.

10. **b.** It will be more profitable to have a low miles-per-gallon engine, and potential producers will spend resources to develop it.

CHAPTER 3

DEMAND, SUPPLY, AND MARKET EQUILIBRIUM

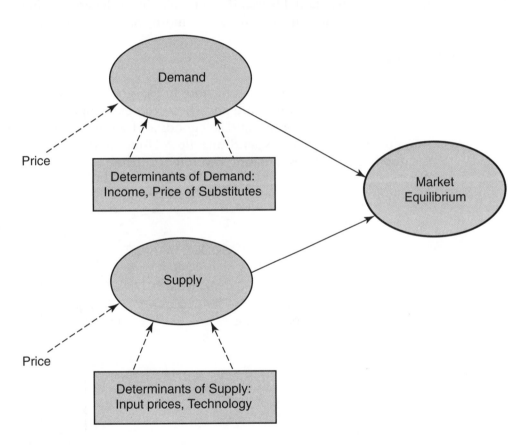

M illions of individuals and companies in a large economy like that of the United States are producing, buying, selling, and investing every day. How can we make sense of all of this?

To understand the macroeconomy, we reduce the large number of relationships, players, and exchanges to a simple model called the circular flow. The **circular flow** gives us an overview of the main pieces of the economy and how it is organized. We then present the concepts of demand and supply, by far the most important tools in the economist's toolbox. We finish the chapter with an appendix on reading and understanding graphs.

THE CIRCULAR FLOW

Our simplified model of the economy has two agents or actors—firms and households—and shows how the participants interact in the economy. Firms are producers and households are consumers. They interact with one another through markets where they exchange goods and services for income and trade labor and other services for wages.

Firms and Households

The goods market is the first market we present in Figure 3.1. In the goods market, firms make revenue by selling goods and services to households. Households spend money in the market to purchase the goods and services for consumption. We know the real world is much more complex than this, but one of the advantages of a simple model is that it can be readily understood. After we understood the basic flows, we can then introduce more complex concepts.

The Goods Market

There are two important flows to note in the goods market. The inside flow is represented by the dotted line and shows the exchange of goods and services. Producers or firms produce and sell goods and services to households. The outside flow represents an expenditure flow. Households spend their incomes on the goods and services, creating revenue for firms.

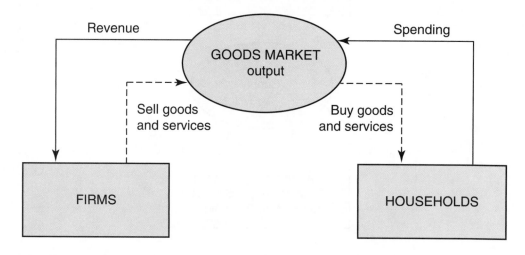

FIGURE 3.1. The goods market.

Firms produce and sell. Households buy and consume.

To complete the circular flow for the whole economy we add a second market, the market for factors of production. In economics the factors of production are land, labor, and capital. These are the inputs that firms use to produce output.

In the factor market the participants switch hats: Households now sell and firms now buy. Households sell their labor and other services, which firms buy. This is shown in Figure 3.2.

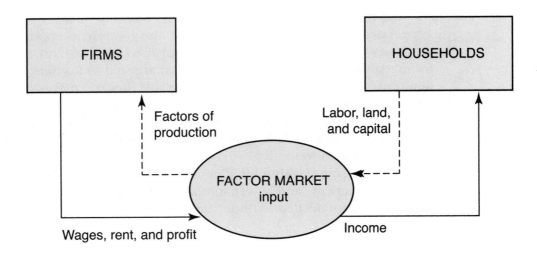

FIGURE 3.2. The factor market.

Firms buy. Households sell.

The inside flow represents the households supplying labor and other services to firms who use them as factors of production. These factors of production are land, labor, and capital (buildings and machines). The exterior flow shows wages and other payments made to households, which become their income.

When we combine the two markets, we have a complete circular flow.

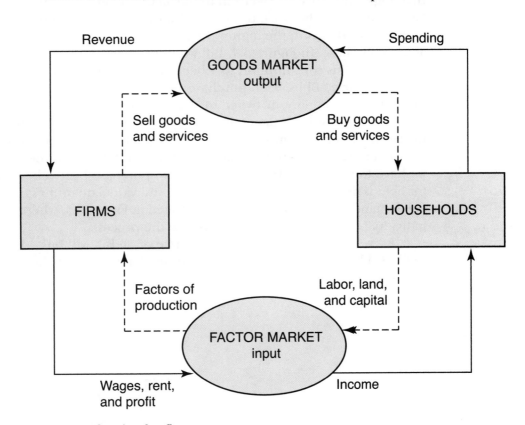

FIGURE 3.3. The circular flow.

Firms and households in both markets.

On the inside flow, locate the "Firms" box. The firms' output of products and services is sold to households through the goods market. They finance these purchases by earning income in the factor market. Firms buy inputs in the factor market in order to produce goods that are sold to households. The outside flow represents the money flow, and the inside flow represents the flow of inputs and outputs. To make cans of tomato soup, firms purchase tomatoes from farmers, hire the labor and equipment, make the cans of soup, and sell them to households. Households earn income by selling their labor and use their wages to buy the tomato soup.

Missing from this simplified circular flow are income that is saved, the role of the government, and international trade. These subjects will be discussed later and are not needed to understand the main parts of the economy and how they are related.

THE DEMAND CURVE: HOW PRICE AND QUANTITY DEMANDED ARE RELATED

A consumer's demand for a product like beer represents one side of the beer market, the demand side. As we saw in the circular flow above, tomato soup is one of the goods sold in the goods market.

Bill is an individual consumer of beer. Bill's demand curve for beer shows how much beer he will buy each month depending on the price. Everything else that might influence his decision to buy beer is held constant, so that we can isolate the effect of the price of beer on how much he is willing to buy. According to **the law of demand**, the higher the price of beer, the less beer he is willing and able to purchase. In Figure 3.4, Bill will buy 4 beers a week if the price is $6. He will increase his consumption to 7 beers a week if the price falls to $3 per beer.

Of course, Bill's beer purchase depends on many more things than its price, but we simplify in order to derive the demand curve. We assume that everything that will influence Bill's demand for beer is held constant. This way we can trace out the amount of beer individual will buy at all different prices.

There are many individuals in a market, and to get to the market demand, we have to include all the individuals who purchase beer. The market demand for beer is derived by adding up all of the individual quantities that each individual demands at each price. This is illustrated in Figure 3.5, where we use only two individuals and a price of $6 to illustrate the process.

As we can see in Figure 3.5, at a price of $6 Bill will buy 4 beers and Helen will buy 3 beers, for a total market quantity demanded of 7 beers at $6.

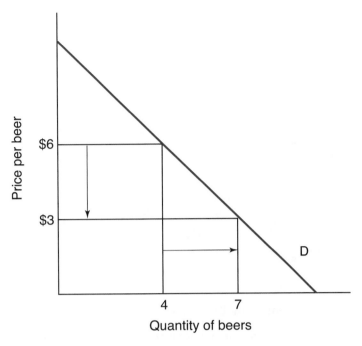

FIGURE 3.4. Bill's demand for beer.

The lower the price, the more beer Bill buys each week.

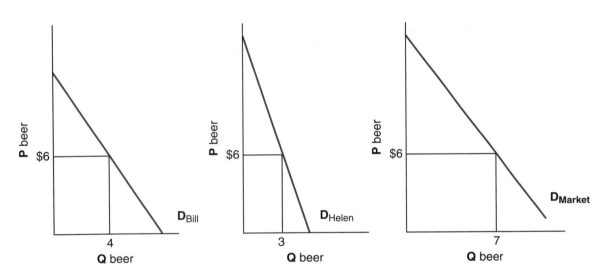

FIGURE 3.5. The market demand for beer.

The market demand is the sum of all the quantities demanded by all the buyers at each price.

A Movement Along the Demand Curve

Consumers will increase the quantity of beer they are willing to buy as the price of beer falls. This is known as the law of demand. As the price increases, less beer will be purchased. If the price of beer rises to $9, consumers will reduce their consumption from 7 beers to 5 beers as in Figure 3.6.

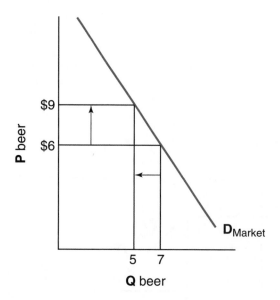

FIGURE 3.6. **A movement along the demand curve.**

As the price of beer increases, consumers buy less beer—the law of demand.

Many other things influence the market demand for beer. To allow for these in our demand analysis, we include them as determinants of the demand for beer. The demand curve is defined as the relationship between the price and the quantity demanded, holding everything else constant. It is these determinants that are held constant. We know they influence the demand, and we want to hold them constant to examine the relationship of quantity demanded to price. However, when any of the determinants of demand change, the entire demand curve shifts.

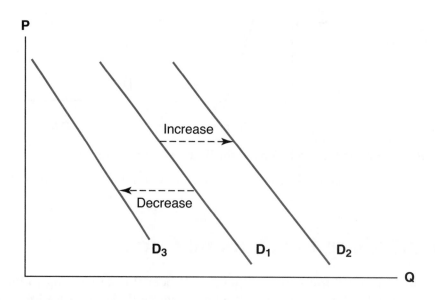

FIGURE 3.7. **Shifts in demand.**

A change in the determinants of demand will shift the entire curve.

The definition of an increase in demand is that at all prices quantity demanded will be greater. The demand will shift to the right from D_1 to D_2 in Figure 3.7. A decrease in demand means that consumers will buy less at all prices. This is shown by the demand curve D_1 shifting to D_3.

The major determinants of consumer demand are income, the price of related goods, tastes and preferences, expectations, and the number of buyers. Income influences our ability to purchase goods and services, and an increase in income normally leads to an increase in expenditures. In fact, **normal goods** are defined as those whose demand increases when incomes increase. We buy more entertainment goods when our income rises. An increase in income increases the demand for a normal good. There are some goods, called **inferior goods**, whose demand decreases when incomes rise. An example of an inferior good might be canned string beans. As your income goes up, you cut back on canned string beans and consume more fresh string beans.

Related goods are goods and services that are substitutes for or complements to the good in question. A **substitute good** is defined as a good whose increase in price shifts the demand for another good rightward. As the price of wine increases, the demand for beer increases because they are substitutes. A **complementary good** is defined as a good that when the price of the complementary good increases we decrease our demand for the good in question. If the price of bacon increases, our demand for eggs will shift leftward because bacon and eggs are complementary goods. Here is a good way to remember the difference: For a substitute good, price and the demand curve move in the same direction; for a complementary good, the price change shifts the demand curve in the opposite direction.

Tastes and preferences are behind whether we like something or not. What determines these tastes and preferences is beyond economics. They are included here because of their obvious influence on demand. For example, if there is an increase in preferences for oatmeal because of its antioxidant characteristics, the demand for oatmeal will increase. Alternatively, if preferences for cigarette smoking decline, the demand for cigarettes will decrease.

Expectations about the future help determine today's demand. If prices for a brand new technology are widely expected to fall as a result of a new research report, today's demand will decrease to incorporate these expectations. If you are expecting a large bonus, you may build this expectation into your current demand for restaurant meals and buy more of them.

Table 3.1 summarizes what we have learned about demand and the determinants of demand. Most importantly, it distinguishes between the changes that will result in a move along the demand curve and those that will shift the demand curve.

To review, any change in the price of beer will change the quantity of beer demanded. A higher price will result in a lower quantity demanded. This is a movement along the existing demand curve. Any change in the determinants of demand will shift the demand curve.

In our beer example the following changes shift the demand for beer inward and to the left

1. a decline in consumer income

2. a drop in the price of wine, a substitute for beer

3. a regulation raising the legal drinking age to 21 in all states, reducing the number of beer buyers.

TABLE 3.1 THE DEMAND FOR A GOOD

The law of demand: Holding everything else constant, the quantity demanded falls when the price goes up.		
		A change will cause a
Defines the demand curve	Price of the good	Movement along the demand curve
Determinants of demand	Income Taste and preferences Prices of related goods Expectations Number of buyers	Shift in the position of the demand curve

THE SUPPLY CURVE AND HOW PRICE AND QUANTITY SUPPLIED ARE RELATED

The supply side of the market is where producers or firms interact in the goods market. Producers hire labor, buy supplies and equipment, and produce goods. In our example the producer is supplying beer. The amount of beer this firm is willing to supply depends on the price of beer, holding everything else constant. The higher the price of beer, the more beer will be supplied. This is shown in Figure 3.8 as the supply curve for firm A.

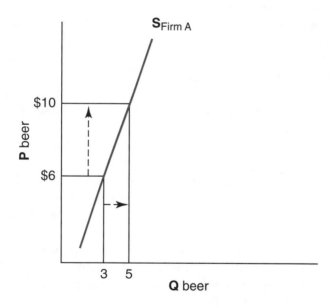

FIGURE 3.8. **Individual firm supply.**

Price increases result in a higher quantity supplied.

How do we get from one company to the whole market? To derive the market supply we use the same process as we did with the market demand—we add up all of the individual firms' quantities supplied at every price. This will result in the market supply curve, and in Figure 3.9 we use a price of $6 as an example. We use only two suppliers, firm A and firm B, to simplify the analysis.

The market supply is the horizontal sum of the quantities for all the sellers at each price. At $6, firm A will supply 3 beers and firm B will supply 4 beers, for a total of 7 beers supplied to the market.

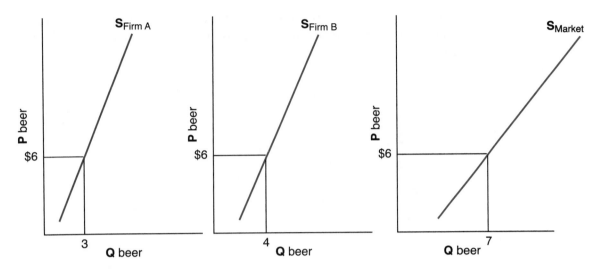

FIGURE 3.9. **Market supply origins.**

The market supply is the sum of the quantities supplied at each price.

The quantities supplied to the market increase with the price, holding everything else constant. This is called the **law of supply**. To see this in action, look at $6 in Figure 3.9 and see that 7 beers are supplied by the market. If the price increases to $12, firms will increase their output and supply 11 beers, as shown in Figure 3.10.

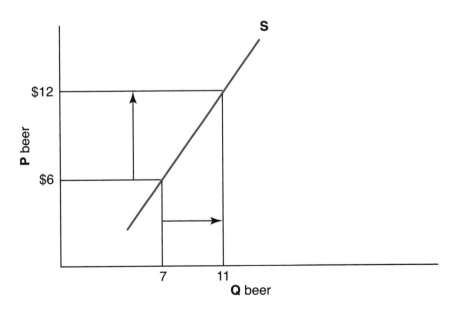

FIGURE 3.10. **Market supply curve.**

As the price increases, more will be supplied—the law of supply.

There are two ways to increase the quantity of beer supplied to the market. One is to increase the price offered to producers which, as we saw above, will cause a movement up the supply curve. Another is to increase the willingness of producers to produce beer at all prices, the definition of an increase in supply. This will shift the supply of beer to the right, so that producers will supply more at all prices.

The difference between these concepts is crucial: An increase in the quantity supplied is very different from an increase in the supply, a shift in the whole supply curve.

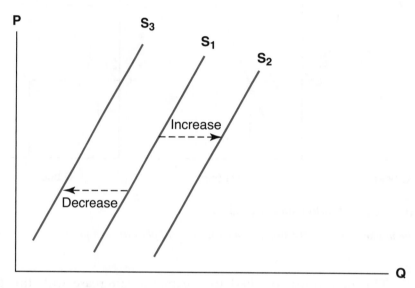

FIGURE 3.11. Shifts in the supply curve.

A change in the determinants of supply will shift the entire curve.

What will shift the supply curve? The variables that will shift the supply curve as shown in Figure 3.11 are called the **determinants of supply** and refer to everything except price that producers use in their decision to produce.

The most common determinants of the market supply of a good are the price of inputs, technology, expectations, and the number of suppliers. Inputs are variables like labor, materials, and electricity that are costs of production. Technology, on the other hand, influences how producers assemble the product. Henry Ford was famous for reorganizing and automating the production line for automobiles so that for the same amount of inputs, more could be produced.

Expectations also play a role in supply decisions of firms because firms base their plans to produce in part on expectations of future prices. For example, if interest rates are expected to go up, firms may take out loans today to purchase more equipment, increasing the current supply of goods. The number of suppliers in the market will also shift the supply curve. If some suppliers leave the market, the market supply will decrease.

We summarize the supply discussion in Table 3.2.

TABLE 3.2 THE SUPPLY OF A GOOD

The law of supply: Holding everything else constant, the quantity supplied increases when the price goes up.		
		A change will cause a
Defines the supply curve	Price of the good	Movement along the supply curve
Determinants of supply	Input prices Technology Expectations Number of producers	Shift in the position of the supply curve

To continue with our beer example, the following changes will shift the supply of beer outward and to the right:

1. a decline in the wages of beer production workers

2. a drop in the price of hops, one of the major ingredients of beer

3. a reduction in the tax on beer production, encouraging individual beer-making companies to supply more at every price and providing incentives for new producers to enter the beer business.

PUTTING DEMAND AND SUPPLY TOGETHER: MARKET EQUILIBRIUM

When we put demand and supply together, we can analyze how both sides of the market interact and under what conditions the quantity supplied will be the same as the quantity demanded. This will occur at what is called **equilibrium**. First we examine equilibrium in the marketplace, and then we intentionally disturb the market to see what happens. We then discuss changes in the allocation of resources as a response to these changes in the markets.

Equilibrium occurs in a market when the price reaches a level where quantity demanded equals quantity supplied. When the market is in equilibrium, there is no pressure to change the price. In our earlier beer market example, this occurs when the price is $6 in Figure 3.12. At this price, consumers are willing and able to purchase 7 beers and suppliers are willing and able to sell 7 beers.

At a price of $6, producers will supply 7 beers and consumers will consume exactly that amount. E_1 in Figure 3.12 indicates the intersection of the demand and supply curves, a point that represents the equilibrium price and quantity. Note that consumers who have a demand for beer would prefer a lower price (they would consume more) and beer manufacturers would prefer a higher price (they would produce more). What the beer market does is to reconcile these competing wishes.

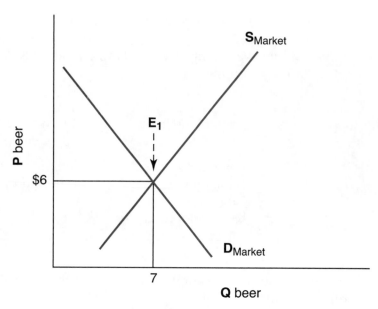

FIGURE 3.12. **Market equilibrium.**

Equilibrium occurs when quantity supplied equals quantity demanded.

Not only does the market work to achieve this compromise, but the price stays at $6 unless the market changes in some way. Both sides of the market are on their respective curves, and neither one will pressure for a change. To see this in a different light we will examine what happens when a market is not in equilibrium. When this is the case, market pressures for the competing claims in the market will lead to an equilibrium that will clear the market.

SHORTAGES AND SURPLUSES

Markets that are not in equilibrium have either a shortage or a surplus because the existing price does not clear the market. Two reasons why prices might not clear the market are that the market has not yet adjusted to a recent shift in the demand or supply or because there is a fixed price that is not allowed to change. If prices are flexible, the market price will adjust to the shortage or surplus until the market is in equilibrium at a price that clears the market.

A **shortage** occurs when consumers want to purchase more than firms are willing to supply at a given price. A shortage is when the price is lower than the equilibrium price. A shortage is also called an excess demand, which means that consumers demand a quantity larger than the quantity suppliers are willing to provide.

A surplus is the opposite. If there is a **surplus**, firms are producing a larger quantity than consumers are willing to buy. This occurs when the price is higher than the equilibrium price. Both of these can be seen in Figure 3.13.

At a price of P_1 in Figure 3.13, consumers are willing to purchase Q_1 and suppliers are willing to supply Q_2, resulting in the surplus shown. This represents an excess supply of Q_2–Q_1, because the price is higher than the equilibrium price. Suppliers, caught with unsold goods, will try to increase sales by lowering the price until it reaches **P*** and there are no more unsold goods.

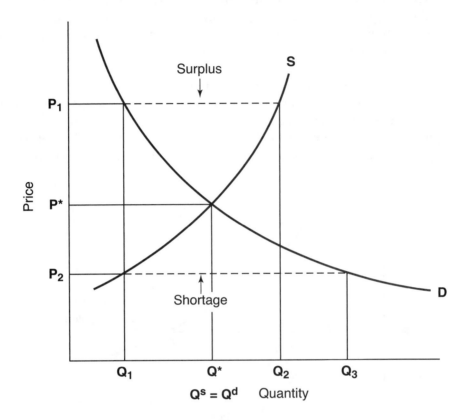

FIGURE 3.13. Shortages and surpluses.

Shortages and surpluses occur when the price does not clear the market.

At a price of P_2, there is an excess demand or shortage. Consumers want to buy Q_3, but producers are producing only Q_1. Consumers will bid up the price because there are not enough goods for everyone who is willing and able to pay price P_2. With prices allowed to move in the market, the price will rise to **P***, the equilibrium price. Once the price is at **P*** we have arrived at an equilibrium price because the quantities demanded are the same as the quantities supplied and there is no incentive for either side of the market to pressure for a change in the price.

Changes in Equilibrium

When the determinants of demand or supply change, the market establishes a new equilibrium price. In the example of the meat market, in Figure 3.14, demand has increased, raising the equilibrium price to P^*_2 and a higher equilibrium quantity produced Q^*_2. Suppose the reason for the demand increase was a change in tastes and preferences for more meat because of a popular diet program, although it could have been another determinant of demand that changed.

At the new equilibrium E_2, note that the result of this change in tastes and preferences is that everyone now pays more for meat and more meat is supplied. Also note that there was no increase in supply but an increase in quantity supplied as consumers bid up the price of meat. None of the determinants of supply changed, so the supply curve maintains its position and does not shift.

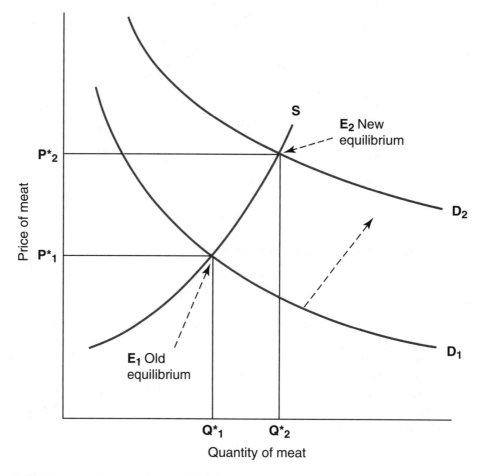

FIGURE 3.14. Changes in equilibrium.

An increase in taste and preferences for meat in diets increases the market demand for meat.

A decrease in the supply will also change the equilibrium price. Suppose that bad weather has harmed the coffee market in South America. The result will be that less coffee is available, a decrease in supply as in Figure 3.15. Remember that a decrease in supply means that producers supply less coffee at all prices.

This new supply is shown as S_2. The result of the decrease in supply is that the new equilibrium price rises to P^*_2 and the equilibrium quantity falls to Q^*_2. As a result of the bad weather, coffee drinkers have to pay more for a cup of coffee and less coffee will be on market shelves.

Because of the increase in the price of coffee, the demand for substitutes like tea will increase, and more tea will be consumed at a higher price.

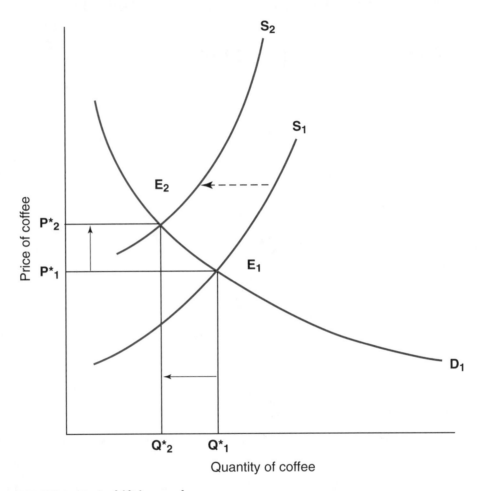

FIGURE 3.15. A shift in supply.

Bad weather ruins much of the coffee crop and the market supply decreases.

CHAPTER APPENDIX: HOW TO READ AND UNDERSTAND GRAPHS

Graphs are very common in the economist's toolbox. Graphs are visual summaries that represent complex ideas simply. They summarize a lot of information and assumptions. One way to get the most out of a diagram or graph is to translate it back into words. To understand a graph more completely, walk around in it and describe what is happening. For example, walk down a line or a curve and explain what is going on. It will helps to label points on a graph such as *A* and *B* in the demand curve example in Figure 3.16.

WALK THROUGH THE GRAPH

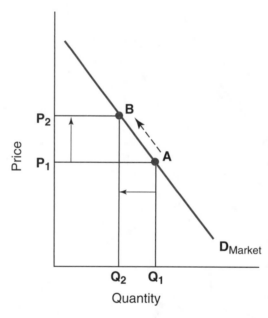

FIGURE 3.16. Demand walk.

As we move from A *to* B, *less is consumed as prices are increasing—the law of demand.*

As we move from *A* to *B*, what is happening? Moving from *A* to *B* shows that the market is reducing its consumption as the price rises. This is the law of demand and assumes that everything else is being held constant. It is a movement along an existing demand curve in response to a change in price.

What is going on in the background away from the diagram? We also need to understand what is going on away from the diagram. As the price increases from P_1 to P_2, consumers will have less income to spend if they continue to purchase the old amount Q_1. Because consumers have many spending choices and limited incomes, they will reduce their consumption of the good whose price has gone up. They will change the mix of goods they consume as a result, consuming less of the good whose price increased.

We also know that nothing else has changed in the market. No determinant of demand has changed. If a determinant had changed, it would have shifted the position of the demand curve. If we see a graph with two demand curves, we know immediately that one of the determinants of the demand has changed, causing the demand curve to shift.

Graphs Show Boundaries

Lines in a graph represent boundaries. Remember our discussion of the production possibilities frontier in Chapter 2? The PPF is called a frontier or boundary because it separates the combinations of goods that can be produced given our current resources from the combinations that are impossible. All the combinations outside the boundary or frontier are impossible to produce.

When we look at the demand and supply curves on a graph, we also find that they represent boundaries or zones. Let's look at the demand curve first.

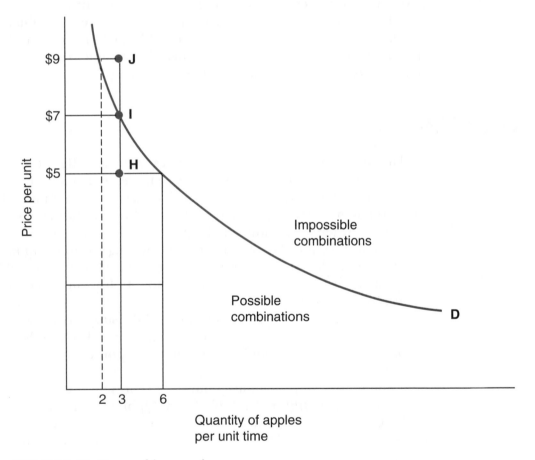

FIGURE 3.17. **Demand is a maximum.**

Points above are not obtainable. Consumers won't pay that much for that quantity.

Using our technique of walking through the graph, begin at *H* in Figure 3.17, which represents the combination of $5 and 3 apples. If this combination becomes available on the market, consumers will buy it. As a matter of fact, consumers are willing to pay $7 for 3 apples (point *I* on the demand curve). If suppliers attempt to charge $9 for these three apples (point *J*), consumers will not pay that amount. There are not enough consumers willing to pay that much, and if a price of $9 is charged in the market, only 2 apples will be sold. Any point on the demand curve represents the maximum amount consumers will pay for that quantity. Alternatively, the demand curve represents the largest quantity that consumers will buy at a given price. To see this, move horizontally at the price of $5. The most apples consumers will buy will be 6. Consumers will not buy more apples at that price. In order to sell more than 6 apples, the price will have to be lower.

What we have discovered is that the demand curve represents a maximum quantity that consumers are willing to buy at a given price, or the most they will pay for a given quantity. When consumers are on their demand curves, they are paying the most they are willing to pay for that quantity.

The demand curve also acts as a boundary between combinations of quantity demanded and price that are acceptable to consumers and combinations that are unacceptable. Later in this appendix demand as a boundary will help us understand the process adjusting to equilibrium.

THE SUPPLY CURVE

Walking up the supply curve shows that as the price offered increases, producers are willing to supply more. As the price increases from P_1 to P_2, quantity supplied increases from Q_1 to Q_2. The supply curve is a minimum. The higher the price, the more firms will supply. Starting at P_2, walk horizontally until you get to point *K*, where firms will supply Q_1. As we continue horizontally, firms will continue to increase the amount they are willing to supply until we reach the supply curve at *L*. Firms will not supply more than Q_2 at a price of P_2. The combination represented by *M* is not obtainable unless the price increases to the point *N* on the supply curve.

The quantity at *M* might be produced if the supply curve were to shift rightward in response to a change in the determinants of supply. Without a change in the determinants of supply, *M* and all other points to the right of the supply curve are impossible.

The supply curve contains points that represent the minimum price necessary to get that quantity produced. Start at Q_1 on the quantity axis and move vertically. Q_1 will not be produced until the price is P_1. As we continue upward, any price higher than P_1 will result in the quantities produced that are on the supply curve.

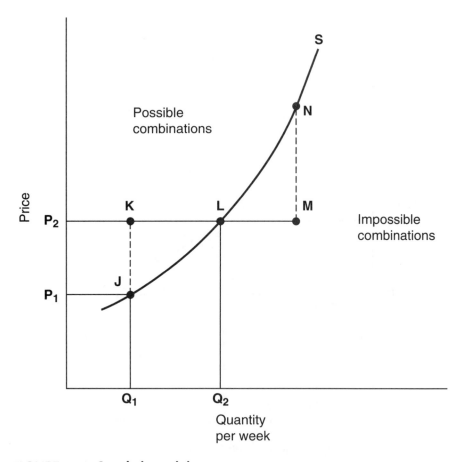

FIGURE 3.18. Supply is a minimum.

Points below the supply are impossible; points above are possible.

THE DYNAMICS OF ADJUSTMENT TO EQUILIBRIUM

One of the most important dynamics in economics is the adjustment to an equilibrium price. This adjustment is one of the main building blocks in understanding changes in the economy and in the allocation of resources. This adjustment process will help us understand the outcomes of policy decisions, for example, where we want to influence the marketplace to produce less smog. Another important use is to understand what happens when there are fixed prices in the economy.

When there is an excess supply, firms or suppliers force the price lower. At a price of P_1 in Figure 3.19, suppliers have surplus goods and lower prices in an effort to sell them. As prices are lowered, consumers increase their consumption, moving along the demand curve until a new equilibrium price is reached. At P_1, the amount sold in the market is determined by the consumer demand and is Q_1, although suppliers are holding quantity Q_2.

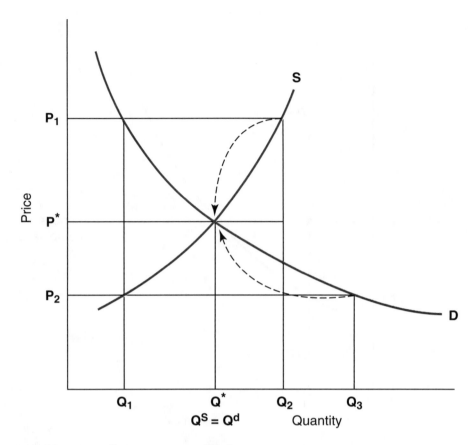

FIGURE 3.19. Adjustment to equilibrium.

The side of the market not on its curve forces the price to change.

When there is an excess demand such as at **P₂**, unsatisfied consumers will force a price change and the amount actually sold in the market will be the amount on the supply curve. As consumers bid the price up, more will be supplied by suppliers who respond to the higher prices by increasing the quantities they supply until the equilibrium price **P*** is reached.

As you move horizontally along the current price, it is the first curve that you encounter in the diagram that determines the amount purchased or supplied in the market. When the market is in equilibrium, the quantity produced is the same amount as the quantity demanded. In an adjustment process, these quantities are different. When the price is higher than the equilibrium price, consumers will buy only the amount on their demand curve, not the amount produced. When the price is lower than the equilibrium price, suppliers will produce only the amount on their supply curve, not the amount that consumers want.

The movement toward equilibrium results from pressure from the side of the market that is not on its curve. This is shown in Figure 3.19 by the curved lines with arrows at the end. In an excess supply suppliers act to force the price down, and in an excess demand it is the would-be purchasers who force the price up.

THE INTERRELATIONSHIP OF MARKETS

One market's outcome affects other markets. A change in the market equilibrium has repercussions in other markets. Let's examine the market for gasoline, a market that is influenced by the global supply of oil. We will do this without the familiar supply and demand graphs, but if you need to, draw them to follow along.

Suppose that the global price of oil rises because of a decrease in supply. This could be due to a wartime shortage, a decision by the Organization of Petroleum Exporting Countries (OPEC) to restrict production, or some other event. The price of gasoline will increase as a result of a decrease in the supply of gasoline in the United States. Because petroleum products are widely used inputs in manufacturing, an increase in the price of oil will also cause the supply curves in these markets to shift inward. Some affected markets are paint, cosmetics, home heating oil and airline travel. It is now more costly to provide these services and manufacture these items, so producers supply less at all prices, raising the prices in these markets.

The higher price of gasoline will affect the market for sport utility vehicles (SUVs). The demand for gas-guzzling SUVs will shift inward, forcing the equilibrium price of these SUVs down, and fewer will be purchased. What caused this decline in the demand? The cost of operating an SUV has increased, and this makes them less desirable than before. Remember that we hold everything else constant to derive the demand curve, and in this case one of the determinants of the demand for SUVs has changed.

The higher price of gasoline will increase the demand for public transportation, as travel by car has become more expensive. If the market for public transportation is not affected by the increase in the price of gasoline, a simplifying assumption, public transportation ridership will increase and there will be upward pressure on public transportation prices.

REVIEW QUESTIONS

Add the word or words that correctly complete each of the following statements.

1. Households exchange labor for wages in the _____ market.

2. In the goods market, households exchange _____ for goods and services.

3. When the demand increases the new equilibrium quantity will be _____ than the old equilibrium quantity.

4. When the supply decreases, the new equilibrium price will _____.

5. The _____ diagram shows the relationship of the factor markets and the goods market.

6. The buyers in the factor market are _____.

7. When a market is in _____, buyers and sellers want to exchange exactly the same amount.

8. When there is an excess _____, producers will force the price lower.

9. If the determinants of supply do not change, the only way to increase the quantity supplied is to _____ the price.

10. A shift in demand for butter will increase the price and _____ the quantity supplied.

Circle the letter of the item that correctly completes each of the following statements.

1. An increase in demand for computers will
   a. be matched with an increase in supply.
   b. lower the equilibrium price of computers.
   c. shift the demand for computers rightward.
   d. shift the demand for computers leftward.

2. If the price of labor decreases, households will
   a. take advantage and offer more hours of work.
   b. hire more labor.
   c. hire less labor.
   d. offer to work fewer hours.

3. If there is an excess demand for beer,
   a. the price is too high.
   b. buyers will bid up the price.
   c. consumers will lower the price.
   d. more beer will sell when the new equilibrium is established.

4. More health care will be consumed at equilibrium if
   a. there is an increase in demand.
   b. there is a decrease in demand.
   c. there is an decrease in supply.
   d. costs of production increase.

5. A natural disaster that reduces the supply of available beef will result in a new equilibrium that has
   a. more beef consumed at a lower price.
   b. more beef consumed at a higher price.
   c. less beef consumed at a lower price.
   d. less beef consumed at a higher price.

6. When a goods market has an excess demand,
    a. prices will fall and more will be consumed.
    b. prices will rise and more will be consumed.
    c. producers will force the price up.
    d. consumers will force the price down.

7. When the market for coffee has excess demand,
    a. producers will force the price up.
    b. producers will force the price down.
    c. consumers will force the price up.
    d. consumers will force the price down.

8. At an equilibrium in the car market,
    a. buyers on both sides of the market are satisfied with the market price.
    b. the price ensures that quantity demanded is the same as quantity demanded. supplied
    c. consumers will pressure and succeed in lowering the price.
    d. producers will pressure and succeed in raising the price.

9. A necessary condition for an equilibrium in a market is that
    a. prices are flexible and allowed to move.
    b. producers have the best interest of consumers in mind.
    c. the demand and supply curves are equal.
    d. the excess demand is the same as the excess supply.

10. If the price of steel increases,
    a. there will be a decrease in the demand for cars.
    b. there will be a increase in the demand for cars.
    c. less steel will be used in the manufacture of cars.
    d. there will be an increase in the supply of cars.

ANSWERS TO FILL-IN QUESTIONS

1. factor
2. money
3. greater
4. increase
5. circular flow
6. firms
7. equilibrium
8. supply
9. increase
10. increase

ANSWERS TO MULTIPLE-CHOICE QUESTIONS

1. **c.** This is the definition of an increase in the demand curve.

2. **d.** This is a movement down the supply curve.

3. **b.** Buyers cannot find enough beer and will force the price up.

4. **a.** The demand curve shifts to the right, forcing the equilibrium price and quantities up.

5. **d.** An inward shift of the supply curve gives this result.

6. **b.** Buyers will bid the price up and suppliers will supply more.

7. **c.** Consumers will bid the price up.

8. **b.** This is the definition of an equilibrium price.

9. **a.** If prices cannot adjust, the markets won't clear.

10. **c.** Suppliers will change the mix of inputs to minimize costs.

CHAPTER 4

THE PRICE SYSTEM AND DEMAND AND SUPPLY

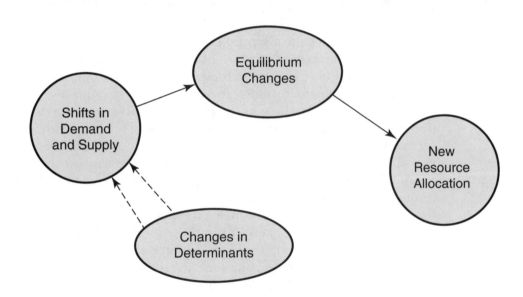

Economics analyzes how resources such as health care services are allocated and how they might be allocated under different economic systems. The crucial decisions are as follows: How much health care gets produced? Who gets it? How much does it cost? How is it produced? How do price changes occur? How do we get more or less health care? Any economic system has to answer all these questions for other products and services.

THE PRICE SYSTEM

The price system is based on a system of competitive markets where there are many consumers and many producers, none large enough to exert a strong influence over the market. Under this economic system it is the marketplace that determines the prices and quantities of goods and services that are produced. This is called **laissez faire capitalism** or **free market economics**.

The **price system** refers to the way the market system works to determine prices and direct the flows of resources. If prices are free to fluctuate, these price fluctuations will send signals through the markets that will change the allocation of resources in the economy. The basic questions of where people work and for what wages, and what goods are produced and consumed and in what quantities are all resolved by the price system, which uses price and profit signals to allocate resources.

For example, in free market economies, prices serve as signals to both sides of the market. High prices encourage consumers to consume less, whereas producers are encouraged to produce more.

As we saw in Chapter 3, an equilibrium price is one that clears the market. Both sides of the market would be better off with a different price. Consumers want a lower price and will consume more if they get it, and producers want a higher price for the goods that they produce.

RATIONING AND ALLOCATING RESOURCES

Prices also influence the allocation of resources. An increase in the price of corn will encourage farmers to produce more corn and less other goods. Rising prices for soy products have increased the acreage devoted to raising soybeans.

Rationing means dividing the existing pie into pieces. The allocation of resources determines who gets the pieces. The price system performs this allocation in a market economy. Macroeconomics is also vitally concerned with increasing the size of the pie, or economic growth and what causes it. One of the measures of social well-being is the quantity of resources available per capita. Economic growth means that more goods and services will be available. How resources are allocated among different players and agents in the economy and how to grow the economy are major themes in macroeconomics.

In competitive markets, rationing goods and services to participants depends on having flexible prices. In later chapters we will examine several important situations where prices are fixed and not allowed to ration products and services are not only rationed among competing claimants. In later chapters we will also examine price ceilings and floors in our treatment of the minimum wage and guaranteed prices for certain products. They are important circumstances where the price system cannot function.

SUPPLY AND DEMAND ANALYSIS: A CASE STUDY OF HOME HEALTH TESTING DEVICES

This case study involves six analytical steps that are used throughout this book:

1. Defining the demand
2. Defining the supply
3. Finding the initial equilibrium
4. Introducing a change that disturbs the equilibrium
5. Examining the new allocation of resources
6. Examining who gains and who loses because of these changes.

The policy and political implications of these economic changes will be addressed throughout the book from two perspectives: how these changes affect the political landscape and how policy decisions affect the allocation of resources in the economy.

The importance of health in the economy comes from the dual roles that consumers play in the economy as workers and as consumers. Their purchases are a source of revenue for producers, and their work hours are inputs for many production processes. Health is a recurring theme in politics and in economics because changes in health policy influence the entire economy. The debates over health care highlight the common ground between economics and politics. The title of a prominent economics journal, the *Journal of Political Economy*, recognizes this connection.

Now let's look at our case study using the six steps.

1. Defining the Demand

The demand for home health testing devices is like the demand for any other good. Following the law of demand, the more costly the devices, the fewer devices will be demanded by consumers.

As seen in Table 3.1, the determinants of this demand for devices are income, the prices of related goods (in this case clinic visits, office visits, and other ways to obtain test results), the number of buyers, expectations, and the tastes and preferences of consumers.

2. Defining the Supply

The supply of home medical testing devices follows the basic rules of the supply curve and the law of supply that we saw earlier in Table 3.2. The law of supply states that holding everything else constant, the quantity of home health testing devices supplied increases when the price goes up. The supply curve shifts when one of the determinants of the supply changes. To review, the determinants of supply are input prices, technology, the number of sellers, and expectations.

3. Finding the Initial Equilibrium

In Figure 4.1, P^*_1 is the market clearing price, because Q^*_1 devices are produced and consumed at that price. We will not see any change in that amount or price until there is a change in the determinants of either the supply or the demand.

One of the major analytical techniques that economists use is to introduce a change in a market and observe how the market changes. "If X then Y" summarizes this approach in abstract terms. An example is "If some event X occurs, then we will see these results Y." We saw this earlier in our analysis of the coffee market, where we found that if bad weather ruins a large part of the coffee crop, then coffee prices will increase and coffee consumption will decline.

We will follow this approach throughout this book. Economists use this technique to test the assumptions behind the analysis. Remember that positive economics means that the analysis must be able to be tested and proven correct or incorrect. "If X then Y" sets up a structure we can use to examine the effects of various policy changes. If the government increases taxes, we will expect these results. We are getting a little ahead of ourselves here, but the technique is so fundamental that it needs to be emphasized early and often.

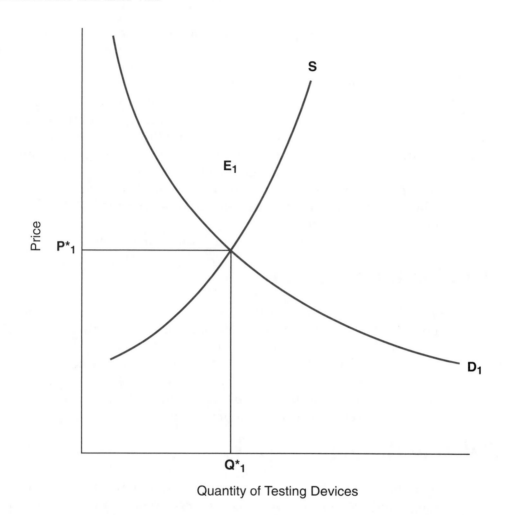

FIGURE 4.1. Equilibrium in a market.

The equilibrium price is the price that clears the market. It is found at the intersection of supply and demand.

We have established the determinants of demand and supply of home testing medical devices and presented the equilibrium in the market.

4. Introducing a Change That Disturbs the Equilibrium

This is the "If X" part. Suppose that a new technological development makes these home testing medical devices cheaper to produce. For example, a microchip processor common to these devices becomes available at half the old cost.

This will change the equilibrium in the device market. See if you can follow the train of thought without looking at Figure 4.2.

Producers are now able to produce more devices at all prices, so that the market supply will increase because of lower input costs. Remember that an increase in supply is defined as more devices being supplied at all prices. The immediate result will be a surplus of devices on the market and as producers try to sell these excess goods, they will force the price lower and lower until a new equilibrium is reached.

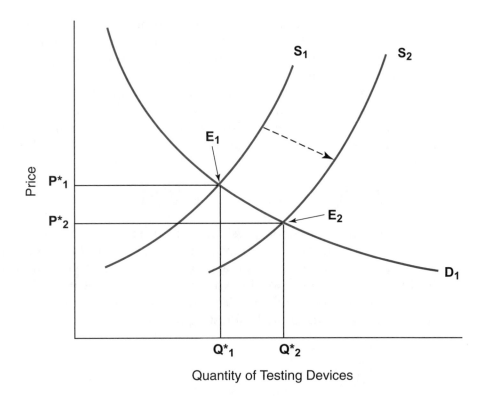

FIGURE 4.2. Better technology increases the supply.

A technological advance increases the supply, lowering the equilibrium price and increasing the equilibrium quantity.

Now comes the "then Y" part. The new equilibrium will be at lower price and a higher quantity consumed and produced. In other words, the result of an innovation that reduces the cost of an input increased the supply of devices, lowering the equilibrium price and increasing the equilibrium quantity. We show this in Figure 4.2.

5. Examine the New Allocation of Resources

So what happened as a result of the innovation? First in the device market, devices became cheaper and more are produced and consumed. Households will use more home testing devices to check on their health.

We also need to examine what happens in related markets to begin to look at how resources might be reallocated. Consumers will use more home testing devices and visit fewer clinics and doctors offices for tests. They will shift the mix of testing services toward more home testing and fewer office visits.

6. Examining Who Gains and Who Loses

Consumers who need tests gain because testing devices are cheaper. If more people get medical tests, society could gain by an increase in the health of the population that might include fewer sick days away from work.

Those who rely on office and clinic visits to perform medical testing will lose. Self-testing by more consumers probably will mean a decline in the demand for office visit medical tests. Since home testing and medical office testing visits are substitutes, the effect will be to reduce the number of office visits for medical testing. This will reduce the equilibrium price and the quantity of office visits for medical testing.

The pattern of the analysis we have used is important. First examine the effects of the change in the market itself and then look at the effects on related markets. One of the characteristics of an economic system is this interrelatedness, which we saw in the circular flow and in our example of the SUV and public transportation.

This Change Would Also Affect the PPF

Remember the production possibilities frontier we covered in Chapter 2? Our example of a technological innovation means that the PPF would shift outward with this new technology. If we assume that the technology affects only home health testing devices, it would expand the PPF only for these devices. In Figure 4.3, society can now produce 5,000 units instead of 4,000 if it devotes all of its resources to producing medical testing devices.

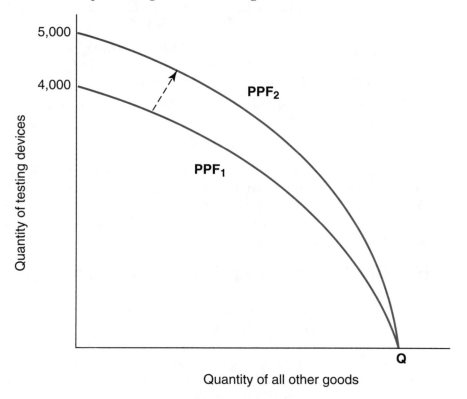

FIGURE 4.3. Shift in the PPF with better technology.

The technology change affects only testing devices.

We have examined an important process in economics. We have set up a framework that allows us to analyze how resources are allocated among competing parties in a competitive market. This six-step process will be repeated often because it is a fundamental tool in economic analysis.

Note: Because this chapter is primarily a case study that reinforces the techniques presented in Chapter 3, there are no questions at the end of this chapter.

PART TWO
MACROECONOMIC CONCEPTS

CHAPTER 5

INTRODUCTION TO MACROECONOMICS

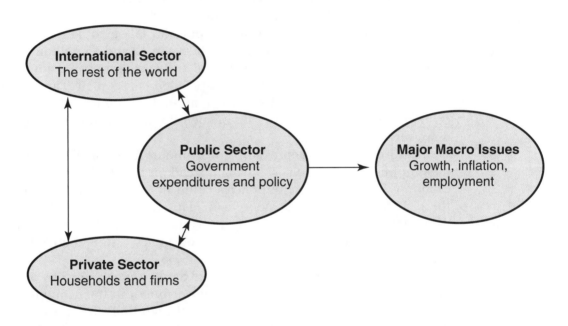

T his chapter introduces macroeconomics and gives an overview of the major concepts and concerns in macroeconomics. Later chapters build on these general points and provide more detail and analysis.

Macroeconomics is the study of the entire economy and its health. The short list that economists use to determine the health of an economy includes growth, the inflation rate, and the level of unemployment. Each one has important consequences about how we live and the opportunities that are available to us. Policy makers want strong growth with no inflation and declining unemployment, an illusive goal. These three goals are hard to achieve at the same time—efforts to achieve one goal often reduce the chances of obtaining another.

Macroeconomics groups all of the participants in the economy together. The private sector (households and firms), the public sector (governments), and the international sector are the main groups in the macroeconomy.

Macroeconomics as a field of study grew as a response to the severe dislocation in the U.S. economy during the depression of the 1930s. A **depression** is a severe recession. Familiar visual images from the Great Depression remind us of how unhealthy the economy was—people jumping out of windows to their deaths, the unemployed on soup lines, and hobos riding freight cars and living in camps are reminders of that chaos. Macroeconomic policies came into being to prevent severe economic downturns.

WHY IS IT CALLED THE GREAT DEPRESSION?

On Black Tuesday, October 29, 1929, the stock market collapsed. On that single day, a record 16 million shares were traded and $30 billion vanished into thin air. Westinghouse lost two thirds of its September value. DuPont dropped 70 points. The "get rich quick" era was over. Jack Dempsey, America's first millionaire athlete, lost $3 million, and cynical New York hotel clerks asked incoming guests, "You want a room for sleeping or jumping?"

By 1932, U.S. manufacturing output had fallen to 54 percent of its 1929 level, and unemployment had risen to between 12 and 15 million workers, or 25 to 30 percent of the workforce. Personal and corporate bankruptcies were common, and two-fifths of the nation's banks failed between 1929 and 1933. The failure of so many banks and the widespread nationwide loss of confidence in the economy led to much lower levels of spending and production, aggravating the downward spiral.

Before the Great Depression, governments traditionally took little action in times of business downturns, relying instead on the market forces to correct the economy. These laissez faire policies could not achieve the needed recovery in the early years of the Great Depression. This painful discovery forced some fundamental changes in the role of government in the U.S. economy. After the Great Depression, government action and policy assumed a central role when the free market economy faltered.

This was true not only in the United States but also in many other free market economies. This increased role of government in the economy took various forms: taxation, industrial regulation (including the insurance of bank deposits), public works, social insurance, social welfare services, deficit spending, and direct government intervention in the market. All of these policies were designed to stabilize the economy and prevent a recurrence of the economic disaster of the Great Depression.

MACROECONOMIC ISSUES

The three main concerns about the health of the economy are inflation, unemployment, and growth. Some policy measures that can tame inflation have undesirable side effects, and some suggested cures for unemployment will be inflationary. These three key macro variables will continue to be our focus from here on. Each chapter will add detail to the models we use, but the basic focus will always be on inflation, growth, and unemployment.

Inflation

Inflation is a rise in the overall price level. If nothing else changes and there is inflation, the dollars you have in your pocket will buy fewer goods. If inflation were completely absent, a 1950 dollar would buy the same goods and services today that your grandfather purchased with it. With a 10 percent annual inflation rate and no other changes, last year's dollar will buy 10 percent fewer goods.

Hyperinflation in Germany

One of the most widely studied periods of inflation occurred in Germany in late 1922 and early 1923, just after World War I. Inflation during the 16 months of this hyperinflation period averaged 322 percent per month. Prices quadrupled each month. People would literally run to the store to buy basic goods before their money lost more value. A can of beans worth 200 marks at the beginning of the month cost 800 marks at the end of the month. People hoarded real goods and tried to get rid of their paper money as soon as possible. Imagine that the stamp on an envelope, which was updated for inflation, was worth more than the check inside to those receiving fixed pensions.

Hyperinflation in Germany is important for our current study. It shows us the importance of controlling inflation to reduce its harmful effects. It also underlines a basic economic principle: People respond to changes in the macro environment. We see the same "flight from paper" whenever there is a period of rapid inflation or the expectation that inflation will soon be rapid. When inflation is strong, firms and consumers transfer their assets from paper money and securities to real or hard goods—food, homes, or gold—to try to maintain the real value of these assets.

One problem with inflation is that it decreases the value of fixed dollar payments. Pensions fixed in their dollar amounts, for example, at $1,000 a month, will continue to be worth $1,000 worth of goods if there is no inflation. With inflation these same pensions lose purchasing power and can buy fewer real goods. The **nominal value** of your paycheck is the number of dollars it is worth. The **real value** is what these dollars can buy in real terms such as loaves of bread or restaurant meals. By controlling inflation, governments are preserving the real value or purchasing power of the currency.

Unemployment

Unemployment is a common result when economic growth slows. Maintaining and increasing employment is one of the major goals of macroeconomic policy. We will examine the toolbox that governments use to maintain and increase employment.

To return to our discussion of the Great Depression, the government approached the problems with a three-pronged scheme to stabilize and protect the economy. This new, more active role took the form of

1. bank and financial sector regulation to require institutions to hold adequate reserves and separate the ownership of financial institutions as well as private business, and mandatory insurance of accounts against loss,

2. a monitoring mechanism to ensure the continual health of the economy, and

3. social policies to protect the unemployed and to tide them over until they could find jobs.

Since the Great Depression, the government's role has become larger. Not only does it act as a regulator in the economy, it also provides and purchases goods and services. An idea of the increase in the government's role in the U.S. economy can be seen in how much more important government spending has become. Total government spending in 1930 accounted for 3.3 percent of GDP. By the year 2000, spending for only one part of total government expenditures—Social Security, Medicare, and Medicaid, was 7.6 percent of GDP.

Today the role of government in the American economy is widespread. It is a regulator of specific industries and manages the overall pace of economic activity, seeking to maintain high levels of employment and stable prices. It uses two main tools: fiscal policy, through which it determines the appropriate level of taxes and spending; and monetary policy, through which it manages the supply of money.

Growth

Growth in the economy refers an increase in the number of goods and services produced. We saw this in earlier chapters as an outward shift of the production possibilities frontier. This is often referred to as increasing the size of the pie. It is also common to view real growth as an increase in national wealth or standard of living.

Maintaining a solid and predictable real growth of the economy is a result that every nation wants to achieve. A rapidly declining economy, as we saw in the Depression and hyperinflation cases, can lead to social chaos and despair.

Economic growth depends on improvements in technology, natural resources, and capital. Capital has two components, human capital—the size, skill, and abilities of the work force—and physical capital in the form of machines and equipment that have a long productive life. Increasing the growth rate of the economy may involve a tax to encourage saving and capital investment, increased government expenditure in basic research, or a major advance in technology.

Whenever we discuss growth, there is a current-versus-future issue. Growth usually has a long-term focus of more than a few years. The issue between current and future periods comes about like this: We may have to reduce today's consumption to increase today's investment so that in the future we will have more productive capability. This is a trade-off that every society faces.

I recall a South American minister of the interior telling his country on TV that "We have to sacrifice now and tighten our belts for the sake of future generations." The next day a cartoon pictured a shoeless peasant holding his hands up in despair, replying to the minister, "I can't tighten my belt, I ate it yesterday."

Supply side policies have as a goal to increase the incentive to work, save, and invest. They have been in U.S. tax reforms beginning in the 1980s and continuing through the 1990s. Their main feature is to reduce the cost of investing in the current economy, which will increase investment and the capacity to supply more goods and services in the future.

Fiscal, monetary, and growth policies are used by the government to maintain a healthy economy. We will look at their interaction and effects on the economy in two ways. The first is to use the circular flow diagram with government and the international sectors added. Another is to look at how these policies affect aggregate demand and aggregate supply.

MAJOR BUILDING BLOCKS: THE CIRCULAR FLOW

To get an overview of the whole economic system, we will look at the four major groups in the macroeconomy: households, firms, the government, and the global economy. We need to include them all to understand the major movements of goods and services, wages, taxes, income, and revenues in the economy. Their interrelationships are also needed to answer basic questions such as: What happens to the economy when imports increase? When government spending increases?

The interrelatedness of all the sectors in the global economy is obvious and has been increasing. When there is a disruption of oil production or a dry season that ruins one country's coffee crop, the rest of the world's economies are affected.

Circular Flow

One of the best ways to understand these complex connections is to examine the circular flow, which now includes the government and the global economy. By adding the government we can now include taxes and government production of goods and services. With the addition of the global economy we can now include the imports and exports of an economy.

In the circular flow, Figure 5.1, we show the money flows as expenditures and receipts. We only show the money flows and not the corresponding goods and services for which they are exchanged. For example, money flows from households to importers, and these imports enter the households as French wines, Italian shoes, and German automobiles. Households also purchase goods and services from domestic firms, but again only the purchases and receipts are shown.

Households earn income both from firms and from the government. Firms pay wages for labor services and interest and dividends on corporate stock. Households also receive payments from the government as wages, interest on bonds, or transfer payments. **Transfer payments** are payments from the government that do not involve an exchange of labor or goods and services. These payments are Social Security benefits, welfare payments, and others. All of these receipts make up the total income received by households.

Household spending, at the upper part of the circular flow, includes purchases from domestic and foreign firms and tax payments to the government. The total of these payments represents total household spending.

Let's look at an example of a household purchase of a bottle of French wine. Money flows to the importer at the top of the diagram, as well as taxes to the government. If it is a bottle of domestic wine, the money flows to the domestic producer.

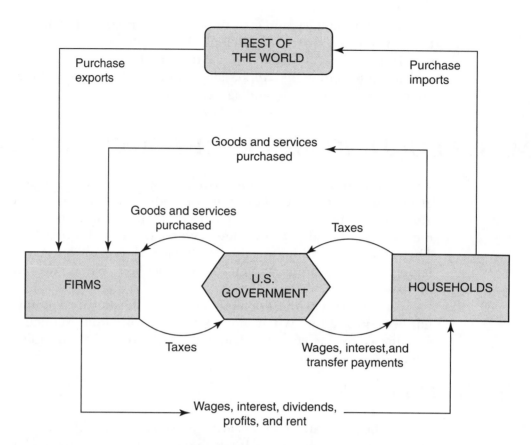

FIGURE 5.1. The complete circular flow.

Adding the rest of the world and the government.

When households save money from their current incomes, it represents a leakage in the circular flow. This money is not spent. Remember that the circular flow shows current expenditures and current income, so savings are monies removed from current consumption. On the other hand, as we will see later, households can spend more than their income through *dissaving* by either drawing down their prior savings or by borrowing. Although this is not shown in the circular flow, it is an important measure that we will return to.

Firms earn revenue from the sale of goods and services to households, from exports, and from sales to the government. Only the revenue from these transactions is shown in the circular flow as flows to firms. At the bottom of the diagram are payments that firms make: to the government in the form of taxes and to households for services.

Look at the government in the center of the circular flow. The government collects taxes from both households and firms. It purchases goods and services from firms and pays wages and transfer payments to households.

The external economy or the rest of the world at the very top of the diagram receives a flow of expenditures from households in the form of payments for imports and sends payments to firms who export.

One of the lessons of the circular flow is that every dollar spent by someone is a dollar received by someone else. This "every transaction has two sides" forms a basis for the way national income accounts and GDP are calculated, as we will see later.

THREE MAJOR MARKETS

The circular flow gives us a simplified overall view of the complete economy. Another view examines the major markets involved in the economy. For each of these markets, there is a foreign or international aspect as well as a domestic one.

The Market for Goods and Services

Goods and services are produced by firms and sold to households and the government. This market also includes services produced by the government, such as roads and highways, and goods produced by firms for sale to other firms, such as factory insurance.

Firms, households, and the government act as buyers in this market. Together they provide the demand for goods and services, whereas firms are the suppliers. The rest of the world also buys and sells in the goods market. The billion of dollars of exports and imports are an important part of the goods market whether the goods are automobiles, agricultural products, robots, or toys.

The Labor Market

Households sell labor services to firms and to the government. They form the supply side of the market, whereas the demand side, the employers, are firms and the government.

The international economy has become more important in domestic labor markets because jobs and their locations can now move very quickly to lower-wage countries. This has been especially true since the 1990s.

We see this more vividly on the supply side, where many countries now have large increases in illegal immigration and large guest worker populations that have made immigration policy a political football. Legal immigration numbers have significantly increased for many countries. It was recently reported that in the 2 years from 2004 to 2006, more than 600,000 eastern European immigrants took up residency in the United Kingdom. This level of immigration and the movement of jobs from country to country will be one of the major international political and economic concerns for the next decade.

The Money Market

Financial or money markets have also become global. Households are on both sides of the money market. They demand or borrow funds from the money market and supply funds to the money market by holding savings accounts and certificates of deposit (CDs) and by purchasing stocks and bonds from firms and from the government.

The government borrows by issuing Treasury bonds, notes, or bills in exchange for money. Firms borrow funds for the construction of new facilities and for other purposes. Firms also borrow by issuing corporate bonds and selling stock. Much of the borrowing and lending is coordinated by financial intermediaries, commercial banks, savings and loan institutions, and insurance companies. As intermediaries, they borrow from some and lend to others.

Interest rates act like prices in the money market whether they are interest rates on 30-year home mortgages, on overnight CDs, or on money market accounts. How interest rates are determined and their role in the macroeconomy will be an important subject for later discussion.

MICROECONOMICS AND MACROECONOMICS

The methodology of macroeconomics is the same as the methodology of microeconomics, only we are looking at aggregates: total output in the U.S. economy and not the total output of corn or oil. We will still use supply and demand (but they are aggregate supply and aggregate demand). As always, there will be trade-offs that have to be made, and we will have to understand the adjustments to a new equilibrium after a significant change.

Macroeconomics is the study of the economy as a whole. Its focus is on the big picture. We will combine or aggregate all the individual consumers, the firms or producers, and the government to arrive at the total demand for goods and services. This total or **aggregate demand** represents the demand in the whole economy. We also combine all of the producers' outputs to determine **aggregate supply**. There will be an equilibrium for the entire economy, but because these outputs and products and services are from different industries, we cannot use individual prices. Instead we will use the **overall price level**. An increase in the overall price level is inflation.

We want to be able to analyze the effects of an increase in European Union (EU) steel exports on the whole economy. Suppose there is a large increase in these imports. In the macro case we examine the effects on inflation, whereas in the micro case we analyze the effects on the price of automobiles and on employment in the U.S. auto industry.

This wider scope of macroeconomics means that we will be dealing with national income and not household income, and with the national price level and not an individual market price level. It is not the demand for coal miners and employment in the coal industry but the demand for labor in the whole economy and overall U.S. employment.

In terms of policy we will be examining the role of government in managing the economy and setting tax rates, not the effects of a specific tax on wheat.

We have the same behavioral assumptions: A higher price means that less is demanded, whether it is automobiles or aggregate output. In other words, the demand curve is negatively sloped: As inflation increases, aggregate quantity demanded declines.

REVIEW QUESTIONS

Add the word or words that correctly complete each of the following statements.

1. _____ economics is the study of the entire economy and its health.

2. _____ is a rise in the overall price level.

3. The _____ value of your paycheck is the number of dollars it is worth.

4. The _____ value of your paycheck is what those dollars can buy in real terms, such as restaurant meals.

5. When an economy _____, more goods and services are produced.

6. The _____ flow gives us a simplified overall view of the complete economy.

7. The methodology of macroeconomics is the same as the methodology of _____.

8. Three major markets—goods and services, labor, and money—make up the _____.

9. A _____ price means that less is demanded whether it is automobile market or total output.

10. _____ is concerned with the overall price level, not individual market prices.

Circle the letter of the item that correctly completes each of the following statements.

1. Macroeconomics is the study of
   a. how different markets like furniture and lumber interact.
   b. individual markets and their supply and demand.
   c. how goods can be substituted for one another.
   d. growth, the inflation rate, and the level of unemployment.

2. Government action and policy assumed a central role in the United States
   a. after the Great Depression.
   b. after World War II, when the free market economy faltered.
   c. after President Woodrow Wilson died.
   d. after World War I.

3. Inflation
    a. occurs when the economy becomes overheated.
    b. is a measure of how strong the economy is.
    c. is the increase in the price of a car.
    d. is a rise in the overall price level.

4. The nominal value of your $1,000 paycheck
    a. is the number of dollars it is worth.
    b. is what the paycheck will buy.
    c. depends on the interest rate.
    d. depends on your income.

5. The real value of a paycheck
    a. depends on your income.
    b. is what those dollars can buy, such as loaves of bread or restaurant meals.
    c. depends on your savings.
    d. depends on the interest rate.

6. Supply-side policies have as their goal
    a. to increase the supply of goods and services.
    b. to balance the increases in demand so there is no inflation.
    c. to increase the incentive to work, save, and invest.
    d. to reduce dependence on foreign supplies of oil.

7. The circular flow gives us
    a. an idea of how the government budget is spent.
    b. a simplified overall view of the complete economy.
    c. an overview of the microeconomy.
    d. an overview of the trade-offs in a large economy.

8. In the circular flow,
    a. firms, households, and the government are buyers in the goods market.
    b. only firms and households are buyers in the goods market.
    c. the government collects only taxes.
    d. each sector has one specific role.

9. In the circular flow,
    a. households exchange only money for goods.
    b. every party buys and sells.
    c. firms exchange only products for money.
    d. only the government collects taxes

10. In macroeconomics, we focus on aggregate
    a. output in the U.S. economy.
    b. output of corn oil.
    c. output of education.
    d. prices and output in manufacturing.

ANSWERS TO FILL-IN QUESTIONS

1. Macro
2. Inflation
3. nominal
4. real
5. grows
6. circular
7. microeconomics
8. macroeconomy
9. higher
10. Macroeconomics

ANSWERS TO MULTIPLE-CHOICE QUESTIONS

1. **d.** This is the definition.
2. **a.** Fear of the Great Depression happening again brought macroeconomic and government policies into a central role.
3. **d.** This is the definition.
4. **a.** Nominal values are not adjusted for inflation.
5. **b.** This is the definition.
6. **c.** Supply-side polices are focused on lowering tax rates and interest rates to stimulate the economy.
7. **b.** Portrays all of the markets and groups in the economy in one diagram.
8. **a.** These three groups are the main domestic buyers.
9. **b.** This highlights the fact that all groups are involved in these two exchanges.
10. **a.** Macroeconomics looks at the whole economy not at individual markets.

CHAPTER 6

NATIONAL INCOME

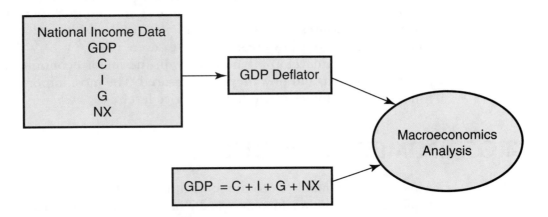

National income and its growth provide the national context in which individuals and companies can prosper or stagnate. Much of the economic world is beyond the control of the individual, and sound decisions made for an expanding economy can be ruinous in a declining economy.

How healthy is the economy? We rely on several measures to help determine its health. These measures have to be aggregate or macro measurements that can tell us how much is produced. We are also interested in how much is earned, consumed, saved, and invested. We want to be able to explain what causes national incomes to rise and fall and economies to grow and decline.

The expression, "A rising tide lifts all boats" describes how everyone benefits when the economy is booming. Overall economic changes are widely reported in the financial and general press because they influence all of us. Total income, unemployment, inflation, trade balances, and the deficit are all **macroeconomic** statistics because they tell us about the entire economy.

MBA enrollments typically increase during lulls or contractions in the growth of the economy and decline during periods of rapid growth. Potential students find the cost of new job opportunities lost to be much lower when national income is contracting, and this encourages them to enroll. As we saw in the last chapter, expansion of the economy means that more goods and services are being produced and that employment is increasing, making it easier for recent graduates to find employment as companies expand.

Because changes in the overall health of the economy affect all of us, economic conditions and forecasts are widely reported and analyzed. A look at the business section of a newspaper quickly tests our ability to understand jargon and terminology of the macroeconomics may include national income, consumer confidence, the latest unemployment figures, or trade deficits. This chapter analyzes the measurement of national income and how the component parts relate to each other. A statement such as "GDP increased by 4 percent over the last quarter" has implications for how successful our individual plans for improvement or starting a new business might be.

If the economy is expanding, how do we measure this expansion? The expansions or contractions of the economy are reported with many other economic statistics. We often need to combine several measures and analyze them together. For example, there is a significant difference between a 4 percent increase in GDP with no inflation and the same increase in GDP with inflation. Because GDP measures the total income of everyone in the economy and the price level measures the rate of inflation, they could cancel each other out. There could be no gain in real income, or even a loss.

We need to develop a familiarity with the major economic statistics, how they are reported, and how they are measured. The most important of these statistics are gross domestic product and price level.

GROSS DOMESTIC PRODUCT

A measure of a family's economic health is the level of income that it enjoys. Families with a higher income usually have a higher standard of living. This is also true for nations. A nation with a higher income can afford to purchase and consume more and enjoys a higher standard of living, including better housing, health care, and automobiles.

Gross domestic product measures both total income and the total expenditure of everyone in the economy. Remember the circular flow in Figure 3.3 that gave a simple overview of the transactions in an economy? On the left side of the flow we tracked revenues, and on the right side we tracked expenditures or spending. GDP remains the same whether we track it from the revenue side or from the expenditure side. Because the economy is viewed as a closed system, all of the expenditures must equal all of the receipts. We will find this same equality of flows built into national income accounts and our models.

Each transaction has a buyer who spends money and a seller who earns income. If Don buys a $100 book, Don's expenditures rise by $100 and the bookstore receipts increase by $100. GDP goes up by $100 whether measured by total expenditures or by total receipts.

Of course the economy is much more complicated than the circular flow. Households don't spend all of their income; they pay some to the government in taxes, and they save some for the future. Households are not the sole purchasers of goods and services. The government is a large buyer. Some goods are bought by firms who want to use them for future production. But since every transaction in the whole economy has a buyer and a seller, total income always equals total expenditures.

Calculating GDP

Gross domestic product is the market value of all final goods and services produced within a country in a given period of time.

It is the favorite measure for comparing different economies and their standards of living. GDP is also the common measure of the development or growth of an economy. Although it has a simple definition, there are many subtleties and important concepts behind the words. It is called gross domestic product partly because it makes no allowance for purchases that are replacing worn-out items. In addition, GDP excludes illegal purchases such as drugs and black market goods and goods that never enter the marketplace.

Goods and services produced in the home are not included, so groceries bought at the supermarket are part of GDP but home-grown vegetables are not. Work performed by family members in the home such as cleaning, cooking, and mowing their own lawn is not part of GDP. If the family hires a maid and a neighborhood kid with a lawnmower, these payments are part of GDP. This does not mean that family work in the home has no value; it means that this value is not calculated into GDP.

We will take each phrase in the GDP definition separately.

Market value means that the goods and services exchanged are valued at market prices. An item that is twice as expensive contributes twice as much to GDP.

All goods and services refer to everything that is sold legally in the marketplace. This includes most purchases such as apples, a new computer, rental of an apartment, and food and groceries.

Final goods are included, and intermediate goods are not. Goods in process are **intermediate goods**, not final goods. For example, a computer chip is an intermediate good in the production of a Dell computer, a final good. The value of the intermediate good is already included in the value of the final good. An exception to this occurs if the chip, an intermediate good, is held in inventory and not sold. When it is sold, it is counted as a final good; otherwise it is counted as "investment" in inventory.

Goods and services include tangible goods such as telephones, books, and ice cream and intangible services such as doctor visits and movie tickets. Watching a concert is an intangible service, and buying the CD is a tangible good.

Produced means currently produced and not produced in an earlier period. This excludes all sales of used homes and cars, as well as eBay transactions.

Within a country refers to production within a country. It is where the production occurs, not who owns the company, that matters. If a Brazilian company produces and sells a CD in this country, it is counted in the U.S. GDP. If the CD is made in a factory in Rio owned by an American company, it is not counted as a part of U.S. GDP.

In a given period of time is usually a quarter or a year. When GDP is reported based on the latest quarter (3 months), it is usually reported as GDP "at an annual rate." It is the quarterly flow of income and expenditures multiplied by 4. This is typically done as a convenience to be able to compare yearly figures.

Seasonal adjustments are always made—whenever you see GDP figures, they are always adjusted for seasonal patterns, and when they are, they are always labeled as seasonally adjusted annual rates. Because such a large volume of sales takes place in the fourth quarter, which includes Thanksgiving and Christmas, the fourth-quarter GDP would seriously exaggerate annual GDP if it wasn't seasonally adjusted.

Components of GDP

There are as many kinds of spending in the economy as there are spenders. At any given time, people are paying their phone bills, having an anniversary brunch, hiring a musician to perform for a corporate event, buying an airplane to carry soldiers, or purchasing a pair of Italian shoes.

To capture all of these purchase categories and to understand to composition of GDP, economists use the following model, where GDP is gross domestic product or **Y**, **C** is consumption, **I** stands for investment, **G** is government purchases, and **NX** represents net exports.

$$Y \equiv C + I + G + NX$$

The model for GDP is expressed as an identity ($\equiv$) or an equation that must be true by definition. Probably the most well-known identity involves debits and credits on a balance sheet. The GDP equation shares this form. We will look at the parts one by one.

CONSUMPTION, C

Consumption is household spending on goods and services not including new housing. It is the largest component of GDP and accounts for about 70 percent of all GDP. Because of this dominance, consumer spending gets a lot of attention. We look at many different measures such as consumer spending plans, consumer confidence, employment expectations, and saving rates.

INVESTMENT, I

Investment is the purchase of goods and services that will be used in the future, not in the current period. It is the total of capital equipment such as machines, inventories, and structures. By convention, the purchase of a new house produced this year is treated as an investment and included in this category because the homeowner will enjoy a flow of housing services over future periods.

Inventory accumulation occurs when Dell purchases a microchip that is not sold in a finished computer and instead is held in inventory. Because the chip was purchased, it has to appear in the expenditure accounts, and because it was not sold, its value is treated as an investment.

Later we will see the important role that inventories play as a buffer in the economy. Inventory accumulation beyond what was expected is a leading indicator that the economy is slowing down. On the other hand, inventory depletion at faster rates than expected is a sign that the economy is gaining momentum.

GOVERNMENT PURCHASES, G

Government purchases are expenditures of state, local, and federal governments. The measure includes spending on goods and services, paper and pencils, public roads, and staff salaries. Payments made for labor services that are made in the current period are treated as wage expenditures and government purchases. The president's salary falls in this category. The government also pays for prior period labor services and calls these **transfer payments.** An example of transfer payments is Social Security. Because transfer payments are not compensation for work done in the current period, they are not counted in GDP.

NET EXPORTS, NX

Net exports is exports minus imports. Because of GDP, gross *domestic* product, the products exported must be produced here and the purchasers of imports must live here. For example, cotton produced in Alabama and sold overseas is an export produced here and sold to an overseas buyer. If more cotton is sold overseas than before, net exports will increase.

A Mercedes made in Germany and sold here is an example of an import. The more Mercedes purchased by Americans, the lower net exports will be.

Because imports are deducted from exports to arrive at net exports, they are not included elsewhere in GDP. When a household or firm buys goods or services from abroad, the purchase lowers net exports but also increases **C**, **I**, or **G** by the same amount. Changes in import purchases do not affect the GDP calculation.

Nominal Versus Real GDP

If GDP is increasing without inflation, then the output of goods and services has increased. If the production of goods and services stays the same but is sold at higher prices, GDP will also increase, but the reason for the rise is the increase in prices not output. Remember that GDP market value depends on the price level. GDP will increase if either or both total output and price level increase.

What we want is a measure of real change, not change influenced by fluctuations in the price level. If you are earning more money this year but it buys only half the goods and services you could buy last year, your have lost real purchasing power. If we are producing the same number of TVs but prices have doubled, GDP will increase solely because of inflation.

Nominal GDP is the quantity of goods and services produced, as valued at current market prices. Real GDP takes changes in price level into account. Real GDP uses nominal GDP and evaluates it using prices that are fixed at a past, base-year level. In this way real GDP represents how the economy's overall production of goods and services has changed over time. It is the real GDP, and movements in it determine whether firms are hiring or firing and whether the economy is expanding or contracting.

Real GDP is the amount of production of goods and services valued at base year prices. It is growth in real GDP that is the goal of most countries. Real growth as a goal depends on policies aimed at controlling inflation. To compare one country's growth with another, the comparison is usually made in terms of real GDP per capita. Remember that real GDP holds prices constant at base year levels, so that real GDP reflects only the quantities produced.

The **GDP deflator**, used to calculate real GDP, is calculated as

$$\text{GDP deflator} = \frac{\text{nominal GDP}}{\text{real GDP}} \times 100$$

The GDP deflator measures the current level of prices relative to the prices in the base year. An example will help us understand how this works.

Suppose that the price level is the same and that the only change in nominal GDP occurs because production has increased. In this case both nominal and real GDP move together and the GDP deflator is constant. Suppose on the other hand that production has stayed exactly the same and prices have increased. In this case, nominal GDP has increased and real GDP has stayed the same. The increase in the price level will be reflected in the rise in the GDP deflator.

Because the quantities of output in the calculation remain the same under all circumstances, the GDP deflator always measures price changes.

Real GDP as a Measure of Recession

Real GDP is also the measure used to examine periods of recession and expansion. During the Depression, real GDP fell by about 30 percent from 1929 to 1933.

Over the last 30 years or so, real U.S. GDP has shown a steady increase with fluctuations around an upward trend. This long-term growth in real GDP averages about 3 percent per year. There are fluctuations around the long-term trend—recessions and expansions as GDP growth responds and adjusts to new circumstances.

Real GDP as a Measure of Standard of Living

GDP measures both total expenditures and total income. Expenditures for goods and services on a per-capita basis show the ability to purchase goods and services by the average citizen. Real GDP/capita comparisons across countries provide a measure of relative economic well-being. Real GDP per capita ranges from about $40,000 per Swiss citizen to about $80 per Mali citizen.

Many noneconomic indicators follow roughly the same pattern as GDP/capita when we compare countries. For example, countries with higher GDP per capita tend to have longer life expectancies and higher literacy rates.

REVIEW QUESTIONS

Add the word or words that correctly complete each of the following statements.

1. Gross domestic product (GDP) measures both total income and the total _____ of everyone in the economy.

2. Gross domestic product is the _____ value of all final goods and services produced within a country in a given period of time.

3. Whenever you see GDP figures, they are always adjusted for _____ patterns.

4. _____ is the purchase of goods and services that will be used in future periods.

5. _____ purchases are expenditures of the state, local, and federal governments.

6. Net exports is exports _____ imports.

7. A Mercedes made in Germany and sold here is an example of an _____.

8. _____ GDP is the quantity of goods and services produced, valued at current market prices.

9. It is the _____ GDP and movements in it that determine whether firms are hiring or firing and the economy is expanding or contracting.

10. The GDP _____ measures the current level of prices relative to the prices in the base year.

11. _____ GDP/capita comparisons across countries provide a measure of relative economic well-being.

Circle the letter of the item that correctly completes each of the following statements.

1. Gross domestic product (GDP) measures
   a. everything that is bought and sold in the United States.
   b. everything that is bought and sold in the United States that is produced here.
   c. the total expenditures of everyone in the economy.
   d. both total income and the total expenditures of everyone in the economy.

2. GDP is the market value of all final goods and services produced
    a. and sold within a country.
    b. and includes investment goods.
    c. within a country in a given period of time.
    d. and consumed within a country.

3. GDP is
    a. always seasonally adjusted.
    b. always in real terms.
    c. always measured on the same day.
    d. never seasonally adjusted.

4. Investment is the purchase of goods and services
    a. to be used in the future as well as in the current period.
    b. that are sold inside the border.
    c. that have a productive period of more than 10 years.
    d. that have a productive period of more than 15 years.

5. Transfer payments, such as Social Security,
    a. are counted in GDP.
    b. are not counted in GDP.
    c. are included in government spending.
    d. are counted in total expenditures.

6. If more U.S. cotton is sold overseas than before,
    a. net exports will increase.
    b. net exports will decrease.
    c. net exports will not change.
    d. the trade surplus will decline.

7. The more Mercedes cars Americans purchase, the
    a. higher net exports.
    b. lower imports.
    c. higher the price.
    d. lower net exports.

ANSWERS TO FILL-IN QUESTIONS

1. expenditures
2. market
3. seasonal
4. investment
5. Government
6. minus
7. import
8. Nominal
9. real
10. deflator
11. Real

ANSWERS TO MULTIPLE-CHOICE QUESTIONS

1. **d.** This is the accounting identity that shows that everyone's purchase is someone else's receipt.
2. **c.** The key here is that it is a flow, that is for a given period of time
3. **a.** Because there is so much seasonal variation, GDP is always seasonally adjusted.
4. **a.** Investments give a flow of services over periods. That is why a home purchase is considered an investment.
5. **b.** This is because they do not represent earnings in the current period.
6. **a.** Net exports is exports minus imports, and exports have increased.
7. **d.** Imports have increased, lowering net exports.

CHAPTER 7

MEASURING UNEMPLOYMENT AND INFLATION

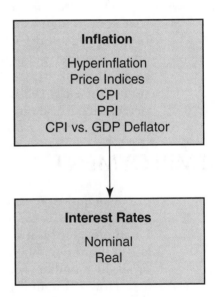

Unemployment

Labor Force Participation Rates
Frictional and Structural
Natural
Costs

Inflation

Hyperinflation
Price Indices
CPI
PPI
CPI vs. GDP Deflator

Interest Rates

Nominal
Real

Periods of recession and slow growth are related to unemployment levels. We now turn our attention to unemployment and inflation measures, two important indices of the health of a nation. We will discuss recessions, expansions, and some rough times. In later chapters, we will dissect this big picture and set up the basic macroeconomic tools we use to model these important concepts.

Recessions and more severe depressions are considered harmful because they are associated with declining output, increasing unemployment, and a falling standard of living. On the other hand, real economic growth per capita means that our standard of living is improving.

After a brief discussion of recessions, we will discuss unemployment and inflation measures and how they are calculated.

RECESSIONS

A **recession** is commonly defined as a period where real GDP declines for two or more consecutive quarters. It is usually accompanied by rising unemployment and falling output. When fewer goods and services are produced, fewer inputs are used, there is some idle capacity, less capital stock is being used and fewer people are employed. Because the measure is real GDP, a recession also means that the standard of living has declined because there are fewer goods and services produced than before. A decline in real output also means a decline in real income.

A much more severe problem occurs in a **depression**, which is defined as a long, deep recession. The length is in years, and the effects are more severe. There is no commonly accepted definition of a depression, but most observers agree that there have been only two in the United States in the last hundred years, the Great Depression that began in 1929 and included the stock market crash, and the milder recession from 1979 to 1982.

The Great Depression, mentioned in Chapter 5, had unemployment rates that went as high as 25 percent of the labor force in 1933. Real output declined between 1929 and 1933 by about 30 percent. A shock of this magnitude brought about the first major macroeconomic policies to prevent it from happening again. In contrast, the highest annual rate of unemployment in the long recession of the early 1980s was 9.7 percent in 1982, and real output declined only 0.2 percent from 1980 to 1982.

UNEMPLOYMENT

Unemployment and the unemployment rate are the key measures of economic health that are widely reported and watched for signs of change. Unemployment is a sign of a weak economy and one that is not fully utilized. It is also more personally felt than just a statistic. We know and see friends laid off or family members without jobs.

How is unemployment defined? The unemployment rate is the percentage of the labor force that is unemployed.

$$\text{Unemployment rate} = \frac{\text{number of unemployed}}{\text{labor force}} \times 100$$

The **labor force** is defined as those adults (older than 16 years of age) who are actively seeking or have jobs. This is not the same as the population, which includes all those younger than 16 as well as many who are not seeking employment. The labor force includes adults who are employed and those who are unemployed.

To be counted as **unemployed**, you must be an unemployed adult who is actively seeking work.

The **unemployment rate** is the number of unemployed workers divided by the entire labor force and multiplied by 100 to get a percentage rate.

Many adults are not in the labor force and are not seeking jobs. The **labor force participation rate** is used to measure how much of the adult population is in the labor force. It is the number of those in the labor force divided by the total population. A relatively low labor force participation rate occurs in some countries such as Italy, where the overall labor force participation rate has historically been among the lowest in Europe.

A 50 percent labor force participation rate means that of all those older than 16 years, half are employed or unemployed and seeking employment. More importantly it means that half of the population older than 16 is not working and is not seeking work.

The labor force participation rate varies a great deal within any nation. In most countries women have lower labor force participation rates than men. In the United States the male labor force participation rate is in the high-80's percentile, whereas the female rate is above 70 percent and climbing.

The rates vary across countries. For example, US and Scandinavian women have labor force participation rates above 70 percent whereas Turkish women have less than half that participation rate. Labor force participation rates increase with education, both across groups and within groups. American women with a higher education have higher labor force participation rates than American women with an average education.

The unemployment rate is an average rate over the entire economy and masks a lot of variation in unemployment, which varies widely by demographic group, industry, and region. The most important of these unemployment differences are those based on regions and demographics. For example, among African-American teenagers, the unemployment rates for the 1982 recession were 52.4 percent for males and 46.3 percent for females. The overall unemployment rate was 9.7 percent.

Lots of variation is also seen on a regional or industry basis, as particular parts of the economy respond differently to a downturn. In the 1982 recession, for example, some states had state unemployment rates of more than 15 percent, whereas the lowest state rate of unemployment was 6.9 percent.

Being unemployed for long periods of time can discourage workers from seeking employment, and they drop out of the labor force. Unemployed workers who stop looking for a job drop out of the labor force altogether. This is called the **discouraged worker effect**. Discouraged workers who leave the labor force increase the measured unemployment rate. If 10 fishermen are unemployed and 90 are employed, the total labor force is 100 and the unemployment rate for fishermen is 10 percent. If 9 of the fishermen become discouraged and leave the labor force, the unemployment rate is now calculated as 1 unemployed to 91 total labor force for an unemployment rate of 11 percent.

Costs of Unemployment

In the Humphrey–Hawkins Act (1978) Congress formally established a specific target rate of 4 percent unemployment. Why is this a policy objective and why is it 4 percent and not 0 percent?

Some unemployment is natural in a dynamic economy that shifts and grows. More jobs are available in the high-tech sector and fewer in agriculture, for example. There are also new entrants such as recent graduates seeking employment for the first time. Until they get a job, these new graduates are classified as unemployed. Also unemployed are those who are switching jobs—for example, someone leaving a sales position and looking for an administrative job. This portion of the unemployment that is due to the normal workings of the labor market is called **frictional unemployment**. It can never be zero because the economy is constantly changing. Some industries and regions grow and others decline. A sales person leaving the upper Midwest to find a job in the same field in California is part of the frictionally unemployed. Frictional unemployment usually lasts for a relatively short period, from a few weeks to 6 months or so, because it takes time to locate a new position.

Structural unemployment is longer-term unemployment due to a change in the structure of the economy. Some jobs will be permanently lost in certain industries. Many countries have experienced a large decline in the number of persons employed in agriculture as they have become industrialized and modernized. Workers who are displaced from agriculture and have not found jobs in the nonagricultural sector are structurally unemployed. For many, their skills are obsolete and do not fit the current economy.

Economists use the term **natural rate of unemployment** to reflect the natural state of the economy as it shifts and grows. It is usually a combination of frictional and structural unemployment. It is "natural" in two senses: It is the expected result of a dynamic economy, and it is **not** related to recessionary or expansionary periods. If there were no current expansion or contraction in the economy, we would still see the natural rate of unemployment. Estimates of the natural rate of unemployment for the United States are in the 5 to 6 percent range.

It is in the context of the natural rate of unemployment that the 4 percent target rate of unemployment chosen by Congress makes sense.

Unemployment usually increases in business downturns. Unemployment related to a business cycle downturn is called **cyclical unemployment**. This unemployment is expected to disappear when the business cycle improves. This means that in a recession unemployment rises above the natural rate but returns to it once the economy comes out of the recession.

INFLATION

Inflation is a general increase in the price level that is measured across all goods and services produced by the economy.

Is inflation harmful? If your wages remain fixed and there is inflation, you will lose purchasing power and can buy fewer goods and services with your wages. If your wages increase exactly the same as inflation, the effect could be neutral. To be perfectly neutral, where there is no harm and no benefit, the exact bundle of goods and services you purchase will have to be purchasable with your newly increased wages. If you think about it, you will realize how difficult this is to achieve. At the same time, you will realize how difficult it is to calculate inflation and to remove its effects. The opposite of inflation is **deflation**, a decrease in the overall price level.

Hyperinflation is a rapid increase in the overall price level that continues over a significant period. Remember our discussion about hyperinflation in Germany, where prices were rising so quickly that checks mailed out to pensioners were worthless by the time they arrived and people were trying to convert all of their money into goods as quickly as possible to preserve its value.

We saw that efforts to preserve the real value of income cause people to switch from holding paper assets like money to holding real assets that will appreciate with the inflation. This "flight from paper" is a common reaction by individuals and firms during rapid inflation.

Remember that we are using the overall price level and that it is a composite. Some prices may go up more than the average and some less than the average increase in price level increase of 5 percent. If you purchase only items that have increased in price, you will be worse off if your nominal wages have not risen an equal or greater amount.

PRICE INDICES

Economists use price indices to measure overall price levels. The price index that covers all the goods and services produced in the economy is called the GDP price index, which we discussed in the last chapter.

The **Consumer Price Index (CPI)** is the most popular index used to measure a the cost of a typical "market basket" of goods and services that consumers buy. It is calculated for the United States and for major metropolitan areas. What goods and services to include in this typical bundle is first determined by extensive surveys at the Bureau of Labor Statistics. Categories include housing, food, and transportation among the major purchase categories. Prices are then found for this basket of items for each time period. For one component as an example, the survey finds out the cost of housing for three different years. The cost of the whole basket is then calculated for the different time periods. The final step is to figure out a base year and compute how the cost of the basket has changed since then.

For example, if the CPI is 125 percent this year and last year is the base period, it means that prices have risen 25 percent since last year.

A similar index that follows the same method is the **Producer's Price Index (PPI)**, which looks at goods and services such as electricity, labor, and insurance that are purchased by firms. Because firms eventually pass their costs on to consumers who buy the finished goods, many observers use the PPI as a predictor of what will happen to the CPI later on. The main advantage of watching the PPI is that it can capture increases in prices earlier in time than the CPI, and for this reason the PPI is considered a leading indicator of future inflation.

Both the CPI and the PPI have some calculation and interpretation problems based on how the indices are constructed. **Substitution bias** occurs when consumers substitute cheaper goods for goods that have risen more in price. Because the measures use a fixed basket of goods, the calculated index overstates what consumers are actually spending. Suppose that the food part of the basket is fixed with a weight or portion for frozen vegetables and a weight for fresh vegetables. If the price of frozen vegetables is relatively cheaper this year than last, consumers will buy more frozen vegetables. The calculated CPI, however, will use the base-year proportions of frozen to fresh vegetables, and therefore overstate what consumers are spending on vegetables.

A second problem with these indices is that they do not include the introduction of **new products** this year that were not available in the base year. The availability of downloadable music at a lower cost than purchasing a CD reduces the cost of listening to recorded music. This reduction in expenditure does not appear in the CPI until it is updated to include downloadable music in its basket of goods.

The third problem is that the **quality** of the goods in the basket may increase and will not be measured. Higher-quality goods that consumers buy that are in the index based on a lower quality will overstate the cost of living. Continual adjustments to account for higher-quality items in the basket are incorporated as the index changes.

Consumers, especially in the last few years, have migrated to nontraditional outlets such as the internet for some of their shopping. When consumers switch to lower-priced outlets, this is called **outlet substitution**. The current assumptions are that all of the these price differences reflect quality-of-service differences. To the extent that this is not true, these price reductions overlook one source of a price decline.

Studies have shown that the upward bias in the CPI is about 1.1 percent per year because of the four factors noted above. By far the most important of the group are the introduction of new products and quality changes.

The GDP Deflator and the CPI

The GDP deflator, which we introduced in Chapter 6, is another measure of overall prices in the economy. The GDP deflator calculates current prices compared to prices in the base year.

The most important difference between the CPI and the GDP deflator is that the GDP deflator covers only goods and services produced domestically, whereas the CPI includes all goods and services purchased by consumers. Consumer import purchases are therefore part of the CPI but not part of the GDP deflator.

Consumer purchases of oil, most of which is imported and sold at the gasoline pump will be a much larger share of expenses in the CPI than in the GDP deflator. Fluctuations in the price of oil will be reflected in the CPI more than in the GDP. Because the CPI includes energy prices, which can be relatively volatile, recent focus has been on a measure of inflation called **core inflation**, that is, the CPI excluding the cost of food and energy.

Another difference between the CPI and the GDP deflator is that the GDP deflator measures the current basket of goods and services actually purchased and is not based on a fixed historical basket. The GDP basket changes automatically each year. This does not cause major differences in the two indices except when prices do not change proportionally. In that case, the fixed weights of the CPI exert undue influence. Remember that the CPI includes only changes in the prices of consumer goods. It does *Not* include changes in the prices of capital goods or military equipment, which are included in the GDP deflator.

For the most part, the CPI and the GDP deflator show a similar pattern of price changes over a long period of years. They mostly move together.

CORRECTING FOR THE EFFECTS OF INFLATION

The purpose of measuring the price level in different periods is to be able to see the underlying real changes in the economy. If inflation adjustments are not made we get a false picture of the real economy, real production, and practically any other measure made in different time periods.

What was the highest grossing movie picture of all time? The answer depends on whether the receipts are adjusted for inflation or not. *Titanic* seems like the clear winner. It was released in 1998 and has grossed roughly $1.98 billion. However, if you adjust for the effects of inflation, *Titanic* drops to number 5 in the rankings and *Gone with the Wind* becomes the highest grossing film in history, after adjusting for inflation, with a world wide gross of $2.69 billion. Comparing unadjusted prices, revenues, or costs in different years can give very different results than when inflation adjustments are made.

Because of the presence of inflation, many contracts have indices for inflation so that real values are preserved over the life of the contract. Many wage agreements have **cost of living allowances** (COLAs), based on the CPI. Social Security payments are also automatically adjusted for the effects of inflation so that recipients can buy the same amount of real goods and services this year as they did 2 years ago.

REAL AND NOMINAL INTEREST RATES

Interest rates are an important economic variable. Interest payments always involve different time periods. Depositing cash today in an interest-bearing account will give you the balance plus the interest next year. Earning 13 percent a year interest on your savings account means that at the end of the year $1,000 deposited today will grow to $1,013 and you will earn $13. Are you any better off than you were a year ago?

You have $13 more than you did a year ago, so you certainly have more money. If prices have risen by less than 13 percent, you are better off than you were. If inflation was more than 13 percent, you have lost purchasing power.

The **nominal interest rate** is the interest rate you earn or have to pay. It is the interest rate that is typically reported in the press or financial news and is reported without taking inflation into consideration. In the above example of the savings account, 13 percent is the nominal interest rate. The **real interest rate** is the nominal interest rate minus the rate of inflation:

Real interest rate = nominal interest rate – rate of inflation

In our savings account example if the rate of inflation is 13 percent, the real interest rate will be zero, and you will not gain or lose purchasing power with the funds in the savings account.

Sometimes the difference between the nominal rate and the rate of inflation can be quite large, making the real interest rate negative. For a 7-year period beginning in 1975, real interest rates were negative in California. The rate of inflation was greater than the nominal interest rate. For home buyers, this meant that the appreciation in the value of a new home due to inflation more than compensated for the interest rate costs of loans to buy the home. During this period, a record number of second homes were purchased in California to take advantage of this negative real interest rate.

Because inflation decreases the purchasing power of the dollar, it is very important to consider dollar figures from different time periods as dollar figures that do not reflect changes in the purchasing power of the dollar. Today's dollar is not the same as the dollar of 20 years ago.

REVIEW QUESTIONS

Add the word or words that correctly complete each of the following statements.

1. The unemployment rate is the percentage of the _____ that is unemployed.

2. The labor force is _____ than the population.

3. Discouraged workers who stop looking for a job are _____ counted as part of the labor force.

4. Those who are unemployed because of the normal workings of the labor market are the source of _____ unemployment. This can never be zero because the economy is not completely labor efficient.

5. _____ unemployment is longer-term unemployment due to change in the structure of the economy

6. Economists use the term _____ rate of unemployment to reflect a normal state of the economy as it shifts and grows.

7. The _____ is the most popular index used to measure the cost of a typical "market basket" of goods and services that consumers buy.

8. A problem with price indices is that they do not allow for changes in _____.

9. The _____ Index looks at the goods and services that are purchased by firms.

10. The nominal interest rate is the interest rate that _____ consider inflation.

Circle the letter of the item that correctly completes each of the following statements.

1. A recession is commonly defined as a period where real GDP
   a. declines by 10 percent or more.
   b. declines by 15 percent or more.
   c. declines for one quarter.
   d. declines for two or more consecutive quarters.

2. The unemployment rate is the percentage of the
   a. population that is unemployed.
   b. labor force that is unemployed.
   c. population that is looking for work.
   d. population that is actively seeking work.

3. When unemployed workers stop looking for a job and drop out of the labor force altogether, this is called
   a. the discouraged worker effect.
   b. unemployment.
   c. cyclical unemployment.
   d. structural unemployment.

4. When workers are switching jobs, for example, leaving a sales position to look for an administrative job, this is called
   a. frictional unemployment.
   b. structural unemployment.
   c. cyclical unemployment.
   d. baseline unemployment.

5. The natural rate of unemployment is represents a combination of
   a. discouraged workers and cyclical unemployment.
   b. frictional and structural unemployment.
   c. structural and cyclical unemployment.
   d. frictional and cyclical unemployment.

6. The Consumer Price Index (CPI) measures the cost of
   a. a typical "market basket" of goods and services that consumers buy.
   b. everything that consumers buy.
   c. everything that consumers buy except gasoline and food.
   d. everything that the economy produces.

7. The CPI does not include
   a. luxury items.
   b. purchases of oil and food.
   c. purchases of imported items.
   d. the introduction of new products this year that were not available in the base year.

8. The Producer's Price Index (PPI) is often used to predict
   a. the future direction of the economy.
   b. the future direction of the CPI.
   c. the future direction of inventories.
   d. the future direction of production.

9. Core inflation
   a. allows for quality changes.
   b. is more volatile that the CPI.
   c. excludes food and energy prices.
   d. does not use a market basket approach.

10. The real interest rate increases when
    a. the nominal rate of interest falls.
    b. the rate of inflation increases.
    c. the rate of inflation falls.
    d. there is less investment.

ANSWERS TO FILL-IN QUESTIONS

1. labor force
2. smaller
3. not
4. frictional
5. Structural
6. natural
7. Consume Price Index
8. quality
9. Producer's Price
10. does not

ANSWERS TO MULTIPLE-CHOICE QUESTIONS

1. **d.** This is the definition.
2. **b.** The key is the denominator of the labor force
3. **a.** This is the definition.
4. **a.** This is the definition.
5. **b.** This is the definition.
6. **a.** This is the definition.
7. **d.** A problem with the CPI is that it will grow as more and more new products are introduced each year.
8. **b.** Producers are ordering for next year's production, so their price changes may have a large impact on the CPI.
9. **c.** This is the definition.
10. **c.** the real rate of interest is defined as the nominal interest rate minus the rate of inflation.

PART THREE
LONG-RUN GROWTH

CHAPTER 8

THE LABOR MARKET AND UNEMPLOYMENT

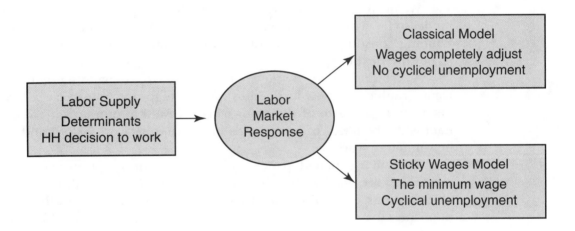

We have just reviewed the measures of unemployment and now turn our attention to the analysis of unemployment, a major topic in macroeconomics. Labor and human capital are key inputs into the production of goods and services.

We will start with a review of some labor market basics, including the determinants of the supply of labor. We then examine the decision that households face in deciding how much to work. We next look briefly at the classical view of labor markets where wages always adjust to clear the market. We then examine some reasons why wages might not adjust, including minimum wage laws, and what this means for unemployment.

SOME LABOR MARKET BASICS

Remember that the **unemployment rate** is the number of unemployed as a percentage of the labor force. The economy is always changing and shifting, and jobs and job opportunities change along with it. Some unemployment in a dynamic economy is an unpleasant fact. People change careers, and many now have second or third careers. This **frictional unemployment** will always be with us. So will **structural unemployment** caused by shifts in the overall structure or pattern of job availability.

We will expand our discussion of unemployment by examining **cyclical unemployment**, a term given to jobs that are lost during a downturn in the economy, whether it is a depression such as the Great Depression or a shorter recession that lasts for 6 months or so. As the economy contracts, less output is produced and fewer jobs are available.

The Supply of Labor

The supply of labor in the economy is positively sloped in relation to the real wage rate: a higher real wage in the economy induces more labor to be supplied. The additional quantity of labor supplied comes both from existing employees working more hours and from additional people entering the work force at the higher real wage.

We need a better understanding of labor supply then we have in our simple model so far. The size and quality of the labor force is very important for understanding consumption, and also for understanding economic growth, the subject of the next chapter.

A growing labor force is one engine for expanding national output. Demographics such as birth rates and immigration rates play a large part in determining the size of the labor force. However, another important determinant is the behavior of households in deciding to work or not and in deciding how much to work.

The labor supply depends on household consumption decisions, and vice versa. They are tied together because most household spending comes from current earnings. In addition to the wage rate, population growth, and immigration, the labor supply as we will see depends on prices, wealth, consumption decisions, and nonlabor income. These additional factors determine the willingness of households to offer labor services at different wage rates.

Prices

The level of prices also influences the decision of households to provide their labor services. Remember that the price level is an indication of the level of prices in the entire economy. Wage earners are concerned with the real purchasing power of their wages. Whatever the **nominal wage rate**, the wage rates in current dollars, households want to know what their wages will buy. That is, what is the real purchasing power of their wages in terms of goods and services? If wages go up 10 percent and so do prices across the board, few households will consider themselves better off because their nominal wage rate has gone up. In this example, **real wages** have stayed the same, and we would not expect households to change their behavior.

To measure the real wage, we adjust the nominal wage rate with a price index, either the CPI or the GDP price index. Whichever index we use, it is clear that households will base their current consumption and labor supply decisions both on current real wages and on expected future real wages.

Wealth and Nonwage Income

Wealth tends to be accumulated during the middle working years, or it can come from an unexpected source—the will of a rich aunt or the lotto. For our analysis, it makes no difference if the wealth is inherited or the result of a windfall gain.

Unexpected increases in wealth and income influence a household's decision to work and how much to work. Consumption will increase and there will be an increase in leisure and a decrease in the labor supply.

Taxes and Transfer Effects on Households

The household labor supply responds to an increase in tax rates by reducing the labor supply. The increase in tax rates lowers after-tax income for any wage rate, and it is the take-home income that is important for households. The marginal benefit of working another hour has declined, so less labor will be offered. Decreasing tax rates, which will raise after-tax income from the same wage, will expand the labor supply.

Transfer payments are payments such as Social Security, welfare, and veteran's benefits. If the government increases these transfer payments, it will increase income to households, increasing consumption and reducing the labor supply.

We can now sum up what we have seen so far.

The supply of labor will increase or shift outward because of

1. a decrease in taxes

2. a decrease in expected future income

3. a decrease in transfer payments and nonlabor income.

Of course, changes in the opposite direction will decrease the labor supply. In every case, the impact will be larger for a change that is viewed as permanent.

Shifts in the labor supply are important, yet how quickly the labor market responds to a recession is a major policy concern.

RESPONSIVENESS OF THE LABOR MARKET IN A RECESSION

We began this chapter with a short discussion of recessions. One of the troublesome questions concerns the responsiveness of the labor market to a recession. If the labor market completely adjusts in the short run to a decline in the demand for labor, then there will be a lower wage and less labor employed. Everyone who wants a job at the lower wage will have one, and according to our definition, there will be no cyclical unemployment due to the business cycle. Wages and the number of employed will rise in periods of expansion and decline in periods of contraction. Under this classical view, there is only frictional and structural unemployment.

As you can imagine, this is a contentious issue in macroeconomics and we need to understand it better.

The Classical View

In this view, wages adjust to changes in the demand for labor. In Figure 8.1, the demand for labor has increased from D_1 to D_2 as a result of an increase in total output because an expansion in the economy is underway.

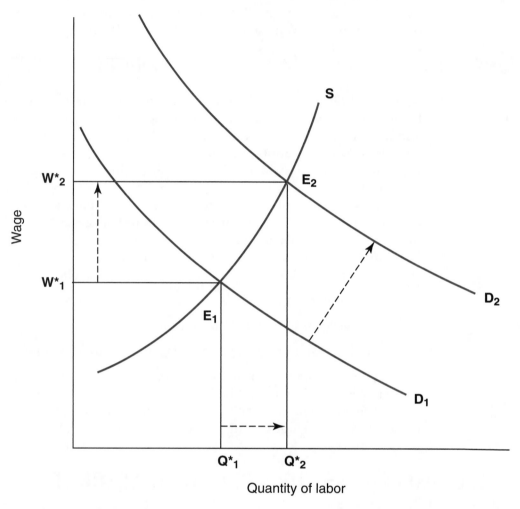

FIGURE 8.1. Labor market.

An increase in demand for labor during an expansion increases wages and employment.

The wage rate will increase to W^*_2, and the number of employed will expand to Q^*_2. Frictional and structural unemployment will not change. We have assumed, of course, that the labor supply curve has not changed. Remember that each point on the labor supply represents the number of people in the economy who are willing to work at various wages. As wages rise, more people are encouraged to enter or re-enter the labor force and give up their leisure time, studies, or nonmarket work.

When the economy slows down, wages will fall and there will be less labor employed. This does not mean that there will be an increase in unemployment. Wages will fall in the market, and everyone who wants to work at this wage can do so. If wages adjust completely, there should be no unemployment due to the cyclical downturn in the economy.

The labor supply curve represents a choice between work for wages and nonmarket work and leisure on the part of households. As wages rise, more people are encouraged to enter the labor force and give up some leisure and non market work. As wages fall during a recession, the opposite is true.

As college and universities know, when wages are declining because of even a mild recession, student enrollments increase because the opportunity cost of going to school has gone down. On the other hand, when the economy is booming, enrollments decline.

In this classical world of perfect adjustment, there is no role for market intervention to correct unemployment caused by the recession—the market takes care of any temporary excess demand or excess supply by adjusting the wages and the number of employed.

To summarize the classical view: A recession results in lower wages, and an expansion results in higher wages, with the unemployment levels determined only by structural and frictional elements. There is no unemployment due to the recession itself.

With unemployment all around us, how can we reconcile this with the classical view that wages adjustments will clear the labor markets? We have to look at some reasons why the labor market may not work perfectly as in the classical view.

Suppose that wages have declined in a particular industry. A person who chooses not to work after these wages have fallen,

1. may believe that it is only a temporary change and that he will soon be reemployed at his old wage.

2. may think he can find a job in another industry and continues to look for a job

If he decides to continue looking for a job, he will be counted as part of the unemployed because he is actively looking for a job. If he has taken the opportunity to go fishing and wait for the economy to rebound, he is not part of the unemployed because he is not actively seeking work.

HOW DO WE ACCOUNT FOR CYCLICAL UNEMPLOYMENT?

One argument is that wages and other input prices do not adjust quickly and are "sticky." The argument goes like this: Following a decline in demand due to a recession, wages are sticky and do remain at their old level W_1 and do not adjust downward in Figure 8.2. The result is that employment is reduced from Q_1 to Q_3, and these workers become unemployed.

Sticky wages are wages that do not quickly adjust in a downward direction leading to unemployment. The strongest example of sticky wages is fixed wages, such as a minimum wage. For the minimum wage to be effective, it must be higher than the market wage. The **minimum wage** is set by federal and state governments and represents a floor that wages cannot go below.

The arguments for a minimum wage tend to be based on a "decent standard of living" that workers should earn. Aside from the normative aspect of this statement, economists find the question of who benefits from a minimum wage a difficult question to answer. In Figure 8.2, we show why this is so difficult to answer. We show an initial equilibrium in the labor market at $W^*_1 Q^*_2$. We assume that the minimum wage is set at W^*_1 in an effort to maintain this standard of living for workers.

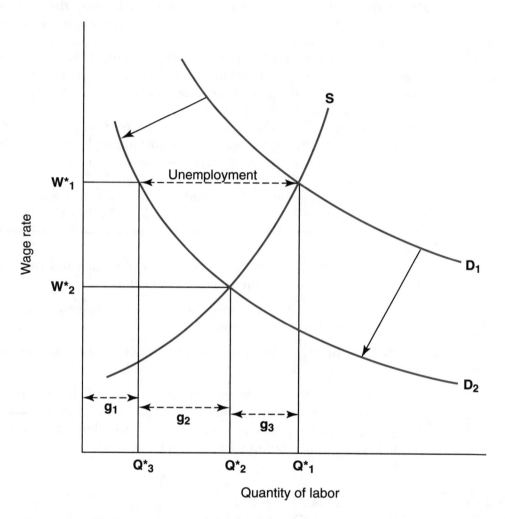

FIGURE 8.2. Minimum wage analysis.

A decline in demand results in unemployment if wages are sticky.

Suppose that the economy enters a recession and there is a decline in the demand for labor as a result. After the decline in demand with a minimum wage of W^*_1, the wage remains where it is and unemployment results in response to the reduced demand. Unemployment is the distance from Q^*_3 to Q^*_1. The big picture is that because wages are sticky or fixed in this case, unemployment results because of the the decline in the demand for labor. The wage does not fall to a new equilibrium wage that clears the market and there is cyclical unemployment because of the reduced demand.

Let us look at the results carefully because the minimum wage is always a political hot potato.

Three groups are affected very differently because of the minimum wage. The three groups in the Figure 8.2 are

1. g_1, workers who have kept their jobs and are now earning above what the market-clearing wage $W*_2$ would be. On the graph, they are represented by the distance from the origin to Q_3. This group clearly gains from the minimum wage that keeps their wage high.

2. g_2, workers who lose their jobs. Firms have to reduce the number of workers they hire. This group is represented on the graph by the distance from Q_3 to $Q*_2$. Note that Q_2* is the number of workers who would be hired if the wage were allowed to fall.

3. g_3, workers who also lose their jobs. They are represented by the distance from $Q*_2$ to $Q*_1$. Because the minimum wage is $W*_1$ and is above the market-clearing wage, these workers want to work but cannot find jobs. In effect, they read the signal of higher wages and want to work at is wage but are unable to. This group would not be seeking jobs if the wage had fallen to $W*_2$.

The answer to the question about who benefits from a minimum wage is not clear. It depends on how one evaluates the relative importance of the three groups. Minimum wage advocates say that the gain in wages by group g_1 is the important thing and that the other effects are minor. Those against a minimum wage say that it increases unemployment, encourages teenagers to drop out of school, and prevents some unskilled workers from getting on-the-job-training.

Empirical studies have shown that higher teenager unemployment is one of the effects of minimum wage laws. Increases in the minimum wage are associated with higher teenage unemployment. Teenagers have little experience and are the least skilled workers. They are attracted by the higher wage, but not all of them can find work.

Why are wages sticky other than in the extreme case of a minimum wage law? There are several explanations, and the issue is still unresolved among economists. Cyclical factors seem to cause unemployment, so it is an ongoing debate.

Sticky Wages

The main arguments for sticky wages have to do with labor contracts and relative wage arguments. **Social or implicit contracts** are agreements between workers and employers that firms will not reduce wages. They are not formal contracts, but implied ones, and have a lot to do with firm attitudes about what is decent behavior in a downturn. In this case the behavior is to retain employees in a downturn. Because less output is produced, retaining employees might mean that they work fewer hours.

Explicit contracts contain wage agreements that can last as long as 3 years. For example, if they are 3-year contracts, the wages will be specified for each of the 3 years. Even if the economy fluctuates, these wages will remain the same.

Another argument for sticky wages is called **imperfect information**. Under this argument, firms have imperfect information about what the equilibrium wage rate really is and they set the wage incorrectly. If the wage is set too high, too many workers will want the available jobs, resulting in some unemployment. Corrections to the misinformed wage may occur in a few months, but the dynamic nature of the labor market may mean that the moving target of the equilibrium wage rate has changed. The labor market is neither a well-organized nor an extremely well publicized or smoothly functioning market, and the contributes to the possibility of missing the right wage and therefore causing some unemployment. Some think that one of the most effective policies to combat cyclical unemployment is to make the labor market more efficient and transparent to eliminate this imperfect information problem.

REVIEW QUESTIONS

Add the word or words that correctly complete each of the following statements.

1. _____ unemployment is a term given to jobs that are lost during downturns in the economy.

2. The labor supply curve represents a choice between work for _____ and nonmarket work and leisure.

3. In the classical view, _____ completely adjust so that there is no unemployment due to a recession itself.

4. _____ wages are wages that do not quickly adjust in a downward direction, leading to unemployment.

5. The minimum wage is set by federal and state governments and represents a _____ that wages cannot go below.

6. One of the effects of the minimum wage is that it _____ people to look for jobs that are not available.

7. Social or implicit contracts are agreements that firms will not reduce wages during a _____.

8. If wages go up 10 percent and all prices do, also, _____ wages have stayed the same.

9. Unexpected increases in wealth _____ the labor supply.

10. Decreasing tax rates _____ the labor supply.

Circle the letter of the item that correctly completes each of the following statements.

1. The supply of labor will increase or shift outward because of
   a. a higher wage.
   b. a lower wage.
   c. an increase in taxes.
   d. a decrease in taxes.

2. The supply of labor will decrease or shift inward because of
   a. a decrease in expected future income.
   b. a higher wage.
   c. a lower wage.
   d. an increase in expected future income.

3. The supply of labor will increase or shift outward because of
   a. a higher wage.
   b. a lower wage.
   c. a decrease in transfer payments and nonlabor income.
   d. an increase in transfer payments and nonlabor income.

4. A shift in the labor supply will
   a. be larger for a change that is viewed as permanent.
   b. be larger for a change that is viewed as temporary.
   c. depend on the nominal wage rate change.
   d. depend on the real wage rate change.

5. As wages rise, more people are encouraged to
   a. reduce their work hours.
   b. seek nonmarket jobs.
   c. give up some leisure.
   d. take more leisure time because they can afford to.

6. Cyclical unemployment refers to jobs that are
   a. lost during downturns in the economy.
   b. lost because of the contraction of some industries.
   c. lost to foreign outsourcing.
   d. lost to a decline in wages.

7. The minimum wage is set by the government and represents
   a. the best wage you can earn.
   b. an attempt to guarantee a minimum standard of living.
   c. a wage tied to the minimum CPI increase.
   d. the maximum wage you can earn for an entry position.

8. A minimum wage will clearly benefit
   a. only one of three affected groups.
   b. two of three affected groups.
   c. everyone.
   d. employers.

9. If wages go up 10 percent and prices also go up 10 percent, the
   a. supply of labor will not shift.
   b. supply of labor will increase.
   c. supply of labor will decrease.
   d. demand for labor will increase.

10. The importance of explicit contracts is that during a recession they will
    a. fluctuate by the amount of the contract.
    b. automatically adjust because of escalator clauses.
    c. not fluctuate.
    d. increase the effects of the downturn.

ANSWERS TO FILL-IN QUESTIONS

1. Cyclical

2. wages

3. wages

4. Sticky

5. floor

6. encourages

7. downturn or recession

8. real

9. decrease

10. increase

ANSWERS TO MULTIPLE-CHOICE QUESTIONS

1. **d.** Lowering taxes gives households more take-home income, so more labor will be supplied at every wage.

2. **d.** Households decide to work today based on today's wage and what they think their future incomes will be. If they expect higher future incomes, they will reduce their willingness to work today.

3. **c.** Households now have less money coming in and will offer more services at every wage.

4. **a.** Jobs are often not easy to change, and if households view the change as temporary, more will stay in their current situations than if the change is permanent.

5. **c.** The gain from working at a higher wage will induce households to give up some leisure (which now costs more).

6. **a.** This is the definition.

7. **b.** This is the rationale most often used in support of a minimum wage.

8. **a.** The only group to clearly benefit are workers who keep their jobs and now are paid a higher minimum wage.

9. **a.** It is the real wage that determines behavior in the macroeconomy and this has not changed.

10. **c.** During a recession employers, are bound by law to honor contracts.

CHAPTER 9

LONG-RUN GROWTH

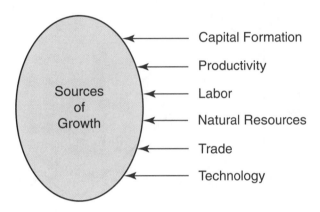

S ustained economic growth is one of the major goals of macroeconomic policy. The United States has grown over the last century at about 2 percent per year in real GDP/capita, the most common measure of the standard of living.

What are the sources of economic growth and what policy measures can governments use to sustain and enhance long-run growth? Increasing real output per capita over time is the definition of long-run economic growth. Some strong advocates of economic growth believe it gives us more choices, more employment, and more freedom. Others feel strongly that economic growth destroys traditional values, increases pollution, and leads to too much power in the business sector. We will not provide an answer to this normative and intense debate, but we will make all of the major issues clear.

We will examine the sources of economic growth and, as we go along, discuss the role of public policies toward growth.

SOURCES OF ECONOMIC GROWTH

Economic growth is an expansion of the ability to produce more goods and services. This expansion can come about through an increase in the labor supply, in capital, in technology, or natural resources, and through trade.

We have two different ways to represent economic growth with our models. The first is an outward shift of the PPF curve in Figure 9.1, which shows that we can produce more goods and services with economic growth because of an increase in technology. In this graph food production per year is on one axis and all other goods produced per year on the other. Remember that the PPF represents production *possibilities* if all the resources in the economy are fully and efficiently used.

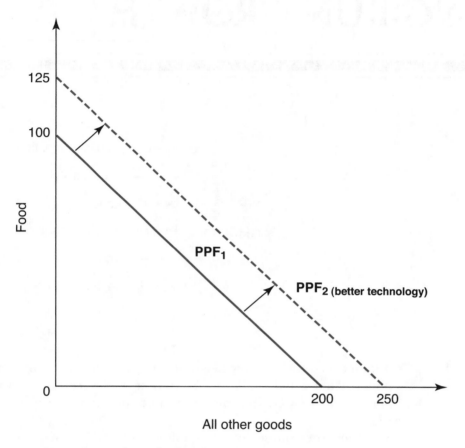

FIGURE 9.1. Growth on the PPF.

A change in technology enables more output each year. Economic growth is shown by the outward shift of the PPF.

An increase in technology increases worker productivity, so that with the same labor force the economy is able to produce more output. Increases in technology have been significant factors in the long record of growth of the U.S. economy.

The Long-Run Aggregate Supply

Another way to show economic growth is to use the concept of the long-run aggregate supply, which we will introduce here and recall later. In the **long run**, there are no fixed factors of production, and resources can enter or exit industries or countries. The elements that determine total output—labor, capital, resources, technology, and managerial skill—are therefore unrelated to the price level. Changes in the price level in the long run have no effect on the long-run supply, so we can portray the long-run supply as a vertical line as in Figure 9.2.

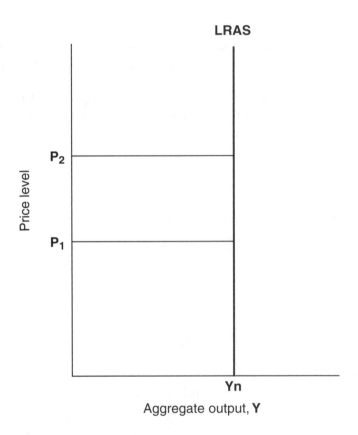

FIGURE 9.2. **Long-run supply.**

Total output in the long run does not depend on the price level.

Whatever the price level, long-run total output remains the same. The position of the long-run supply curve is called full employment output or the **natural rate of output** at **Yn** because it shows what output is produced when unemployment is at its natural or normal rate. This rate of output is what the economy moves toward in the long run.

This is classical macroeconomic theory, where prices and changes in prices do not affect real values. In other words, real values do not depend on nominal values. The vertical long-run supply is consistent with this view because output, the real value of goods and services, does not depend on the price level, a nominal value. Most economists believe that the long-run supply curve is vertical.

Why are individual market supply curves, such as the supply of accountants, upward-sloping in microeconomics? These supply curves show a larger quantity supplied at a higher price. The answer is that these supply curves assume that all other prices are constant. In microeconomic analyses the price is a **relative price**, holding all other prices constant. A higher price in these markets means a higher relative price, which encourages more workers in a particular industry. In the macroeconomics models, when all prices rise together, there is an increase in the price level, or inflation. There is no change in the overall quantity of goods and services supplied.

Economic Growth

Increases in the availability or amount of labor, capital, natural resources, and technology leads to economic growth and a rightward shift of the long-run supply curve.

The following changes increase the long-run supply and raise the natural level of output. They are grouped in various categories, and they look like a wish list for long-term development.

Changes in labor
  Immigration
  Population growth
  Increased labor force participation rate
  Increased quality of labor force

Changes in capital
  Increases in the capital stock

Changes in technology
  Advances in technical knowledge

Changes in natural resources
  Newly discovered resources, oil reserves
  Advantageous shift in the weather

Others
  Increase in foreign trade
  Easier environmental regulations.

This growth is shown in the continual rightward expansions of the long-run aggregate supply curve in Figure 9.3. It is the natural rate of output, which is increasing over time.

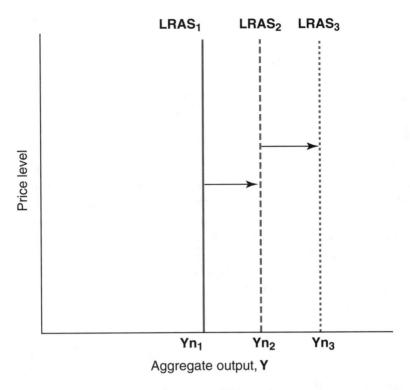

FIGURE 9.3. Economic growth.

Increased long-run growth over time.

Does real output growth over time ensure an increasing standard of living?

To make the link between increases in total output over time and the standard of living, we have to look at real output/capita. Not only do we need inflation rates to arrive at this number, we also need population growth. Simply increasing output or output potential is not enough to guarantee an increase in the real standard of living.

Many countries with large population increases each year face a declining standard of living—not because they are not increasing output but because they are not increasing output fast enough. The increase in output is swamped by population increases. For many of these countries, slowing down population growth is a major policy tool for increasing the standard of living.

The growth policies that are most important depend on what the local circumstances are in the country. A well-developed country may choose adjustments in tax rates to stimulate investment as its high-priority item. This solution would not be a high priority for a developing nation with a weak judicial system and an ineffective tax collection process.

MAJOR COMPONENTS OF LONG-RUN GROWTH

The major components of long-run growth are the labor supply, human and physical capital, natural resources, technology, and productivity. They are the same elements that increase the long-run aggregate supply.

Labor Supply

The labor supply represents a relationship between higher wages and the number of people willing to work at these wages. At higher wages, more labor will be available, coming from new entrants, people re-entering the labor force, and immigrants in addition to those already working who may increase their hours of work. About 20 percent of the growth of the U.S. economy since 1929 has come from labor force growth.

What will shift the labor supply so that more workers are available to work at all wages? We will assume that the willingness of households to enter the labor force is constant.

TABLE 9.1 INCREASES IN THE LABOR SUPPLY

An increase in the labor supply can be caused by

- An increase in population
- An increase in immigration
- An increase in labor force participation rates

With no other changes, population growth will add to the supply of labor, as will an increase in immigration and an increase in labor force participation rates.

It is not only the growth in population that is important in the long term. The quality, training, skills, and labor force participation rates also contribute to real long-term growth.

The **labor force participation rate** is the ratio of the labor force to the total working-age population, those 16 and older. It is a measure of the willingness of the population to work. These rates do not change very much on a national basis, but major changes within certain sectors can have a large impact. For example, in the United States, the labor force participation rate for women tripled between the end of World War II and the end of the century to about 75 percent. This tripling of the labor force participation rate is a measure of a major demographic shift caused by more women entering the labor force.

Efforts to increase labor force participation rates, if successful, increase in the supply of labor. Some examples of general efforts are education and health policies that make employment easier and more stable. Specific policies focus on the incentives to work. Female participation rates can be increased by modifying the flexible working-time rules that keep many women out of the labor force. Many older workers leave the labor force, even though they want to continue to work, because of elements in the tax codes that penalize them for working by harming future pension and social benefits.

Capital

Capital or physical capital is the stock of structures and equipment used to produce goods and services. An increase in capital stock increases output growth. About 14 percent of U.S. output growth since 1929 has been due to increases in capital stock.

Remember that capital stock yields a flow of services over time. Houses and office buildings provide benefits over their lifetimes. On the government side, government investment in highways and bridges and other infrastructure investments contribute services over many years. Highways and bridges, for example, lower the costs of transportation over their lifetimes. The value of the flow of these services provides the incentive for investment in capital goods.

Government also acts to increase private investment by offering tax incentives to invest and subsidies to investment projects. These actions increase investment and add to the capital stock and growth.

Direct foreign investment can also contribute significantly to output growth. An inflow of direct foreign investment increases capital stock and leads to higher productivity and an increase in economic growth. Some of the profits will go to overseas investors, but the effects of increased capital stock remain in the receiving country.

The addition of physical capital can increase the productivity of labor in addition to its direct contribution. Accountants with computers can process more balance sheets with computers than by hand, and the use of scanners can speed up checking out groceries, recordkeeping, and inventory management with fewer errors.

Adding more and more capital to an existing labor force shows large gains in productivity when there is very little capital. When there is a lot of capital per worker, each additional unit of capital investment added yields a smaller increase in output per worker, known as **diminishing returns**. This is shown in Figure 9.4.

Imagine four people doing a manual task that can be computerized. Adding the first computer can significantly increase output. Adding the fifth computer does not have as dramatic an addition to output.

This is an important consideration for many developing countries with little physical capital. Dramatic spurts in output per worker (productivity) can be achieved with modest additions of capital. When there is lots of capital per worker, other avenues may be more effective.

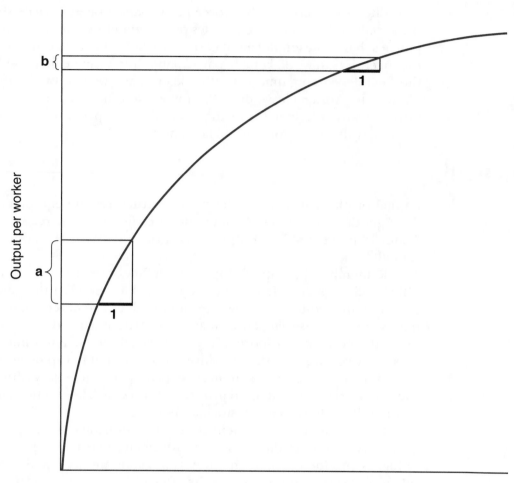

FIGURE 9.4. Production function.

Diminishing returns: as more and more capital per laborer is added, the additional output gained gets smaller and smaller, (b < a).

Human Capital

Human capital is the knowledge and skills that workers acquire from education, experience, and training. Increases in human capital add to long-term growth. About 19 percent of U.S. economic growth since 1929 has been attributed to increases in human capital.

How do we increase human capital? Increasing the training of a worker this year will have a long-term effect on the worker's ability to produce. Many MBA degrees are paid for by companies whose employees are MBA students. Improving the health of the population adds to productivity because healthy people are more productive than sick people. On-the-job training, vocational skill training, job experience, and schooling make individuals more productive whether the investment is made by firms, the government, or the individuals themselves.

If there is a significant "brain drain" from overseas countries to the United States, then this will add to our capacity to produce, just as the exporting country will suffer a loss in human capital.

Natural Resources

Natural resources are land, rivers, and minerals that are used in production. They are classified as *renewable*, like forests, and *nonrenewable*, like oil which cannot be reproduced easily or quickly.

Differences in natural resources are responsible for some of the differences in standards of living around the world. The OPEC countries are rich today because of the large deposits of oil within their borders.

Japan, however, with few natural resources, enjoys one of the highest standards of living in the world. The Japanese have pursued an aggressive international trade policy and have imported many of the natural resources they need to produce and export manufactured goods. They are a major oil importer.

Most economists argue that natural resources do not impose a strong limit on economic growth. Technological progress has often increased rapidly, especially when scarcity and rising prices seem to indicate that we will run out of something. In addition, international trade offers an opportunity to acquire someone else's abundant natural resources.

When we were faced with a copper and tin shortage about 50 years ago, developments in plastics replaced many items formerly made of copper, among them copper telephone lines. Phone calls now travel not only over copper lines but increasingly over fiber-optic lines. Plastic containers for many food products have replaced the tin cans they used to come in.

Increasing prices of raw materials provide a very strong incentive to develop new products that will replace them in the market. This is a combination of two of our basic economic principles: People respond to economic incentives, and prices and profits act as signals.

Many of the arguments claiming that "We will run out of X by 2020" do not take into account the effect that rising prices have on incentives to develop new products. Some of the analysis has been very simplistic. For example, "We are consuming 10 units a year and have only 100 units, so we will run out in 10 years." This leaves no role whatsoever for the effect of rising prices, which work in two ways to lessen these crises related to declining supplies. Rising prices reduce the current rate of consumption per year and rising prices and profits spur more discoveries—even for a nonrenewable resource like oil. The recent growth of biofuels and non-gasoline–powered automobiles is a result of the increase in of oil prices in the present decade. Rising prices also encourage the development of more efficient engines.

Steel prices have risen for many years, and the response from the automobile industry has been to reduce the of content steel and increase the content of substitutes like aluminum, magnesium, plastic, and fiberglass.

The capacity to produce depends on a country's natural resources—land, weather, and minerals. Finding new oil reserves can increase the capacity of a country to produce oil. For many countries, important natural resources are imported.

Increases in Productivity

About 50 percent of the growth in the U.S. economy is due to increases in productivity. This is by far the most important element in our growth. The major component of this increase in productivity has been the growth of knowledge. **Labor productivity** is output per hour worked, or the amount of output produced by an average worker in an hour.

Technology

One of the major reasons the United States is able to produce more today than 30 years ago is the tremendous advance in technology. The invention of the computer has meant that we can produce more with the same level of capital, labor, and natural resources.

As an example, in 1981 Apple computers had 5 megabytes (Mb) of storage, and in 2006, the storage in a laptop was 122,880 Mb. This change from a desktop to a laptop that operates faster, with more storage, and on a wireless network, gives a representative sense of the magnitude of the changes in computers. Other areas have had similar major advances.

IMPORTANCE OF INVESTMENT

One way to raise productivity is to invest more current dollars and resources and consume less in the current period. We referred to this as the current versus future consumption choice. The growth will come from capital accumulation or an increase in capital stock. This enhanced future growth will come at a cost of less current consumption.

Different countries evaluate this loss of current consumption differently. If a country cannot feed its citizens, cutting back on food production to invest in infrastructure and capital investment means that less food will be available. The costs of cutting back on consumption and food production can be measured in the increase in deaths. For countries at this level of subsistence, cutting back on current consumption will be among the last choices for increasing economic growth.

On the other hand, a wealthy country with a healthy population that is exporting food to the rest of the world will probably view a curtailment of current consumption with very different eyes.

OTHER EVENTS

Advances in knowledge and know-how are the largest contributors to advances in productivity. Because of these improvements, we can better manage inventories, schedule and track individual packages around the world, and find the cheapest place to buy an item on the internet. The increases in cost saving and efficiency add to our productivity. Trade and the ability to trade have similar effects on growth as inventing new production processes.

Regulations such as mandatory controls on water and air quality or restricting some production process to ensure worker safety can reduce growth. These trade-offs between more production and a cleaner or safer environment need to be evaluated with a measure that can compare the marginal gain to society of a cleaner environment with the marginal cost to society of less growth. The choice is never full growth versus complete environmental protection, but finding the right mix of the two. These debates go on in every country.

Industrial policies to encourage growth tend to focus on sectors of the economy that are deemed to be more important than others. Governments who chose a particular sector in their industrial policies have chosen that sector to be one of the major engines of growth. Japan's focus on developing the automobile industry is a good case in point.

Most industrial policies in the United States are on the state level, where states give special considerations to what they feel are "clean" industries, like financial services, in order to attract them to that state. So far, on a national level the United States has not singled out any particular industry and relies more on consumer sovereignty and the marketplace to make these decisions.

Changes in weather can have major effects on growth. A prolonged drought in some countries has severely limited the amount of food they can produce themselves and has resulted in population decline, famine, and a need for international humanitarian relief efforts. Some African countries have had so little rainfall that their subsistence farmers are unable to grow corn. To tackle this difficult problem, seed specialists have recently introduced a variety of corn that requires very little water.

We sum up the major determinants of an increase in long-term growth in Table 9.2.

TABLE 9.2 LONG-TERM GROWTH DETERMINANTS

Countries can increase their GDP if they

- Increase the labor supply
- Increase human and physical capital
- Increase productivity
- Increase natural resources

REVIEW QUESTIONS

Add the word or words that correctly complete each of the following statements.

1. The elements that determine total output are labor, capital, resources, and _____.

2. Changes in _____ in the long run will have no effect on the long-run supply.

3. Decreases in the availability or amount of capital will lead to economic _____.

4. The labor force participation rate will _____ when the working-age population declines.

5. Many older workers leave the labor force because of elements in the _____ that penalize them for working.

6. Increasing the capital stock will lead to an _____ in economic growth.

7. About _____ percent of if the growth in the U.S. economy is due to increases in productivity.

8. _____ is the knowledge and skills that workers acquire from education, experience, and training.

9. One of the major reasons the United States is able to produce more today than 30 years ago is the tremendous advance in _____.

10. Industrial policies to encourage growth tend to focus on _____ of the economy that are deemed more important than others.

Circle the letter of the item that correctly completes each of the following statements.

1. An increase in the skill level of workers will
   a. decrease the demand for these workers.
   b. have no effect on the long-run supply.
   c. decrease the long-run supply.
   d. increase the long-run supply.

2. A decrease in foreign trade will
   a. decrease the long-run supply.
   b. increase the long-run supply.
   c. have no effect on the long-run supply.
   d. usually lower the price level.

3. The long-run supply curve will shift to the right in response to
    a. a decrease in immigration.
    b. an increase in wages.
    c. a decrease in the capital stock.
    d. an increase in the capital stock.

4. The long-run supply curve will shift to the left in response to an
    a. increase in regulation.
    b. increase in foreign trade.
    c. increase in immigration.
    d. increase in net exports.

5. Changes in the price level in the long run do not affect the long-run supply.
    a. However, changes in inflation will.
    b. So we can portray the long-run supply as a vertical line.
    c. But an increase in the money supply will increase the LRAS.
    d. But a decrease in the money supply will decrease the LRAS.

6. Increases in the availability or amount of labor and capital will
    a. shift the long-run supply curve to the right.
    b. not change the position of the long-run supply curve.
    c. shift the long-run supply curve to the left.
    d. decrease the output potential of the economy.

7. Capital is
    a. domestic money available for investment.
    b. annual investment in buildings and equipment.
    c. the stock of structures and equipment used to produce goods and services.
    d. foreign money available for investment.

8. An inflow of direct foreign investment will
    a. replace U.S. investment.
    b. increase the long-run supply curve.
    c. decrease the long-run supply curve.
    d. not change the long-run supply curve.

9. Diminishing returns occurs when will
    a. each additional unit of capital per laborer does not increase output.
    b. each additional unit of capital per laborer increases output by larger and larger amounts.
    c. each additional unit of capital per laborer increases output by smaller and smaller amounts.
    d. You cannot increase output per laborer by adding capital.

10. One of the major reasons the United States is able to produce more today than 30 years ago is
    a. the availability of skilled labor.
    b. our strong agricultural sector.
    c. our aggressive expansion of exports.
    d. the tremendous advance in technology.

ANSWERS TO FILL-IN QUESTIONS

1. technology

2. the price level

3. decline

4. increase

5. tax codes

6. increase

7. 50

8. Human capital

9. technology

10. sectors

ANSWERS TO MULTIPLE-CHOICE QUESTIONS

1. **d.** This is an increase in worker productivity.

2. **a.** A decrease in foreign trade means less access to the productivity, resources, and skills of other countries.

3. **d.** Capital stock increases increase the productive capacity of the economy in the future.

4. **a.** Regulation increases costs.

5. **b.** The LRAS will not change with a change in inflation, which is on the vertical axis, so we portray the LRAS as a vertical line to show this.

6. **a.** These represent an increase in the productive capacity of the economy.

7. **c.** This is the definition.

8. **b.** An increase in investment, regardless of the source, will increase the productive capability of the economy.

9. **c.** This is the definition.

10. **d.** This is a historical fact.

PART FOUR
MONEY AND PRICES

CHAPTER 10

THE MONEY SUPPLY AND THE FEDERAL RESERVE SYSTEM

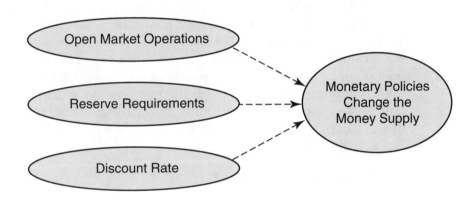

AN OVERVIEW OF MONEY

In this chapter, we begin with a discussion of money and different kinds of uses for it. We will look at the process of money creation and the role that banks play in it and finally examine the role of the Federal Reserve (the Fed). We will finish the chapter with an examination of the money supply and the tools the Fed has to control it. We will wait until the next chapter to discuss the demand for money.

What Is Money?

We are all familiar with money and use it every day of our lives. We rarely think about money except to complain that we do not seem to have enough. However, money has three special characteristics: It is a medium of exchange, a store of value, and a unit of account. All three of these terms together encompass what we mean when we say "money."

Without a commonly accepted method of payment like money, people can barter. **Barter** is an exchange of certain goods and services for others. To complete a barter exchange means you have in exchange to find someone who wants exactly what you have in exchange for exactly what you want. Having a commonly accepted medium of exchange eliminates this matching problem. For money to be a **medium of exchange**, both buyers and sellers must accept it. Money is something that is widely accepted as a medium of exchange.

Imagine how difficult it would be for you to find a person who wants to exchange their ham and eggs for your paperback mystery book? How and where do you find such a person? What will happen if you don't find them until midnight? Because money is a medium of exchange, using it makes the exchange much easier. You can exchange your paperback for money today, and the money for ham and eggs tomorrow or whenever you wish.

Money also acts as **a store of value** over different time periods. Money must be durable to last over time and it cannot be fragile or temporary. Many things are stores of value: Rembrandt paintings, gold ingots, and real estate. However, these items are not portable, easily divisible, or easily usable in exchange, whereas money is.

Among different kinds of assets, money is considered **liquid** because it is a means of payment that is easily exchanged for goods and services at all times.

Money does have a big disadvantage: Its value falls when prices increase. Your $10 bill buys 5 cans of beer at $2/can but only 2 cans of beer when the price is $5/can. When beer prices are rising, it is better for you to buy the beer and hold on to it as a store of value instead of keeping the money. This decline in the value of money when prices rise is the main reason we are concerned with inflation. When prices are rising rapidly and people expect more inflation, we see them changing their holdings and assets. They hold as little money as possible and as many real goods.

A Standard Unit of Account

Money also serves as a way of keeping books and quoting prices. Prices are quoted in monetary units such as $5.50, not in 20 pages of a paperback. Because the price of an item is quoted in a standard unit, everyone attaches the same meaning to it in their decisions to purchase it or not.

LEGAL TENDER, COMMODITY, AND FIAT MONEY

Historians love to tell us about the different things that have been used as monies in different parts of the world. Shells, cattle, cigarettes, beads, and tulips in seventeenth century Holland have all been used as monies. These monies are usually divided into different classes: fiat and commodity.

Fiat money or token money is something that has little worth by itself. Our U.S. dollar bill is an example of fiat money. The actual value of the paper is practically zero.

Commodity money, on the other hand, has some intrinsic value. Cattle have intrinsic value as food or as a source of milk. Gold and platinum are other examples of commodity money. They have other uses as jewelry or industrial precious metals.

The dollar bill is **legal tender**, legal for the satisfaction of debts and payments. In fact, the government passes laws declaring that it must be accepted. All U.S. bills contain the phrase "This note is legal tender for all debts, public and private."

In order to protect the value of a currency, governments also assure the public that they will not debase it. One way for the government to pay its debt obligations would be simply to print an extra amount of money and be done with it. Unfortunately, resorting to the printing press to pay debts would **debase the currency** by reducing its value for all holders, public and private. One of the key issues for any economy is how to control the supply of money, and not try to solve debt problems by printing more money.

THE SUPPLY OF MONEY

There are many different ways to pay a bill in the United States: by cash, by a checking or demand deposit account, by a credit card, or by a debit card. All of these methods are widely used to settle accounts.

What do we mean when we talk about the money supply? Which of these different ways to pay a bill are included and which are not? Whether a method of payment is included as money has to do with various measurements of the money supply. We will review these measurements and then look at the important role that the money supply has in the economy.

Economists and the government use several different measures of the money supply, depending on what they are trying to measure. **M1** is **transactions money** and includes monies that can be used to pay debts or purchase items.

M1 is defined as currency held outside banks and also includes demand deposits (checking accounts), traveler's checks, and other checkable deposits.

Currency is the same as cash, and demand deposits are monies held in checking accounts that are payable "on demand." Other checkable deposits are any deposit accounts held in a financial institution that can be withdrawn using a check. These include negotiable order of withdrawal (NOW) accounts , essentially checking accounts that pay interest, and automatic transfer savings (ATS) accounts, which automatically move funds from checking to savings accounts, and vice versa, when a certain balance is reached.

M1 is a stock variable that is measured at a point in time such as a specific day, for example, October 1. The importance of the components of M1 seems to be changing. Cash seems to be declining among the components as more and more people take advantage of electronic and other noncash ways to satisfy their purchase and debt repayment needs.

M2 is another measure of money that is used when a broader measure is needed. It includes near monies that are close substitutes for transactions monies. They are not as liquid in some cases, and in others have some restrictions on their check-writing capability. M2 includes M1 and these near monies. Examples of these are savings accounts and accounts that you can write a check on, such as money market funds and money market mutual funds.

M2 = M1 + savings accounts + money market accounts + other near monies. M2 is often four times the size of M1, which it includes. Having the broader M2 definition provides a more stable, less fluctuating view of the money supply. When people switch from a transactions money account to a near money account, M2 stays the same, whereas M1 declines. This usually occurs when a new near money account is developed.

Although some argue for an even broader definition of the money supply than M2, which for example might include credit card accounts, for our purposes we will use M1, transactions money, when we discuss "the money supply."

PRIVATE BANKING SYSTEM

Because most of the money in the United States is held in banks or passes through them, we need to understand the structure and operation of a private banking system like ours.

Banks are **financial intermediaries** for lenders and borrowers, collecting excess cash from households and firms, and storing as deposits in various accounts. Loans are made from these deposits for car and home purchases and for commercial purposes. Banks are called financial intermediaries because they connect or link lenders to borrowers. Commercial banks, savings and loan associations, life insurance companies, and pension funds are the main types of financial intermediaries. Recent financial market deregulations have increased the kinds of intermediaries and greatly expanded the entities that can offer checking accounts and make loans.

How Banks Create Money

U.S. accounting practices use a dual-entry system, where assets and liabilities are defined to be equal or in balance. The simplest balance sheet is a **T-account**, which we will use to show how banks create money.

Assets are owned items that are worth something. For a bank, these include the building it is housed in, its furniture, the cash it holds in its vaults, stocks, and bonds, and so on. Loans are an important asset of a bank because they represent an obligation to pay the bank. A borrower has a contract to repay the loan by a certain date, and this contract has value. Banks can sell this loan in a secondary market or to another bank for cash.

Other assets that we need to understand are Federal Reserve deposits, which are held by the Fed. These reserve deposits are held by the Fed and, along with vault cash held in the bank, make up the reserves required by the Fed. **Reserves** in our example below are a combination of vault cash and reserves held on deposit at the Fed. As we will see later, changing the reserve requirement forces banks to adjust these reserves and changes the money supply.

Liabilities are what the bank owes, the obligations the bank has to pay.

The most important of these are bank deposits, which the owner can write a check on or withdraw at any time.

Banks are required to hold a certain percentage of their total deposits as reserves. This is known as the **required reserve ratio**. If the ratio is 15 percent, then a bank with deposits of $200 million must hold reserves of $30 million, either at the Fed or as vault cash. Reserve requirements became the law after the Great Depression to assure depositors that the bank would have enough reserves to pay its obligations.

How do banks create money? Banks lend out their excess reserves to others who then use these funds. **Excess reserves** are the difference between actual reserves and required reserves. It is from these excess reserves that new loans can be made. If there are no excess reserves, banks cannot make loans.

Suppose that First Bank opens its doors, accepts $900 in deposits, and holds all of these deposits as reserves. **Reserves** are deposits that have not been loaned out. Because all of the reserves are being held, this means the bank is operating with a 100 percent reserve requirement. Table 10.1 shows this initial T-account.

TABLE 10.1 T-ACCOUNT FOR FIRST BANK

Assets		Liabilities	
Reserves	$900	Deposits	$900

Before the bank opened, the money supply in the economy was $900 and was all held as cash. After the bank opens, all of the currency is deposited in the bank, with $900 set aside as reserves. The money supply is still $900, but now it is all held inside the bank. If each bank holds all its deposits as reserves, banks cannot influence the money supply.

Money be created can only in a fractional-reserve system where banks can lend out excess reserves. Excess reserves are the difference between actual reserves and required reserves. First Bank made no loans because it believed in keeping all the reserves.

Suppose that First Bank is approached by people who want to borrow some of the money and are willing to pay interest for the use of these funds. They want to build a new home or start a business. The bank has to keep some reserves on hand to serve customers who ask to make withdrawals. If the flow of new deposits from the loans is about the same as the withdrawals, the bank can lend out the funds and needs to keep only a small percentage on hand as a reserve. This is called a **fractional–reserve** system. A fractional-reserve banking system is one where banks hold only a fraction of deposits as reserves.

The **reserve ratio** is the fraction of deposits held as reserves. The amount that a bank holds in reserves depends on its internal policies and on the Fed reserve requirement. The Fed uses the **reserve requirement** to ensure that there are sufficient reserves in the banking system to meet withdrawals. Banks can have reserves greater than those required by the Fed, and these are called **excess reserves**. If the reserve requirement is 10 percent and banks are holding 20 percent in reserve, these 10 percent excess reserves can be lent out or kept at the discretion of the individual bank.

What happens to the T-account as First Bank changes its required reserves to 10 percent? It now has $810 in excess reserves and can lend it out if it wants to. If First Bank lends the excess reserves out, its T-Account will look like this:

TABLE 10.2 T-ACCOUNT FOR FIRST BANK

Assets		Liabilities	
Reserves	$900	Deposits	~~$900~~ 90
Loans	$810		

Note that its liabilities have not changed. First Bank still has to pay its depositors. What has changed is that the bank now has two kinds of assets, reserves and loans.

The money supply increases when the loans are made. If they are made in cash, the money supply is now $900 in deposits plus $810 in cash. Before the loans, the money supply was only the $900 deposited in the bank. The money supply has grown because the bank made loans from their excess reserves. When banks hold only fractional deposits on reserve, they create money.

This seems unbelievable. Banks making loans create money but also create obligations to pay them back. There is no increase in wealth in the system, but more money is in circulation. If the loan was for building a house, the proceeds will be spent by the borrowers who purchase contractor's services, lumber, and appliances. The bank has added more money to the system and more money is available for transactions, but the economy as a whole is no wealthier than before.

The Money Multiplier

First Bank's actions are repeated throughout the banking system. Suppose that the loan is deposited in another bank, creating a liability for that bank of $810. On the asset side of the balance sheet, there is an increase in deposits of $810. With a reserve requirement of 10 percent, $729 can be loaned out. These new loans of $729 start the process all over again, with an additional $656 created. Every time money is deposited, a new loan is made creating more money. Because only 90 percent can be lent out in our example, the process eventually ends, as each new deposit can put only 90 percent of the deposit into the system again as a loan.

The **money multiplier** is the amount of money the banking system generates with each dollar of reserves, and it is defined as the reciprocal of the reserve ratio.

The total amount of money created in the system depends directly on the reserve ratio. In our example, how much money will be created throughout the economy? If the reserve requirement is 10 percent (1/10), then its reciprocal is 10/1 or 10. With a multiplier of 10, our original deposit of $900 will increase the money supply to $9,000 when all the dust has settled.

Original deposit × multiplier = 900 × 10 = $9,000

The banking system can increase or decrease the money supply, as we have seen. Because the multiplier is directly related to the reserve requirement, we need to examine what the Fed has to do with money creation.

THE FEDERAL RESERVE SYSTEM

The Federal Reserve acts as a central bank in the United States. and is responsible for monetary policy. In other countries, the central bank performs many of the functions of the Fed in the United States. The Federal Reserve is an independent agency that does not take orders from Congress or from the president. It was set up that way so this monetary policy would be independent of the legislature and the White House. The main tools of monetary policy are open market operations, reserve requirements, and the discount rate. All of these tools affect the economy by changing the money supply.

Monetary policy is formally set by the **Federal Open Market Committee** (FOMC). The regular meetings of the FOMC are watched very closely, and there is much speculation before each meeting about what it will decide. That is because the FOMC sets goals regarding the money supply and interest rates and directs **open market operations** through the Open Market Desk. Open market operations are the buying and selling of government securities.

In the U.S. economy the Fed operates as a central bank. It is the bank for banks. It holds deposits, makes loans, and ties together the nation's banks. Only banks can hold accounts there. As a central bank, the Fed clears interbank payments between members, regulates and audits the banking system, and aids banks in trouble. It also manages foreign exchange rates and foreign currency reserves.

As globalization and the interdependency of financial market have increased, the Fed now acts more frequently on international economic issues and advises on intercountry negotiations. Notable areas they have contributed to are debt reduction for developing countries and easing the monetary problems of eastern Europe.

They also have responsibilities and authority to control bank mergers, conduct bank examinations, and set reserve requirements. To assist failing banks they act as a lender of last resort. Acting as a **lender of last resort** means that when a bank cannot find any other sources of funds, the Fed provides it with funds to prevent it from failing.

How the Fed Controls the Money Supply

The Fed influences the money supply with three tools that work on the amount of reserves that banks have. They are open market operations, the required reserve ratio, and the discount rate. Any action the Fed takes to increase reserves creates more money. As more reserves are created, banks are able to lend more, increasing the money supply in the economy.

Open Market Operations

Open market operations are the most significant of the Fed's tools for controlling the money supply. These operations involve buying and selling existing government securities (bills and bonds) in the market.

When the Fed buys bonds, more money is put into the banking system, as sellers now have funds that were inside the Fed and outside the system. These funds enter the banking system and expand the reserves and therefore the money supply. On the other hand, when the Fed sells bonds, it takes funds out of the system, reducing reserves and the money supply.

If the Fed buys $100 million worth of bonds, this $100 million will result in an expansion of the money supply, the size of which is determined by the money multiplier. If the reserve rate is 10 percent, then the $100 million injection of funds into the market will expand the money supply by $1,000 million or $1 billion.

The Required Reserve Ratio

There is an easy way to change the supply of money: Change the reserve requirement. If the Fed increases the required reserve ratio, banks will have fewer available reserves to lend out and will have to hold more deposits to meet the requirement. The end effect will be to reduce the money supply. If the Fed lowers the required reserve ratio, banks will have more available reserves to lend out, increasing the money supply.

The Discount Rate

Banks can borrow from the Fed as their bank and are charged an interest rate called the **discount rate**. As banks borrow money from the Fed, more deposits enter the system, some are loaned out, and the supply of money increases.

A decrease in the discount rate encourages more borrowing from the Fed because the cost has gone down. As loans from the Fed enter the financial system, deposits increase and more loans can be made. The supply of money increases.

As a policy tool, changing the discount rate has two main problems. The effects are hard to know in advance with any precision. The effects need time to work completely through the system, and the system is complex. A second problem with the discount rate as a policy tool is that there are many other sources of loans in the economy. Because there are so many other sources of funds for banks, changes in the cost of these substitute sources can largely offset changes in the discount rate.

As monetary policy tools, open market operations, the reserve requirement, and the discount rate all affect bank reserves. To understand how bank reserve changes affect the money supply and eventually the interest rate is our eventual goal. Before we can model how interest rates are determined, we have to examine the supply of money and, in the next chapter, the demand for money.

THE SUPPLY OF MONEY

We have discussed the monetary policy tools and their effect on the supply of money. We treat the supply of money as though it is completely determined by the Fed and not influenced by the interest rate. In our simple model, this means that we can represent the supply of money as a vertical line as shown in Figure 10.1.

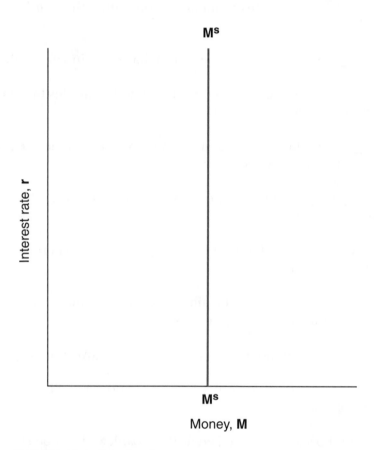

FIGURE 10.1. Supply of money.

Money supply when Fed policy is not influenced by the interest rate.

The following is a quick review of our discussion so far. All the actions listed shift the money supply to the right, making more money available to the economy.

- Open market purchases of bonds and government securities
- A decrease in the reserve requirement
- A decrease in the discount rate

When we add the demand for money in the next chapter, we will be able to understand the interaction of both sides of the money market in determining the equilibrium interest rate.

REVIEW QUESTIONS

Add the word or words that correctly complete each of the following statements.

1. _____ money or token money is something that has little worth by itself.

2. _____ money, on the other hand, has some intrinsic value.

3. _____ is transactions money and includes monies that can be used to pay debts or purchase an item.

4. _____ is a broader measure of money that includes near monies that are close substitutes for transactions monies.

5. The _____ ratio is the percentage of total reserves that banks are required to hold.

6. Money can be created only in a _____ system where banks can lend out excess reserves.

7. The money _____ is the amount of money the banking system generates with each dollar of reserves.

8. Open market operations are buying or selling government _____.

9. If the Fed increases the required reserve ratio, this will _____ the money supply.

10. Banks can borrow from the Fed as their bank and will be charged the _____ rate.

Circle the letter of the item that correctly completes each of the following statements.

1. The U.S. dollar bill is an example of
   a. commodity money.
   b. transactions money.
   c. fiat money.
   d. exchange money.

2. Open market purchases of bonds and government securities will
   a. take money out of the system.
   b. shift the money supply to the left.
   c. not shift the money supply.
   d. shift the money supply to the right.

3. A decrease in the reserve requirement will
   a. create more money.
   b. decrease the supply of money.
   c. not affect the supply of money.
   d. force banks to call in some loans.

4. If the Fed increases the discount rate,
   a. the money supply will shift to the left.
   b. the money supply will increase.
   c. the money supply will not be affected.
   d. more money will be available.

5. Banks in a fractional reserve system can create money by
   a. holding more than the reserves required.
   b. lending out excess reserves.
   c. depositing all their excess reserves in the Fed.
   d. holding all the excess reserves as vault cash.

6. If the Fed increases the required reserve ratio,
   a. banks will have more available reserves.
   b. banks will have fewer available reserves.
   c. it will increase the money supply.
   d. banks will be able to loan out more deposits.

7. If the reserve requirement is 10 percent, a new deposit of $800 will increase the money supply by
   a. $10,000.
   b. $8,720.
   c. $8,000.
   d. $18,000.

ANSWERS TO FILL-IN QUESTIONS

1. Fiat

2. Commodity

3. M1

4. M2

5. required reserve

6. fractional reserve

7. multiplier

8. securities

9. reduce

10. discount

ANSWERS TO MULTIPLE-CHOICE QUESTIONS

1. **c.** Fiat money means that a dollar bill has no value except as a dollar bill.

2. **d.** Purchase put money into the banking system.

3. **a.** Banks now will have excess reserves that they can lend out.

4. **a.** It will cost banks more to borrow, so they will borrow less.

5. **b.** If they have to keep all their reserves, they cannot lend out any. As they lend out excess reserves, the impact is multiplied.

6. **b.** Banks will have to hold more reserves and lend out less.

7. **c.** The multiplier is 10, so the final impact is $8,000.

CHAPTER 11

MONEY DEMAND AND THE INTEREST RATE

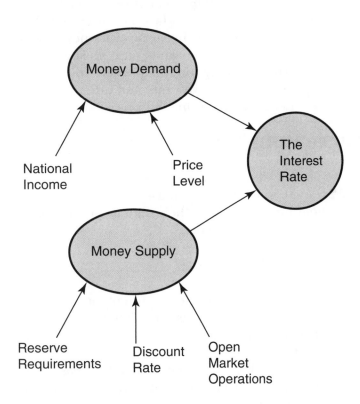

How the Fed influences the money supply was explored in the last chapter, and we now turn to the other side of the market—the demand for money. After we examine the demand for money and its determinants, we will look at how the equilibrium rate of interest is determined. What causes interest rate changes will become a key link in understanding how Fed monetary policies can work to restrict or stimulate the economy.

In the next chapter the interest rate will also provide a key bridge to link the money market and goods market.

First, we have to cover some basic concepts. **Interest** is a fee that a borrower pays for use of the lender's funds and represents earnings to the lender. The **interest rate** is the annual interest payment on a loan expressed as a percentage of the loan. If the lender is paid an annual interest rate of 10 percent on a $1,000 loan, the lender will receive $100 in interest each year.

Interest rates act as signals to participants in the market: Rising interest rates make it more costly to hold money as cash and at the same time more advantageous to hold interest-bearing bonds. To simplify our analysis, we will assume there is only one interest rate and that this interest rate determines how much money and how many bonds we are willing to hold.

THE DEMAND FOR MONEY

The demand for money is a central concept in macroeconomics. By money, we mean cash and non-interest-bearing deposits that households are willing to hold. We make a simplifying assumption that the only asset choice households have is to hold money or bonds, where bonds refers to any interest-bearing security. Money includes money on deposit (non-interest-bearing), as well as currency in circulation. Households face an either/or choice with their money: They can choose to hold it in the form of money or as an interest-bearing bond. As we expect, these money balances are sensitive to the rate of interest because interest is what you have to give up when holding money. How much money we hold depends on the interest rate and other determinants.

Let us look at some reasons why we hold money.

The Transactions Motive

One of the major reasons we hold money is to facilitate purchases and transactions—to buy things. This is called the **transactions motive**. Households hold money to make their regular purchases—to pay food, electricity bills, and many other transactions.

The Speculative Motive

Another reason why the amount of money households are willing to hold is related to the interest rate is the relationship between the interest rate and the value of bonds. The interest rate is inversely related to the price or market value of bonds.

A **bond** is a loan that earns a *fixed rate of interest* over a fixed time period. For example, Peter buys a 1-year bond for $1,000 with a fixed interest rate of 11 percent. This will return 11 percent interest and $1,000 at the end of the year. Bonds are bought and sold in bond markets, and the price of bonds fluctuates in the market. The **yield** on a bond is the interest you actually earn on your investment, which depends on a bond's price or market value. When the bond price fluctuates, the yield or actual earnings change.

Returning to our example, suppose the interest rate falls to 9 percent right after Peter buys the bond. If he now wants to sell his bond, he will have to sell it in the bond market. Potential bond buyers now have to compare a new 1-year $1,000 bond with a fixed interest rate of 9 percent to Peter's older bond offering a fixed rate of 11 percent. Peter's bond is now worth more than he paid for it: potential buyers will bid up the price of Peter's bond until it reaches

$1,222.22—exactly the bond price that will give the same yield as the new interest rate of 9 percent. (Peter's fixed interest on the bond is $110 divided by the price of the bond at $1,222.22, which equals a 9 percent yield.)

Buyers have bid up the price of Peter's bond to the point that the yield on the bond now equals the now lower interest rate of 9 percent. Remember, because the bond interest rate is fixed, it is the bond price that rises or falls to equate the yield to the interest rate.

The value of a bond and its relationship to the market interest rate is this: When the market interest rate falls, the market value of bonds rises, and when the market interest rate rises, the market value of bonds falls.

If Peter thought that interest rates were too high, his purchase of the bond would have been speculative—he bought the bond in the hope that interest rates would fall and it would increase in market value. This is called the **speculative motive**—investors hold bonds in anticipation of lower interest rates, which increase the value of their bonds.

Holding Money or Bonds

In our simplified model, each household faces a trade-off between holding money and holding interest-bearing assets. Changes in the interest rate affect this mix. Higher interest rates reduce the amount of money that is held, and lower interest rates increase the amount of money.

We see a common economic decision—if the costs of holding money rise, people will hold less money. In other words, as the interest rate rises, it will cost more to hold currency as cash and less will be held (and more bonds).

These choices between holding bonds and money at all possible levels of interest define the demand for money. As the interest rate increases, households will hold less money. When the interest rate is higher, less money will be held, and when the interest rate is lower, more money will be held.

This inverse relationship is represented by the negative slope of the demand for money in Figure 11.1. As the interest rate increases from 3 percent to 5 percent, it costs more to hold money and households change the mix of their holdings by holding less money (M_A to M_B).

The Demand for Money

The money demand in the economy includes checking account balances and cash held by households as well as by firms. Firms have to meet payrolls, make purchases, and have cash on hand for transactions just as people do.

The trade-off that firms face is identical to that faced by households—foregone interest earned is the cost of holding money. Firms also wish to hold interest-bearing assets and not all of their assets in money. A higher interest rate implies that firms will hold less in cash balances and more in bonds.

The total quantity of money demanded at any given time in the economy will includes that demanded by both households and firms and depends on the interest rate.

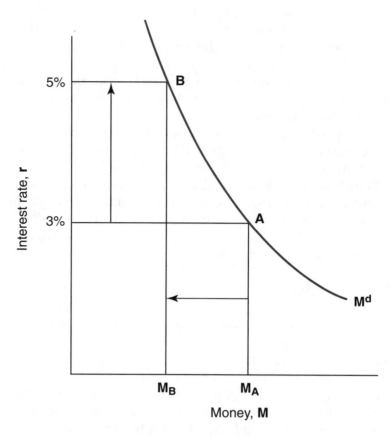

FIGURE 11.1. The demand for money.

The higher the interest rate, the less money people want to hold.

Shifts in the Demand for Money

In Figure 11.1 the quantity of money that firms and households want to hold depends on the interest rate—any changes in the interest rate will change the amount of money held, holding everything else constant. A higher interest rate induces people to hold less money and can be seen as movement along the money demand curve M^d from A to B.

However, there are other things that influence the quantity of money we want to hold at a given moment, and a change in any one of these determinants will cause the M^d curve to shift. We first examine the volume of transactions in the economy.

An increase in total output or real GDP means there is more economic activity—more goods and services are being produced, incomes are higher, firms are selling more and hiring more—and in short more transactions are made by both firms and households. This increase in transactions increases the demand for cash balances at all interest levels.

This is shown as an upward shift in the demand curve in Figure 11.2.

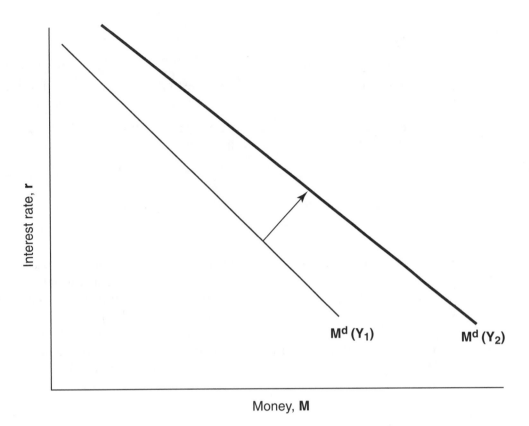

FIGURE 11.2. An increase in money demand.

Money demand increases as aggregate output Y increases.

Money demand shifts upward when aggregate income **Y** increases, resulting in a higher quantity of money demanded at every interest rate; money demand shifts downward when aggregate income **Y** decreases.

The amount of money needed for transactions also depends on the price level **P**. If the price level doubles, twice as many cash balances will be needed for the same volume of transactions. If everything you purchase costs twice as much now you will have to carry twice as much cash as before.

An increase in the price level also shifts the demand for money upward—firms and households will need to hold more balances at all interest levels. A decrease in the price level causes the demand for money to shift downward—less money will be needed to buy the same number of items.

The Determinants of Money Demand: A Review

The amount of money held depends on the cost of holding money as cash balances—the interest rate. A higher interest rate costs firms and households more in foregone interest earned to hold the same level of cash balances, so they will reduce their money balances. This relationship describes the demand for money.

TABLE 11.1 MONEY DEMAND

	Description	A change will cause a
Defines the demand curve	**r**, interest rate	Movement along the demand curve
Major determinants	**Y**, aggregate output (income)	Shift in the demand curve
	P, price Level	Shift in the demand curve

An increase in aggregate output in the economy increases employment, income, and transactions so that the demand for money increases (shifts upward) in response to an increase in aggregate output. When aggregate output declines, the demand for money shifts downward and to the left.

An increase in the price level implies that more balances are needed to meet the usual level of transactions, and this increase in the price level shifts the demand for money upward. A decrease in the price level shifts the demand for money downward.

THE EQUILIBRIUM INTEREST RATE

Now that we have covered both the demand and supply of money, we can answer one of the most important macroeconomic questions—How is the interest rate determined in the economy? This determination is vital because interest rates and interest rate changes act as signals and incentives throughout the economy. As interest rates change, households and firms change their behavior not only in the money markets but in the goods markets as well.

An equilibrium rate of interest results when the quantity of money demanded equals the quantity of money supplied. This is best understood when we examine the adjustment dynamics that lead to the equilibrium rate of interest.

SUPPLY AND DEMAND IN THE MONEY MARKET

We introduce the supply of money curve **M^s** from the last chapter, remembering that the money supply is assumed to be independent of the interest rate and therefore is shown as a vertical line. The money supply is, however, dependent on the three Fed tools: the discount rate, the required reserve ratio, and open market operations. The money supply is added in Figure 11.3.

What is the equilibrium interest rate? Suppose that no one knows and someone calls out "r_1" to see if this is the market-clearing rate—where the quantity of money demanded equals the quantity of money supplied. What will happen?

At r_1 in Figure 11.3, there is an excess supply of money—households and firms hold more money than they want. So they will turn to the bond market to buy bonds.

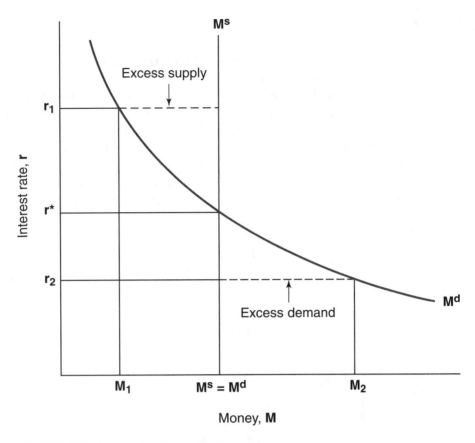

FIGURE 11.3. Interest rate equilibrium.

This graph shows adjustments to equilibrium.

As they try to buy bonds, they drive up the price or market value of bonds, lowering the yield, and as bond prices rise and the yield keeps going down, the interest rate falls, lowering the cost of holding money and encouraging people to hold more.

As the price or market value of bonds is bid up, the yield falls as does the rate of interest until it is equal to r^*, where everyone holds the amount of money they would like to. r^* is the equilibrium rate of interest because at this rate $M^d = M^s$. To sum up, if the interest rate is too high, causing an excess supply of money, the interest rate will fall, encouraging people to hold more money.

Suppose that the interest rate called out is r_2. What would happen? At r_2 there is an excess demand for money; people want to hold more money than is available. In order to hold more money, they offer to sell bonds, driving the market value of bonds down and the yield higher. Yields on bonds will increase until they are the same as r^*, where no more bonds will be offered for sale and firms and households have just the right amount of money and bonds.

If the interest rate is too low, causing an excess demand for money, people will go to the bond market to sell bonds, causing the interest rate to rise, and encouraging people to hold less money.

Money Supply Shifts

Because we now have both sides of the market, we can evaluate how the Federal Reserve influences interest rates.

Suppose the Fed feels that interest rates are too high at 12 percent and want to lower them to encourage the economy to expand. To lower interest rates, they increase the money supply. The Fed can increase the money supply by lowering the required reserve ratio, by buying securities through open market operations, or by lowering the discount rate.

After the increase in the money supply there is an excess supply of money at the old rate of 12 percent, as shown by the dotted line in Figure 11.4.

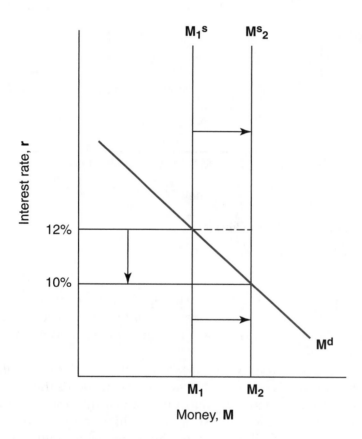

FIGURE 11.4. An increase in the money supply.

The Fed increases the supply of money, lowering the interest rate.

The adjustment process to the lower equilibrium interest rate should be familiar. With an excess supply of money, people adjust by trying to purchase bonds, driving up their market value and forcing the yield and the interest rate lower until the interest rate reaches 10 percent, where the money market is at a new equilibrium. The results of the expansion in the money supply are that more money balances are held at lower interest rates.

Money Demand Shifts

The equilibrium rate of interest also changes in response to shifts in the demand for money. As we saw earlier in this chapter, the demand for money shifts when either the level of aggregate output changes or the price level changes.

Because the demand for money depends in part on the transactions demand, we use the level of total output (Y) to represent an increase in the transactions demand. An increase in the level of total output shifts the demand for money upward and increases the equilibrium interest rate to r^*_2 in Figure 11.5.

At the old interest rate, there is an excess demand for M (shown by the dashed line in Figure 11.5), and people sell bonds to get more money balances. In the bond market, this lowers the price of bonds, increasing their yield and the interest rate to r^*_2.

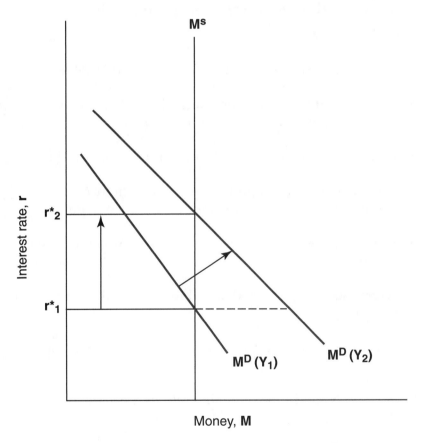

FIGURE 11.5. The effects of an increase in income on the interest rate.

An increase in total output increases the demand for money and causes r* *to increase.*

An increase in aggregate output **Y** shifts the demand for money upward and raises the equilibrium interest rate.

The price level also affects the demand for money. Remember that for a given price level, people decide how much money to hold based on the interest rate and other factors. When the price level increases, people need more money to handle their payments and transactions. The increase in the price level shifts the demand for money upward, causing the equilibrium rate of interest to increase.

So far, we have examined the mechanics of how the Fed can influence the money supply and therefore the equilibrium rate of interest.

In Chapter 12 we will examine the effects of money growth on inflation.

REVIEW QUESTIONS

Add the word or words that correctly complete each of the following statements.

1. When the market interest rate falls, the market value of bonds _____.

2. The demand for money shows that the higher the interest rate, the _____ money people want to hold.

3. If the price level increases, the demand for money will _____.

4. If there is an excess supply of money, the interest rate will _____, lowering the cost of holding money and encouraging people to hold more.

5. Holding money to pay everyday bills is an example of the _____ motive.

6. When there is an excess demand for money, the equilibrium interest rate will _____.

7. When the Fed increases the money supply, the equilibrium interest rate will _____.

8. Holding bonds in the hope that interest rates will fall is an example of the _____ motive.

9. When the Fed wants to slow down the economy, it follows a _____ money policy.

10. What a bond actually earns is called the _____.

Circle the letter of the item that correctly completes each of the following statements.

1. The higher the interest rate,
    a. the more money will be demanded.
    b. the less money will be demanded.
    c. the more money will be supplied.
    d. the more investment will occur.

2. The demand for money will increase when
    a. the interest rate falls.
    b. the interest rate increases.
    c. total income increases.
    d. total income decreases.

3. An increase in total output (Y) will
    a. shift the demand for money outward.
    b. increase the money supply.
    c. lower the equilibrium interest rate.
    d. shift the demand for money downward.

4. If the price level (P) decreases, households and firms will
    a. increase the supply of money.
    b. increase the demand for money.
    c. decrease the supply of money.
    d. demand less money.

5. If there is an excess supply of money,
    a. the interest rate is too low.
    b. people will sell bonds.
    c. people will buy bonds.
    d. the money supply will automatically adjust.

6. If the Fed wants to stimulate the economy, it can
    a. raise the Fed funds rate.
    b. increase the money supply.
    c. decrease the money supply.
    d. pursue a policy of tight money.

7. As the interest rate rises,
    a. it will increase the supply of money.
    b. less cash will be held.
    c. more cash will be held.
    d. it will decrease the supply of money.

8. Holding money to pay everyday bills is an example of
   a. dissaving.
   b. the speculative motive.
   c. M1.
   d. the transactions motive.

9. When there is an excess demand for money,
   a. households will buy bonds.
   b. the equilibrium interest rate will fall.
   c. the money supply will increase.
   d. the equilibrium interest rate will rise.

10. When the Fed increases the money supply,
   a. the equilibrium interest will fall.
   b. fewer bank loans will be made.
   c. the demand for money will increase.
   d. the demand for money will decrease.

ANSWERS TO FILL-IN QUESTIONS

1. rises

2. less

3. increase

4. fall

5. transactions

6. rise

7. fall

8. speculative

9. tight

10. yield

ANSWERS TO MULTIPLE-CHOICE QUESTIONS

1. **b.** The interest rate represents a cost of holding money. When it rises, people want to hold less in cash.

2. **c.** An increase in total income will mean more consumption and therefore an increase in the demand for money.

3. **a.** An increase in total output will mean more consumption and therefore an increase in the demand for money.

4. **d.** With a drop in the price level, the same goods will require less money to purchase them.

5. **c.** Holding more money than they want, people will buy bonds in our model.

6. **b.** Increasing the money supply will lower the interest rate and stimulate consumption and investment.

7. **b.** The cost of holding money has increased, and people will want to hold less.

8. **d.** Money is a medium of exchange, and people use it to cover their usual purchases.

9. **d.** Selling bonds to get money will raise the interest.

10. **a.** At the old interest rate, there is an excess supply of money that will go to bond purchases, lowering the interest rate to a new equilibrium.

CHAPTER 12

LONG-RUN INFLATION AND MONEY GROWTH

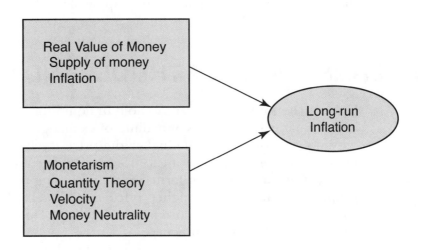

I nflation reduces the value of nominal goods and services, lowering their real value in terms of what goods they can buy. In Chapter 7 we discussed both the measurement of inflation and the costs that it imposes. Some monetary policy decisions can be inflationary, and we now want to examine these circumstances.

We begin with an examination of how changes in the money supply influence the real value of money. We will look at the supply and demand in a traditional market-determined value of money. In our analysis we will rely on the link between the money supply and inflation. Then we will analyze the effects of an increase in the supply of money.

The quantity theory of money is the basis of the monetarist view, which we will examine in this chapter. We will close with some important policy links between long-run inflation and the supply of money.

THE VALUE OF MONEY

When we introduced money in Chapter 10, we made the point that one of the drawbacks of fiat money is that it has value only in terms of what it can purchase. Inflation and rising prices mean that money is worth less in real terms.

Inflation is a rise in the general level of prices that affects the value of money. We think of inflation as an increase in the price of the average basket of goods that households purchase. The real value of money can be expressed as $1 divided by the price level, or $1/P$, where P represents the inflation rate. If there is no change in inflation, the value of money has not changed. If there is deflation, or a decline in the price level, your dollar is worth more in terms of the real goods it can buy in the market. If inflation increases, the value of your money, $1/P$, declines in terms of what real goods it can buy in the marketplace.

We will examine what determines the value of money in traditional demand and supply terms. In Figure 12.1, we show the value of money as $1/P$ to include the effects of inflation. The money supply M^s is determined by the Fed and at the moment is at M.

THE DETERMINANTS OF THE DEMAND FOR MONEY

How much money do we want to hold in liquid form for transactions? Money is held primarily because it is a medium of exchange. How much is held depends on the prices of goods. The higher the price level of the basket of goods, the more money households want to hold. At higher and higher price levels, the less each dollar is worth in terms of its purchasing power and the more money people want to hold. A higher price level lowers the real value of money, and people want to hold more nominal dollars. This is shown in Figure 12.1 as a negatively sloped demand curve.

If we take the money supply as determined by the Fed, what determines the equilibrium in the market? What determines the value of money that will result in the quantity demanded being the same as the quantity supplied? Since the value of money depends on the rate of inflation, it will be the price level that adjusts to find the equilibrium in the long run.

The interest rate plays a key role in the short run, as we will see in later chapters. But in the long run, the overall level of prices adjusts to the level where the demand for money equals the supply. If the price level is too high and the value of money is below the equilibrium value (below point A in Figure 12.1), there is an excess demand for money. People want to hold more money than the Fed has created, and so the price level must fall to balance supply and demand. In the opposite case, there is an excess supply of money (above point A). People want to hold less money than the amount available, and the price level must increase to balance supply and demand.

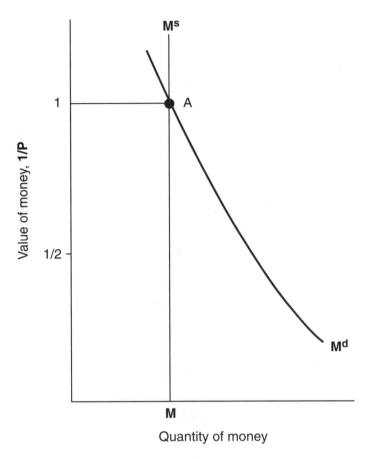

FIGURE 12.1. The real value of money.

The value of money determined by supply and demand.

THE EFFECTS OF AN INCREASE IN THE MONEY SUPPLY

Suppose that the Fed decides to increase the money supply. What happens? In Figure 12.2, this is shown as a rightward shift in the money supply from M^s_1 to M^s_2. At the old equilibrium **A**, there is now an excess supply of money. People try to get rid of this extra supply of money by buying goods and services. This results in an increase in the demand for goods and services. Even if people put some of the money in a bank, the bank can lend out part of it, and so the effect is to increase the demand for goods and services. Whichever path is taken, the increase in aggregate demand bids up the price level in the economy. There has been no change in the ability of the economy to produce goods and services, so the increase in the demand for goods and services pushes the price level upward. Remember that the ability to produce goods and services depends on capital, technology, labor, and the other determinants of production discussed in Chapter 9.

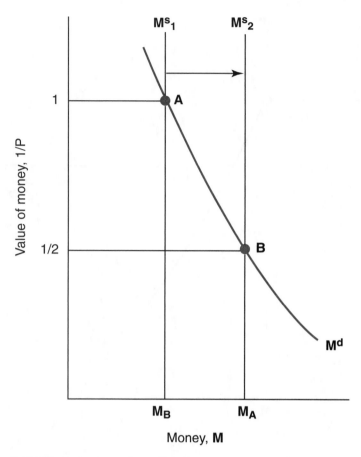

FIGURE 12.2. The value of money.

The Fed increases the money supply, causing inflation, which reduces the value of money.

As the price level increases, so does the amount of money demanded. The adjustment moves down the demand curve until the new equilibrium is reached at **B**. The result of money being injected into the system is a higher rate of inflation, a lower value of money, and a higher amount of money demanded.

The adjustment comes to an end when the price level has increased just enough to lower the value of money to **B**, the new equilibrium. The new money supply has been absorbed in the system, resulting in a higher price level and a correspondingly lower value of money.

MONETARISM

The importance of money in the economy is not a debated point. Almost all economists agree that money is important in the economy. An increase in the supply of money in the **AD/AS** framework results in an increase in **AD**, which leads to an increase in aggregate output **Y** and the price level **P**.

One of the central concepts in the monetarist approach is the velocity of money:

**The velocity of money is the average number of times
a dollar bill changes hands during a year.**

If I pay $5 for groceries, the grocery store owner may hold on to that particular bill for a while or so until it is paid out to the Coca-Cola supplier, who later uses it to pay for gasoline, and so on. If during the period of a year this particular bill changes hands four times, its velocity of circulation is 4 and the average time each owner keeps it is 3 months.

To measure velocity in the economy, we use GDP because it is a measure that is widely available. We define velocity as

$$V \equiv \frac{GDP}{M} \text{ , where M is the stock of money}$$

If the amount of final goods and services for the year, GDP, is $8 trillion and the stock of money **M** is $1 trillion, then the velocity of money **V** is 8.

Since GDP is price level **P** times real output **Y**, we can substitute **P** × **Y** for GDP:

$$V \equiv \frac{P \times Y}{M} \quad \text{or} \quad M \times V \equiv P \times Y$$

This is an identity because it is a definition. The equation tells us nothing about what happens to **P** and **Y** when **M** changes. The final value of nominal output (**P** × **Y**) depends on what happens to **V** when there is a change in the money supply. If **V** falls and **M** increases, there can be no change in **P** × **Y**, so that changes in the money supply have no effect on nominal output.

The Quantity Theory of Money

The core assumption of the quantity theory of money is that the velocity **V** is a constant or changes so little that we can consider it relatively constant. We show this with a bar over **V** in the equation

$$M \times \overline{V} = P \times Y$$

The equation is no longer an identity because if **M** changes, there will be a change in **PY**. If the equation represents the real world, then we have an easy explanation of changes in nominal output. Because **M** is a policy variable of the Fed, a change in **M** will result in an equal percentage change in **PY**. If **M** doubles, **PY** will double, and if **M** remains the same, so will nominal output.

This result clearly depends on whether **V** stays put and does not change very much. Measurements using M_2 as the measure of the money supply have shown that velocity has been relatively stable over time relative to GDP.

If velocity is constant, then Fed actions will affect only the price level and will not change real output. Real output of goods **Y** is determined primarily by all of the factors that influence aggregate production and growth: labor, physical capital, human capital, natural resources, and available technology. Because money is neutral, it does not affect output levels **Y**. This is called **money neutrality**—changes in the money supply do not affect real variables.

Money neutrality gives us some additional insight into the question of the harmful effects of inflation. It is not clear that inflation harms everyone; it depends on what is happening to your wages. If your wages grow at the same rate as inflation you are not worse off, and if they grow faster than the rate of inflation, you are better off.

Because velocity is stable when the Fed changes the quantity of money **M** in the system, proportion changes in the nominal value of output **PY** occur. With output **Y** determined by the factor supplies and technology, the Fed changes the money supply **M** and induces proportional changes in the nominal value of output **PY**, these changes are reflected in changes in the price level **P**.

There are two major lessons to be learned from our analysis.

1. There cannot be sustained long-run inflation without increases in the money supply.

2. As we will see in Chapter 13, supply shocks can cause stagflation and falling output. Fiscal and monetary policy measures cannot restore both output and the old price level. Policy measures that increase the aggregated demand to accommodate the supply shock can restore the output levels but lead to higher inflation in the short run.

The monetarist's major contribution is that inflation cannot continue indefinitely without increases in the money supply. This forces us to examine how to increase the money supply to accommodate real growth without inflating the economy. Monetarists argue that the money supply should be increased by just enough to sustain long-term real growth in the economy (growth in **Y**), and no more. If the money supply grows faster than **Y**, inflation will be the result. In fact, they say it even more strongly: Sustained inflation is strictly a monetary phenomenon.

REVIEW QUESTIONS

Add the word or words that correctly complete each of the following statements.

1. The real value of money can be expressed as $1 divided by the _____ level.

2. A higher price level _____ the real value of money.

3. The _____ adjusts to find the equilibrium value of money in the long run.

4. If there is an _____ in inflation, the value of money will fall.

5. The _____ of money is the average number of times a dollar bill changes hands during a year.

6. The quantity theory of money is expressed as **MV** = _____.

7. The _____ output of goods **Y** is determined primarily by all of the factors that influence aggregate production and growth.

8. Nominal output is determined by real output times _____.

9. Money _____ is when changes in the money supply do not affect real variables.

10. There cannot be sustained long-run inflation without _____ in the money supply.

Circle the letter of the item that correctly completes each of the following statements.

1. The real value of money can be expressed as
   a. $1 divided by the price level.
   b. $1 multiplied by the interest rate.
   c. $1 multiplied by the rate of inflation.
   d. $1 divided by the interest rate.

2. A higher price level
   a. raises the nominal value of money.
   b. lowers the nominal value of money.
   c. raises the real value of money.
   d. lowers the real value of money.

3. The real value of money has a negatively sloped demand curve because
   a. the nominal value of money increases with inflation.
   b. inflation reduces the real value of money.
   c. inflation increases the real value of money.
   d. a higher price level increases the value of money.

4. When the Fed increases the money supply,
   a. it reduces the value of money.
   b. it increases the value of money.
   c. it doesn't change the value of money.
   d. the demand for transactions balances decreases.

5. The velocity of money is
    a. how fast you can exchange money for goods.
    b. the number of times each year that households use money for bills.
    c. the average number of times a dollar bill changes hands during a year.
    d. very unstable compared to changes in GDP.

6. The quantity theory of money implies that
    a. if velocity is constant, **PY** will not change when the money supply changes.
    b. if **M** doubles, **PY** be half as large.
    c. if **M** doubles, **PY** will stay the same.
    d. if **M** doubles, **PY** will double.

7. Because money is neutral,
    a. only increases in the money supply will affect the real economy.
    b. only decreases in the money supply will affect the real economy.
    c. changes in the money supply will affect not real variables.
    d. all changes in the money supply will only affect real variables.

8. There cannot be sustained long-run inflation without
    a. decreasing the money supply.
    b. increases in the money supply.
    c. increasing the reserve requirement.
    d. decreasing the reserve requirement.

ANSWERS TO FILL-IN QUESTIONS

1. price

2. lowers

3. price level

4. increase

5. velocity

6. **PY**

7. real

8. the price level

9. neutrality

10. increases

ANSWERS TO MULTIPLE-CHOICE QUESTIONS

1. **a.** Nominal money, a dollar bill, is adjusted for inflation (**P**) to derive the real value of money.

2. **d.** The higher the denominator, the lower the real value of money.

3. **b.** The more inflation, the more money we want to hold.

4. **a.** Increasing the money supply increases consumption and investment and raises prices, reducing the value of money.

5. **c.** This is the definition.

6. **d.** **MV** = **PY** with velocity fixed gives this result.

7. **c.** This is the definition.

8. **b.** The major conclusion about long-run inflation.

PART FIVE
AGGREGATE
DEMAND AND SUPPLY

CHAPTER 13

TOTAL EXPENDITURE AND OUTPUT: C + I + G + NX

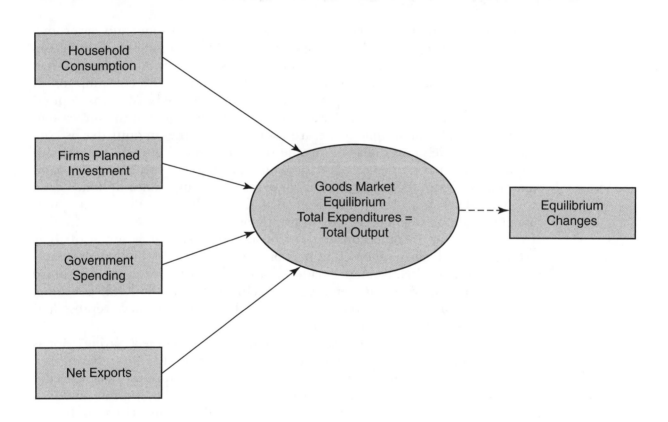

T he diagram shows the basic concepts we will cover in this chapter on the goods market. The equilibrium real output level, think real GDP, is determined by total expenditures, **C** + **I** + **G** + **NX**, which include consumption by households, planned investment by firms, government expenditures, and net exports. Total expenditure must equal total income in our simple model.

We then derive total expenditures and discuss equilibrium and equilibrium changes in the whole economy. This chapter is the first one to model how total income is determined in the goods market. In Chapter 6 we reviewed how GDP is measured, and in this chapter we establish the macroeconomic model to explain and analyze the changes in GDP.

Consumption plays a major role in the economy because about 70 percent of GDP originates with consumers. The United States is often called a consumer-led economy for this reason. Consumer spending and attitudes are watched closely to determine how confident consumers are about the economy and what they plan to buy and do in the future. There are several "consumer confidence" indices whose new surveys always make the financial news.

The statement "Consumer confidence is way up" means that consumers view job possibilities as increasing and that there will be good times ahead. In this atmosphere, consumers are more willing to undertake purchases of automobiles and other items that may commit them to making payments over several years. When consumer confidence is down, most consumers are reluctant to enter into long contracts.

TOTAL INCOME AND CONSUMPTION

In our model households receive income, and they spend some and save some. We will use **C** to represent the total spending of all the households in the economy. In Figure 13.1 the consumption function **C** shows that the higher the real income that households receive, the more they spend on the consumption of goods and services. In our example, when incomes increase by ΔY, consumption expenditures increase by a smaller amount ΔC because some of the increase in income is saved. For simplicity, we are assuming that the amount that is consumed out of each new dollar of income stays the same. Figure 13.1 shows this simple consumption-to-income relationship. Moving upward along the consumption function, higher levels of income result in more consumption.

Note that not all income is spent. If that were the case, the consumption function would be a 45-degree line drawn through the origin.

Why isn't all income consumed? Consumers decide how much of their income they will consume based in part on what they think will happen tomorrow. In each period consumers decide to save some of their income for future needs. We are assuming that even with no real income, households will consume. Households will draw down their savings in order to live. We have represented this amount of consumption by *a* in Figure 13.1.

In each period, consumers set aside some of their income as savings, not as saving. Remember the earlier distinction between stocks and flows. Saving is a flow, in this case an amount set aside in each period for future use. *Savings* is the accumulated total of all these saving efforts. Saving can be at a rate of $40 a month or a year, and savings can be in the thousands of dollars or zero. If consumers are fearful about the future prospects of the economy or of holding on to their jobs, the will consume less today and save more.

What determines how much household consumption results from a given amount of income? The major determinants of the consumption function, those variables that will shift the consumption function, are household wealth, the rate of interest, and household expectations about the future.

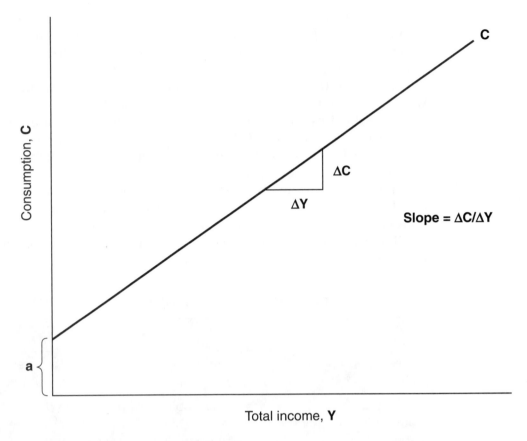

FIGURE 13.1. The consumption function.

Higher consumption with higher real income.

As total **household wealth** increases, the consumption function shifts upward, resulting in more consumption at all levels of income. Total income is a flow, an amount per time period such as a year. From this flow of income, households purchase the goods and services that they want. Wealth on the other hand, is a stock. Think of it as a house that contains a cookie jar with money in it. If the real value of the house increases or your favorite aunt puts money into your cookie jar, you will spend more on goods and services this month than before, even though your income has stayed the same. If this happens to all Americans, the consumption function will shift upward. When the stock market is booming, stockowners have more wealth and consume more.

How do **interest rates** affect household consumption? Our initial discussion of interest rates indicated that they always involve different time periods. When interest rates increase, saving becomes a more attractive option for households and they save more and consume less. The opportunity cost of consumption has increased. A dollar spent on consumption when the interest rate was 5% costs the consumer the opportunity to earn 5% on her money. When the interest rate is 10%, that same dollar spent on consumption costs more in terms of lost earnings.

If interest rates increase, the consumption function shifts downward. At every level of real income, there will be less consumption. If the opposite occurs, a decrease in interest rates will make saving a less attractive use of real income, and consumers will spend more out of their real income and save less. In Figure 13.1, this would be represented as an upward shift in the consumption function. At every level of income, more consumption would occur.

Household expectations about the future help determine the position of the consumption function. If households expect the economy to worsen, they will consume less this month because of the uncertainly of maintaining their jobs and income flows. If consumer expectations worsen, the consumption curve will shift downward. On the other hand, if they expect the economy to soar, along with their job prospects, this will shift the consumption function upward. At all levels of real income, there will be more consumption.

Table 13.1 provides a review of the consumption function and its major determinants.

TABLE 13.1 THE CONSUMPTION FUNCTION

		A change will cause a
Consumption per unit time	Real income	Movement along the consumption curve
Determinants of household consumption expenditures	Household wealth Interest rates Household expectations about the future	Shift in the position of the consumption curve

Consumers are not the only participants in the goods market. Firms are actively purchasing supplies, hiring labor, and producing output.

PLANNED INVESTMENT I

As we build the model, we add **I**, planned investment in the economy by business firms. We assume for the time being that planned investment is a fixed amount for the period and show this as a horizontal line in Figure 13.2. In macroeconomics, investment always means investment in capital, machinery, or equipment. That is, investment is investment in capital goods, goods that will provide a stream of output over several years. This is an important difference from the way that some people view investments, which they often think of as stocks and bonds.

We have added two additional items to Figure 13.2, a line labeled **C** + **I** and a 45-degree line. **C** + **I** now represents total expenditures in the economy. The total expenditure is now for both consumption and investment. We have also added a 45-degree line to show the equality between total expenditure (**C** + **I**) and total income or output **Y**. Because by definition total expenditures must equal total income, all of the equilibrium positions are along the 45-degree line. Points that are off the 45-degree line represent temporary positions in the economy before it can adjust to a new equilibrium.

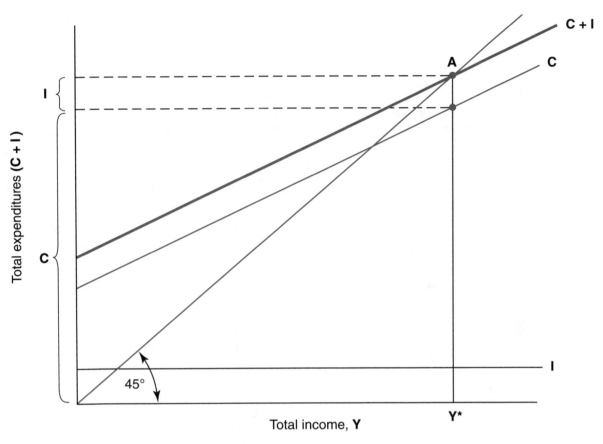

FIGURE 13.2. Total expenditures, C + I.

Adding investment to consumption.

At point *A*, total income or output is the same as total expenditure. This is the macroeconomic definition of equilibrium in the goods market. Recall that in economics an equilibrium means that there is no incentive or tendency to change. In microeconomics, when quantity demanded is the same as quantity supplied, both sides of the market are satisfied at the market-clearing or equilibrium price.

THE ADJUSTMENT TO EQUILIBRIUM

Firms hold inventories as a buffer so that they can accommodate shifts in demand and supply for their goods. Since inventories have to be purchased in advance, firms plan for a level of inventories that they think will tide them over. This is an investment for them, and sometimes they hit the planned level of inventories just right and sometimes not.

In Figure 13.3, planned investment and actual investment are the same at point *A*. At a higher level of output Y_3, to the right of Y^*, total expenditure by consumers and firms (**C + I**) is less than the amount of output, **AE < Y**. Some goods produced for sale are now unsold because total expenditure is less than output. Because expenditures fall short of the amount of output, firms are forced to retain some of their output as an unplanned investment in inventory. Because of this unplanned addition, actual investment in inventories is larger than what was planned.

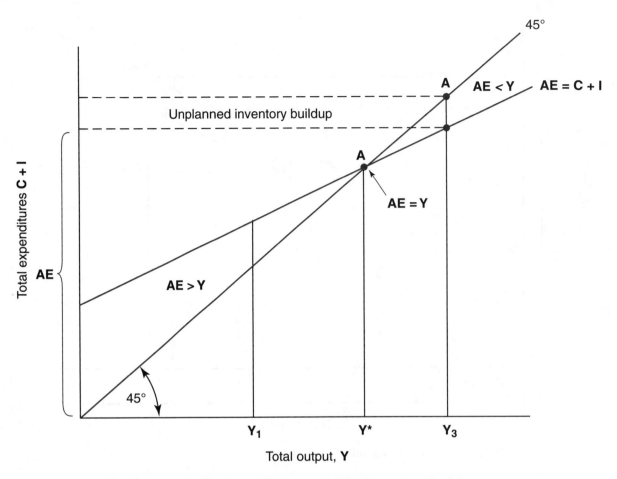

FIGURE 13.3. Equilibrium adjustments.

Unplanned inventory changes force equilibrium.

Inventories of final goods are goods that are held to produce final output during the period. Firms have a planned level for these inventories based on what they think sales will be. If sales are lower than what the firms expected, they firms will not be able to use all of the planned inventories set aside and will have more inventory than planned. Their actual inventories will be larger than their planned inventories. For example, if we are at Y_3, the amount of the unplanned inventory investment is indicated by the distance between the dashed lines in Figure 13.3. Because firms have some unsold goods and unwanted inventory buildup, they will produce less output.

As firms produce less output, output falls, incomes fall, and consumption falls until an equilibrium is finally reached at Y^*. These are all movements along the existing total expenditures $(C + I)$ curve. This is not an immediate adjustment but a series of adjustments over time. At Y^*, on the 45-degree line, there are no unsold goods and there is no unplanned inventory buildup. Planned investment in inventories is equal to actual investment in inventories, and there is no tendency to change. Y^* is the equilibrium.

Suppose that output is at Y_1, below the equilibrium. If this is where the economy is, how does an equilibrium come about? At Y_1, total expenditure is greater than output. Inventories will be drawn below planned levels. There will be an unplanned decrease in inventories because consumers and businesses want more output than has been produced. Firms will respond by increasing output until Y^* is reached.

Inventory investment levels and inventory adjustments are commonly watched and reported statistics indicating what the future direction of the economy may be like. Inventory depletion is a sign that sales are more rapid than anticipated, and if the outlook for the economy stays the same, firms will order more goods to replace the depleted inventory. Whether inventories are accumulating or depleting is often interpreted as a leading indicator of the future direction of the economy.

THE MULTIPLIER

Changes in total income affect many people in the economy. If my income goes up, I will spend more, increasing someone else's receipts and income. Their higher income will go through the same process, generating more income for someone else. This will result in a total impact on the economy of more than the amount that my income increased.

In a similar way, when we added planned investment by firms to total expenditure, the change in total income and output was larger than the amount of planned investment **I**. In Figure 13.4, we have increased planned investment by ΔI. Note that the change in output ΔY is larger than ΔI because of the multiplier.

The **multiplier** is the ratio of the change in the equilibrium level of output or income to the change in total expenditure. In this case, the planned investment multiplier results in a change in output that is greater than the change in planned investment. If there had been a change in consumption, it would be called the consumption multiplier. In any case, a multiplier allows a change in spending to produce an even larger change in income.

The multiplier is an important concept in macroeconomics, and we will use it in many ways. The process works like this. Suppose that firms feel the economy will be stronger and increase their planned investment expenditures by ΔI in Figure 13.4. As soon as they do, Y_1 is no longer the equilibrium. Firms now have unplanned depletions of their inventory and will increase output. In order to increase output, firms increase employment. Incomes increase as a result, and this leads to a higher level of consumption. This increase in consumption leads to another increase in production/output, which leads to another increase in employment and income, causing yet another increase in output, and so forth. The final effect of the change in planned investment levels will be a new equilibrium level of output at Y_2. Note that both consumption and planned investment have increased to higher levels.

What determines how large the multiplier is? The size of the multiplier in the diagram is dependent on the slope of the total expenditure ($C + I$) function. Since we have assumed that planned investment is a constant, the slope of the total expenditure function is the same as the slope of the consumption function, or $\Delta C/\Delta Y$. We call this slope the **marginal propensity to consume (MPC)**, and it is the fraction of a change in additional income that is consumed.

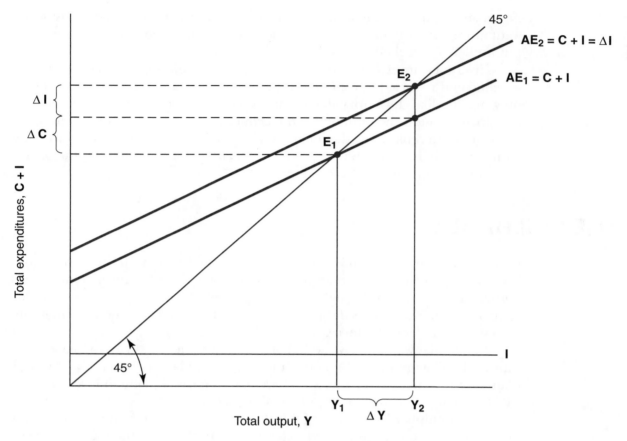

FIGURE 13.4. The AE multiplier.

An increase in investment increases total output by a multiple.

Because we are allowing consumers only to spend or save from their incomes, we can express how extra income is spent and saved:

$$MPC + MPS \equiv 1$$

The **marginal propensity to save (MPS)** is the fraction of additional income that is saved.

When incomes go up by $100 and consumption increases by $75, the MPC is 0.75. For every $100 that incomes go up, consumers will spend $75. We are assuming that the remaining $25 of the increase in income is saved and the MPS is 0.25.

We are using a very simple model to describe the multiplier and how it works. Studies of the U.S. economy have found the actual multiplier to be about 1.4. This means that for a sustained increase in total spending in the economy of $10 billion, the eventual result will be to raise GDP over time by about $14 billion.

$$(\Delta Spending) \times multiplier = (\Delta equilibrium\ GDP)$$
$$\$10\ billion \times 1.4 = \$14\ billion$$

We have not dealt with all of the major groups in the economy and we still have to add government spending and net exports.

GOVERNMENT SPENDING IN THE ECONOMY

Let us introduce government spending **G** into the model for total expenditures, remembering that **G** is government expenditures on goods and services.

$$AE = C + I + G$$

An increase in **G** will increase total expenditures. If government spending increases by \$10 billion, total expenditures will increase by \$10 billion. As a result, equilibrium GDP will increase, but it will increase by more than \$10 billion. A \$10 billion increase in government expenditures will increase equilibrium GDP by \$10 billion times the multiplier.

In Figure 13.5 **G** represents government spending and is shown as a parallel upward shift in the **C + I**. Note that total expenditures increases by **ΔAE** in the diagram.

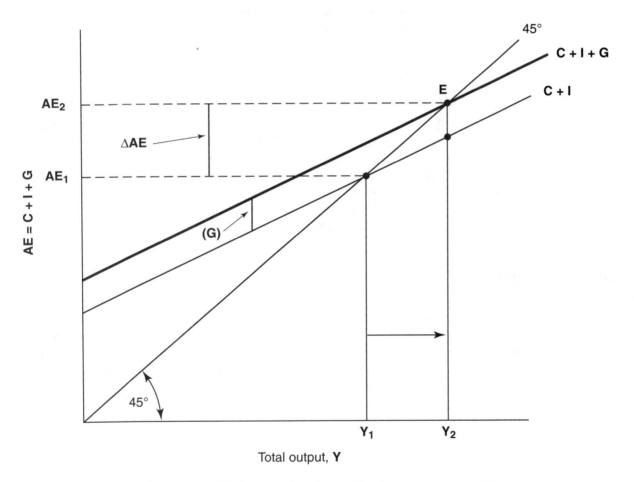

FIGURE 13.5. Equilibrium total output with government expenditures.

Total expenditures increase more than the addition of government expenditures.

The equilibrium output in the economy goes from Y_1 to Y_2 with the addition of government expenditures **G**. Both total output **Y** and total expenditures **AE** have increased by equal amounts because they represent the equilibrium condition. Even more importantly, note that the increase in **AE** labeled **ΔAE** in Figure 13.5 is much larger than the increase in total expenditures represented by **G**, the familiar multiplier in action.

The increase in government spending has stimulated the economy and resulted in more total output **Y** and along with it more employment and income.

The amount of the final increase in total income is determined by the increase in government spending times the spending multiplier. The government spending **G**, for example, $100 billion, in the economy will eventually increase total income by $400 billion. The initial increase in spending then becomes someone else's income, and if consumers spend 75 percent of this income, then $75 billion will be respent in the second round. This process continues, and each time 75 percent is respent. The final impact on the economy will be determined by the multiplier.

If consumers spend 75 percent of each additional dollar of income they receive, the MPC will be 0.75 and the multiplier will be 4:

$$\text{Multiplier} \equiv \frac{1}{1 - \text{MPC}} = \frac{1}{\text{MPS}} = \frac{1}{0.25} = 4$$

The final effect of the injection of $100 billion is the amount of government spending times the multiplier: $100 billion × 4 = a $400 billion increase in **Y**.

The multiplier applies to a change in spending by any of the components of total expenditures. Suppose there is a boom in the stock market, increasing the wealth of households and stimulating their consumption spending by $20 billion. If the spending multiplier is 4, then this increased wealth will result in an increase in total income of $80 billion.

NET EXPORTS

An increase in net exports will has an effect similar to that of an increase in government spending. The increase will have a multiplier effect of the increase times the spending multiplier, and the calculation and analytics will be the same. An increase in net exports will expand total output and a decrease in net exports will reduce total output and expenditure.

REVIEW QUESTIONS

Add the word or words that correctly complete each of the following statements.

1. If consumer expectations worsen, consumption will _____.

2. If total household wealth increases, the consumption function will shift _____.

3. If households expect the economy to worsen, GDP will _____.

4. When interest rates _____, households will save more.

5. The opportunity cost of consumption is _____.

6. Firms hold _____ to accommodate shifts in demand and supply for their goods.

7. The _____ is the ratio of the change in the equilibrium level of output or income to a change in total expenditure.

8. The _____ is the fraction of a change in additional income that is consumed.

9. An increase in total government spending of $100 billion will raise GDP by $100 billion times _____.

10. If households spend $0.50 of each additional dollar they earn, the multiplier is _____.

Circle the letter of the item that correctly completes each of the following statements.

1. When total expenditures are greater than total output,
   a. total expenditures will decrease.
   b. unplanned inventories will accumulate.
   c. total output will decrease.
   d. total output will increase.

2. When consumer confidence drops,
   a. planned inventories will be depleted.
   b. household will increase consumption.
   c. households will reduce consumption.
   d. households will increase their saving.

3. As total household wealth increases,
    a. households will save more.
    b. the consumption function will shift upward.
    c. households will still consume the same amount.
    d. firms will decrease investment.

4. If households expect the economy to improve,
    a. they will consume less this month.
    b. they will save more this month.
    c. they will consume more this month.
    d. they will not buy large-ticket items.

5. When interest rates increase,
    a. consumers will spend more and save less.
    b. the opportunity cost of consumption has decreased.
    c. firms will invest more.
    d. consumers will save more and consume less.

6. Unplanned inventory accumulation in the economy is a signal that
    a. the economy will be stronger in the future.
    b. consumer demand is larger than anticipated.
    c. total output will decline in the future.
    d. total output will increase in the future.

7. When government spending increases, the result will be
    a. an increase in total output.
    b. a decrease in total output.
    c. a decrease in total expenditure.
    d. a decrease in consumption.

8. The multiplier is
    a. 5 when the MPC is 0.2.
    b. 3 when the MPC is 0.5.
    c. the ratio of the change in consumption due to a reduction in saving.
    d. the ratio of the change in the equilibrium level of output to a change in total expenditure.

9. If the MPC is smaller than we expected, an increase in government spending will
    a. have more of an impact on total income.
    b. less of an impact on total income.
    c. have a larger multiplier.
    d. cause the MPS to be smaller.

10. An increase in net exports will
    a. increase GDP by the amount of the increase.
    b. decrease GDP by the amount of the increase.
    c. increase GDP by the amount of the increase times the multiplier.
    d. decrease GDP by the amount of the increase times the multiplier.

ANSWERS TO FILL-IN QUESTIONS

1. decrease

2. upward

3. decline

4. increase

5. the interest rate

6. inventories

7. multiplier

8. marginal propensity to consume

9. the multiplier

10. 2

ANSWERS TO MULTIPLE-CHOICE QUESTIONS

1. **d.** Planned inventories are being depleted, and producers respond by increasing output.

2. **c.** Consumers will reduce current consumption because they anticipate rougher times ahead.

3. **b.** More wealth complements income and leads to an increase in consumption.

4. **c.** Expected better times in the future will increase current consumption.

5. **d.** A higher interest rate makes saving more attractive, and consumers will save more and consume less.

6. **c.** Producers will reduce their orders because they have an inventory buildup.

7. **a.** An increase in government spending will expand output by the multiplier.

8. **d.** This is the definition.

9. **b.** A smaller multiplier means that more of each additional dollar spent by the government is saved, so the final increase in consumption will be smaller.

10. **c.** An increase in net exports is like any other increase in total expenditures.

CHAPTER 14

AGGREGATE DEMAND, AGGREGATE SUPPLY, AND SHORT-RUN INFLATION

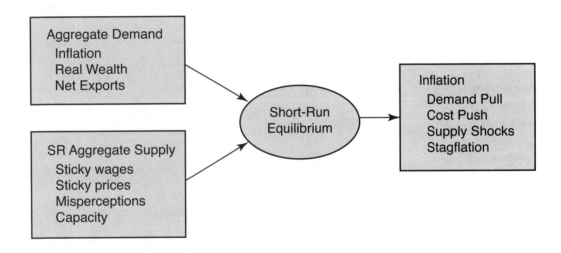

W hy do prices rise in the overall economy? How can we control inflation? These basic questions and their answers are the basis for this chapter.

Inflation is a rise in the general level of prices. An inflation rate of 5 percent means that most prices will rise 5 percent. Inflation harms those who have fixed incomes based on dollars. If your grandmother receives $500 a month from a pension that is not automatically adjusted for inflation, when inflation rises by 5 percent, her pension is worth less. Her clothing, food, water, and other goods are now more expensive, and she will have to buy less to stay within her budget.

In Chapter 6 we discussed how inflation is measured and analyzed some of the costs of inflation. In many earlier chapters we assumed that the price level was fixed. Now we will look at the causes of changes in the price level.

180 MACROECONOMICS THE EASY WAY

We will follow our usual pattern, examine the aggregate demand and then the aggregate supply, and discuss equilibrium and equilibrium adjustments. We will see how the price level and the real economy influence each other.

AGGREGATE DEMAND

To examine the effect of aggregate demand and supply on the price level, we will begin with the relationship between total expenditures and the price level.

How does the price level affect total expenditures? At higher price levels, the demand for money is higher. With given incomes, an increase in the price level means that more money balances will be needed to cover the normal transactions in the economy. If the price level doubles, households and firms will want to hold twice as many money balances to cover their usual purchases.

In Figure 14.1, we show this increase in the demand for money on the left-hand side. With no change in the money supply, the impact on the money market will be an increase in interest rates from 4 percent to 8 percent. On the right-hand side of Figure 14.1, we show that less planned investment will occur because of the rise in the interest rate. This is a response by firms to the increased cost of planned investments. Because planned investments cost more, firms will invest less.

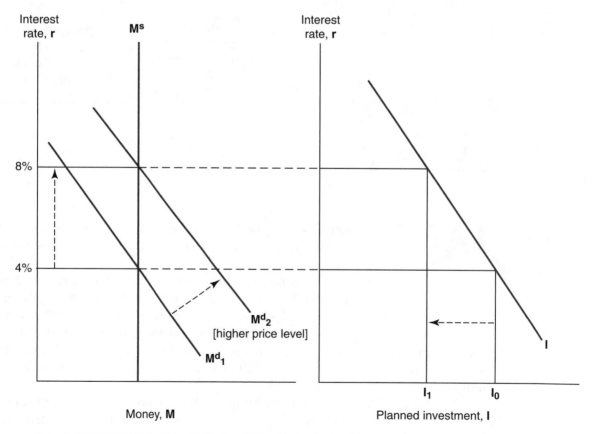

FIGURE 14.1. How inflation influences planned investment.

A higher price level leads to an increase in the demand for money, raises interest rates, and reduces planned investment.

One of the main components of total expenditures is planned investment **I**, and this has just been reduced from I_0 to I_1. This drop in planned investment will result in a new and reduced demand for total output as seen in Figure 14.2 by the downward shift in the total expenditure curve.

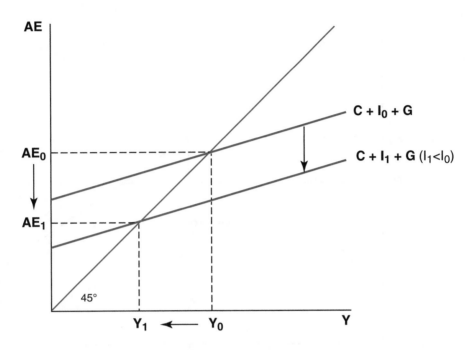

FIGURE 14.2. A decline in planned investment.

Total expenditure declines because of reduced planned investment, reducing total expenditure and income.

The result of the increase in the price level is a reduction in equilibrium output and income **Y**. As the price level increases, the amount of total income and output declines, revealing a negative relationship between the price level and total output.

The aggregate demand curve, which we have just derived, is downward-sloping in relation to the price. Let's review the chain of reasoning. We first started with the money market and showed how the demand for money increased because of the increase in the price level. This drove up the equilibrium interest rate. In the goods market, the response to this increase in the interest rate resulted in less planned investment, resulting in less total expenditure as $(C + I + G)$ shifted downward.

All of the points on the aggregate demand curve shown in Figure 14.3 represent possible equilibria in the goods market. The example we just saw was a rise in the interest rate, which lowered total expenditures and resulted in a new lower equilibrium level of output in the goods market. Total expenditure equaled total income at this lower output level Y_1 in Figure 14.2. Both levels of total income, Y_0 and Y_1, are on the aggregate demand curve in Figure 14.3; Y_0 is associated with a lower level of inflation, and Y_1 is associated with a higher level of inflation.

To repeat, both the money and goods markets are in equilibrium along the new aggregate demand curve, shown in Figure 14.3. Note that the vertical axis is now the price level.

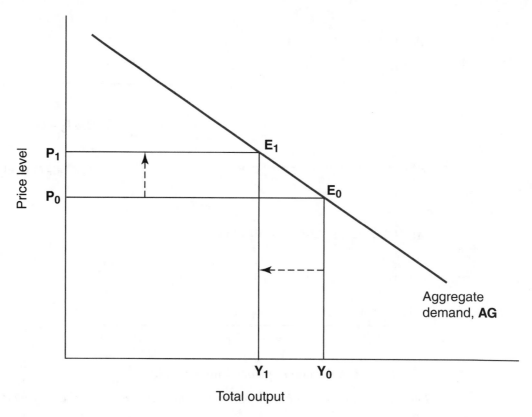

FIGURE 14.3. Aggregate demand.

The higher the price level, the less total output demanded.

WHY DOES THE AGGREGATE DEMAND CURVE SLOPE DOWNWARD?

So far, we have just looked at the effect of rising prices on the money market and traced the effect through the goods market to the aggregate demand. There are other reasons why the aggregate demand is downward-sloping.

When we examined how consumers behave, we looked at their choice of saving and consumption and the role that the interest rate played in that choice. The same increase in the interest rate that led to a fall in the level of investment spending encourages consumers to spend less and save more. This lowers consumption expenditures **C** and reduces total expenditures. A higher interest rate increases the cost of current consumption, and households consume less at all price levels. The combined effect of an increase in the price level, delivered through an increase in the interest rate, is that **both** the **I** and the **C** components of total expenditures will be at lower levels.

The Real Wealth Effect of Inflation

When we first introduced the consumption function, we discussed how changes in wealth would shift the consumption function. If the price level increases, the real value of some forms of wealth will decline. Any financial assets in nominal terms such as a savings account balance of $100,000, will decline in real purchasing power. If wealth is held in stocks or real estate, then whether the real value declines or not depends on whether the nominal prices of these goods increase at the same rate as inflation or faster.

When the price level rises, the real wealth effect suggests that some asset categories will see a decline in real value and that this will reduce consumption in the economy. This is a third factor that can explain the negatively sloping aggregate demand curve.

The Effect of Inflation on Net Exports

Remember that our definition of GDP is

$$GDP = C + I + G + NX$$

Holding government expenditures constant, how will a change in the price level affect net exports, which we have held constant so far? An increase in the U.S. price level will result in higher interest rates and less planned investment, as we saw above. These higher interest rates will attract more foreign investment. The demand for dollars will increase, bidding up the value of the dollar in foreign exchange markets. This higher value of the dollar reduces the cost of imports, which increases as a result, and exports will be more expensive for foreigners to buy and will decline. The result of these changes will be to reduce net exports (exports minus imports). The rise in the price level (inflation) in the United States will reduce U.S. net exports and total output **Y**.

To review: the aggregate demand curve is negatively sloped (the price level is negatively related to the quantity of goods and services demanded) because a higher price level

1. increases the demand for money balances, raising the interest rate and discouraging planned investment,

2. leads to a higher interest rate, which encourages consumers to save more and spend less,

3. causes some paper assets to decline in real value, reducing consumption expenditures,

4. leads to a currency appreciation, which results in more imports and fewer exports.

Shifts in the Aggregate Demand Curve

What causes the aggregate demand curve to shift? The simple answer is any change in the economy that shifts or alters the money and goods markets. We have assumed that all of the determinants of the demand for money—the supply of money, planned investment, government spending, and net exports—have remained constant in the above examples. If any of these change, the aggregate demand curve will shift.

For example, if consumers become more optimistic, consumption will increase for all levels of income and the aggregate demand will shift outward. We have summarized the determinants of the aggregate demand in Table 14.1.

TABLE 14.1 SHIFTS IN THE AGGREGATE DEMAND

Shifts to the right—more is demanded at every price level	Shifts to the left—less is demanded at every price level
↑ C Tax cut or stock market boom	↓ C Tax increase or stock market decline
↑ I Higher profit expectations or ↑ Money supply that lowers r	↓ I More pessimistic outlook or or ↓ money supply that increases r
↑ G More defense spending	↓ G Less highway spending
↑ NX Rapid overseas growth, dollar depreciation	↓ NX U.S. boom, dollar appreciation

SHORT-RUN AGGREGATE SUPPLY

We now shift focus to the short-run aggregate supply. The short-run aggregate supply represents the total goods and services available at all possible price levels. There is significant discussion and disagreement among economists about the short-run aggregate supply and its shape.

In the introductory chapters, we discussed how economists use a scientific framework described as "If X, then Y." This is a perfect opportunity to recall that approach. Because there is no strong consensus among economics professionals, we will see in the coming pages that if the **short-run aggregate supply curve (SRAS)** has a certain shape, some policies will not work. As a beginner in economics, you will have to realize quickly, if you have not already done so, that many answers or results depend on the assumptions you make. This is especially true about the shape of the short-run aggregate supply curve. We will make these arguments and discussions as clear as possible so your ability to analyze them will not be affected. However, you must remember that the results of your analysis will depend on the assumptions you make.

We will also discover another barrier to determining clear-cut implications of policy decisions. If we believe that a specific policy action will shift both the supply and the demand curves, the outcome will depend on the magnitude of these shifts. We cannot examine with precision some issues because we will see the possibility of both curves shifting at the same time, resulting in an indeterminate answer that depends on how much each curve has shifted.

Short-run aggregate supply is the positive relationship between the price level and total output in the economy. The higher the price level, the more output is produced. This is different from the supply curve in a particular market like the automobile market. In that case, an increase in the price of automobiles will encourage automobile producers to supply more cars. An individual market supply curve is positively sloped in relation to the price of that market's good.

What about the shape of the economy's short-run supply curve? The short-run aggregate supply curve slopes upward. The higher the price level in the economy, the more goods and services are supplied. In our discussion of economic growth, we used a long-run aggregates supply curve that was completely vertical. Why isn't the short-run aggregate supply curve vertical? Why does it slope upwards? There are three explanations why it could be upward sloping in the short-run.

The first is **sticky wages**, where nominal wages that are slow to adjust to price changes. If the wage adjustment to an increase in the price level is not quick, employment and output will be more profitable and firms will produce more output in response to the higher price level.

The **sticky prices** explanation suggests that firms are slow to adjust prices or that firm price adjustments lag behind economy wide price changes. If there is a fall in the overall price level, some firms will maintain their prices while they are changing their announced price lists. These firms will suffer a decline in sales as a result. They will then cut back on output and employment. In this case, the fall in the price level will result in less output.

The third explanation has to do with **misperceptions** and a lack of perfect information. When firms see their product prices increasing, they incorrectly assume that it is not a price level increase but a change in their particular markets. They perceive the increasing price level as an increase in the relative prices they face. Their response is to increase production.

Note that all three of these explanations rely on a temporary change, one that in the short run corrects itself over time. Wages and prices will adjust and misperceptions will be adjusted by better information if there is enough time.

Figure 14.4 shows a short-run aggregate supply curve.

The shape of the short-run aggregate supply curve in Figure 14.4 is relatively horizontal at low levels of output and relatively steep as output approaches capacity at Y^*. This is because the response of firms in the economy to an increase in the price level depends on how close to capacity they are operating and on how rapidly wage rates adjust to price changes. If the economy has ample excess capacity and the price level rises, the response will be to increase output with existing machinery and employees. When capacity utilization is very high, increases in the price level lead to relatively small increases in output. This difference in responsiveness is the difference between the output responses of ΔY_1 and ΔY_2 to the same ΔP price change in Figure 14.4.

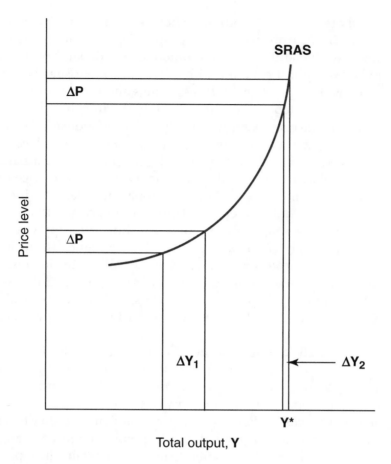

FIGURE 14.4. Short-run aggregate supply.

The same price increase has less effect on output in the more vertical part of the supply curve.

Shifts in Aggregate Demand

We can now analyze shifts in aggregate demand. We detailed the factors that could shift aggregate demand above, and now we want to trace their effects on the price level.

Figure 14.5 shows increasing aggregate demand shifts and the results.

We have shown the upper part of the aggregate supply curve **SRAS** vertical at **Y***. In the short run, there are physical limits to the amount of output a country can produce. In the short run it is usually assumed that some inputs are fixed and cannot be changed rapidly. Technological change, improving labor force skills, or the movement of resources from one country to another can be a lengthy process. Because of this short-run inability of the supply curve to completely adjust, any demand shifts above **AD$_4$** will result only in forcing up the price level, with no change in real output. On the other hand, when the economy has excess capacity and underutilized resources, public policies to increase employment and output have more impact on output and relatively less impacts on inflation.

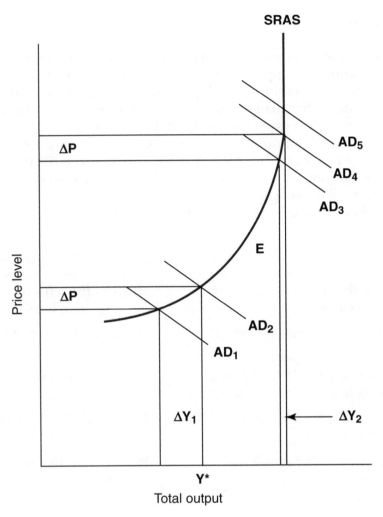

FIGURE 14.5. Short-run aggregate supply and increasing AD shifts.

AD increases add less and less to output Y as the SRAS *becomes more vertical.*

The importance of the shape of the **SRAS** and the heated debates about it are based on the effectiveness of public policies to combat inflation. The effectiveness of policies to stimulate aggregate demand have less and less impact on output, and more on prices, as the SRAS becomes vertical. In other words, the larger the excess capacity in the economy, the greater the impact of expansionary monetary and fiscal policies on real growth and employment. As the economy gets closer to capacity in the short run, the effects of stimulating aggregate demand will be mostly inflationary, with very little change in employment and real output **Y**.

Shifts in the Short-run Aggregate Supply Curve

Changes in the determinants of the short-run aggregate supply curve will shift the position of the supply curve at all price levels. The major determinants of SRAS are a change in the cost of inputs including wages, economic growth, public policy efforts that change taxes for firms or change the pattern of regulation and changes in firm expectations about the economy.

With regard to input costs or any of the determinants of the short-run aggregate supply curve, we have to remember that this **SRAS** is for the entire economy, not just one industry. In this case, the increase or decrease in input costs affects all firms operating in the economy.

We have summarized these shifts in Table 14.2.

TABLE 14.2 SHIFTS IN THE SHORT-RUN AGGREGATE SUPPLY

Shifts to the right—more is supplied at every price level	**Shifts to the left**—less is supplied at every price level
Lower costs of inputs including wages	**Higher costs** of input including wages
Economic growth, more labor, technological change, and so on	**Economic decline**
Public policy, tax cuts, and deregulation	**Public policies**, tax increase, and more regulation
Expectations of future sales, optimistic	**Expectations** of future sales, pessimistic

THE EQUILIBRIUM PRICE LEVEL

The short-run equilibrium is shown in Figure 14.6. Aggregate demand and aggregate supply intersect at 1 in the short run.

How are changes in equilibrium resolved? We will see three successive points of equilibrium (1, 2, and 3) as we examine the effects of an increase in aggregate demand and how that plays out over time. Starting at the natural rate of output equilibrium shown by point 1 and Y^*, suppose that aggregate demand shifts from AD_1 to AD_2. The economy will feel upward pressure on production costs or prices because it is moving up $SRAS_1$ in the short run at point 2. When input costs are bid up, $SRAS_1$ shifts inward to $SRAS_2$, reflecting these higher costs. In the long-run equilibrium at point 3, output is at the natural rate of output Y^*, but with a higher price level.

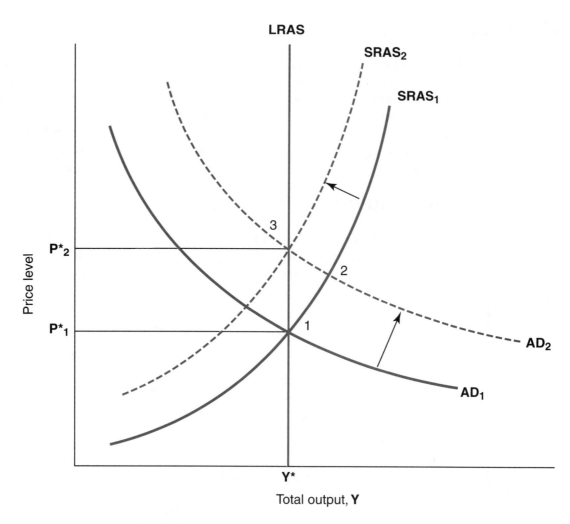

FIGURE 14.6. Classical view.

Aggregate demand increases cause the short-run aggregate supply curve to shift upward as input prices increase.

Figure 14.6 is labeled the classical view because the long-run aggregate supply does not change with a change in the price level. It changes only with economic growth.

CAUSES OF SHORT-RUN INFLATION

We now turn our attention to two basic causes of short-run inflation. Remember that inflation is an increase in the overall price level. An important distinction is whether there is a persistent rise in prices, called **sustained inflation**, or a one-time bump in the price level.

Changes in the short run such as an increase in aggregate demand or a decrease in aggregate supply will lead to a short-run increase in the price level. The short-run causes of inflation are classified as demand-pull or cost-push inflation, indicating which side of the market has initiated the increase in prices.

Demand-pull Inflation

Inflation caused by an increase in aggregate demand is called **demand-pull inflation**. As we have seen, any increase in consumption spending, planned investment, government expenditures, or a reduction in taxes shifts the aggregate demand curve outward. Expansionary monetary and fiscal policies also shift the aggregate demand outward. Because of the shape of the SRAS, continual increases in aggregate demand initially spur output increases with some inflation, but as the economy gets closer to capacity, the main result will be inflation.

Cost-push or Supply-side Inflation

Cost-push inflation or supply-side inflation is caused by an increase in costs of production. Often it is caused by a supply shock such as a sharp increase in the price of oil, an input that many industries use to produce output. We have illustrated this in Figure 14.7.

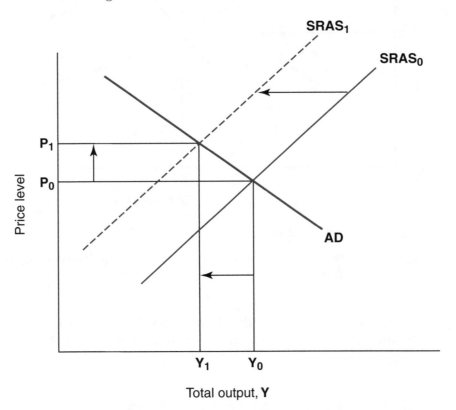

FIGURE 14.7. OPEC supply shock.

OPEC restricts output of oil, increasing inflation and reducing output and employment.

When OPEC member nations agreed to restrict output in the 1970s, this produced a supply shock, which we show in Figure 14.7 as a decrease in supply from **SRAS$_0$** to **SRAS$_1$**. This sharp increase in the price of oil caused cost-push inflation in the United States and many other countries, as well as total output declines. This is called **stagflation**—the economy experiences rising price levels (inflation) and falling output (stagnation) shown in Figure 14.7.

Stagflation causes a real policy dilemma. Efforts to stimulate aggregate demand shift aggregate demand upward and to the right, but the short-run result will be even more inflation accompanying the growth in output. However, efforts to lessen inflation cause a decrease in aggregate demand, which will lead to less employment and even less output being produced.

Expectations and Inflation

Expectations play an important role in inflation. If households expect prices to rise next year, they will increase this year's demand for goods and services to take advantage of prices that are lower now. Their actions will increase the demand for current goods, causing their prices to rise. This can be a self-fulfilling prophesy.

If all the firms in the economy expect inflation to rise by 12 percent next year, they will increase their prices by 12 percent. The effect of these inflationary expectations will shift the short-run SRAS curve to the left. The result: Inflation will increase because consumers and firms think that inflation will be higher next year.

Edmund Phelps won the Nobel Prize in economics in 2006 for his work on the importance of expectations about future inflation. Because of his work, central banks now focus on inflationary expectations as well as on the money supply and demand.

REVIEW QUESTIONS

Add the word or words that correctly complete each of the following statements.

1. A higher price level leads to an _____ in the demand for money.

2. An increase in the _____ will encourage consumers to spend less.

3. With a price level rise, the _____ effect suggests a decline in consumption.

4. A higher value of the dollar will _____ imports.

5. Demand shifts in the _____ portion of the short-run aggregate supply curve lead only to inflation.

6. When there is excess capacity, _____ in aggregate demand will have more impact on output and relatively less impact on inflation.

7. The short-run aggregate supply will shift to the _____ because of a new oil discovery.

8. Sticky _____ are nominal wages that are slow to adjust to price changes.

9. The sticky _____ explanation suggests that firm price adjustments lag behind economywide price changes.

10. _____ inflation is caused by an increase in costs of production.

Circle the letter of the item that correctly completes each of the following statements.

1. A higher price level raises interest rates and
   a. encourages consumption.
   b. encourages more planned investment.
   c. reduces inflation.
   d. reduces planned investment.

2. Sticky wages
   a. are wages pegged to an inflation level.
   b. are one argument for demand pull inflation.
   c. are real wages that are slow to adjust to price changes.
   d. are nominal wages that are slow to adjust to price changes.

3. Along the new aggregate demand curve,
   a. demand equals supply.
   b. the goods market is in equilibrium.
   c. both the money market and the goods market are in equilibrium
   d. the money market is in equilibrium.

4. Aggregate demand will shift to the right when there is a
   a. lower rate of interest
   b. higher rate of interest.
   c. decrease in the money supply.
   d. dollar appreciation.

5. In the flatter, more horizontal part of the short-run aggregate supply curve,
   a. there is no unemployment.
   b. aggregate demand increases will impact real output.
   c. aggregate demand increases will be purely inflationary.
   d. the economy is working at full capacity.

6. When the short-run supply curve is vertical, decreases in aggregate demand will
   a. influence the employment level.
   b. reduce employment.
   c. reduce total output.
   d. reduce only inflation, not the employment level.

7. Demand-pull inflation
   a. can be caused by more favorable consumer expectations.
   b. can be caused by a decline in wealth.
   c. can be the result of a supply shock.
   d. can lead to stagflation.

8. A currency appreciation will result in
   a. a decline in GDP.
   b. no change in GDP.
   c. fewer imports and more exports.
   d. more imports and less exports.

9. Cost-push inflation or supply-side inflation can be caused by
   a. an increase in aggregate demand.
   b. an increase in the costs of production.
   c. a decrease in aggregate demand.
   d. a decrease in the cost of production.

10. A stock market boom will
    a. shift the aggregate demand curve to the right.
    b. cause the economy to move down the aggregate demand curve.
    c. shift the aggregate demand curve to the left.
    d. cause the economy to move up the aggregate demand curve.

ANSWERS TO FILL-IN QUESTIONS

1. increase

2. interest rate

3. real wealth

4. increase

5. vertical

6. increases

7. right

8. wages

9. prices

10. Cost-push

ANSWERS TO MULTIPLE-CHOICE QUESTIONS

1. **d.** Higher interest rates increase the cost of planned investment, which reduces planned investment.

2. **c.** This is the definition.

3. **c.** That is how the aggregate demand is defined so that *both* markets are in equilibrium.

4. **a.** A lower rate of interest stimulates both consumption and investment, shifting the aggregate demand curve to the right.

5. **b.** Real output can increase more easily when there is excess capacity.

6. **d.** The economy is overheated and at full capacity, so a decline in aggregate demand will reduce only inflation in this case.

7. **a.** The aggregate demand will increase, increasing the price level.

8. **d.** A stronger local currency will by more imports than before and cost more for those who receive exports.

9. **b.** The OPEC supply shock decreased the SRAS because of the higher costs that a higher price of oil imposed on the economy.

10. **a.** An increase in wealth will encourage more consumption and an increase in the aggregate demand curve.

CHAPTER 15

MONETARY AND FISCAL POLICY

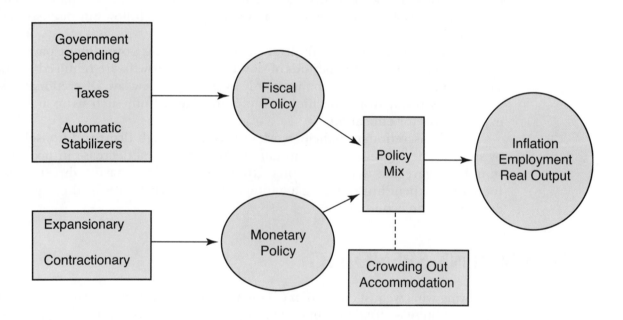

The main topics in this chapter concern how the government hand is felt in the economy. We will look at the effects of taxes on the economy, as well as at changes in government spending. These two aspects of fiscal policy affect inflation, real output, income, and employment in the whole economy.

There are very few topics that are more heated than taxes and government spending. Behind the heat are some strongly held normative judgments about what the role of the government should be. Most conservatives want as small a government as possible, lower taxes, and a strong reliance on the market system to allocate resources. They maintain that laissez faire or a free market is the best way to organize economic activity.

On the other hand, liberals want to make sure that government corrects for the faults of the market economy and provides the necessary social and physical infrastructure. These corrections take the form of efforts to ensure a more competitive business environment and a more equitable distribution of wealth and resources.

Because these are normative arguments, there is little that economics can add to the debate. However, if the debate changes to a decision about whether a tax cut to the poorest one-third of the population will have a greater impact on aggregate demand than a tax cut to the top 5 percent of income earners, this becomes an empirical question and right up the economist's alley. The answer involves how these extra funds are spent and invested by each group and which impact is larger. But we are getting ahead of ourselves.

The government plays several roles in the economy at the macro level. Some are automatic, some are discretionary, and some are regulatory. The purpose of these policy tools is to stabilize the economy and permit stimulation and dampening actions to maintain a healthy economy with real growth, low inflation, and low unemployment.

The major policy tools are fiscal policy and monetary policy. Fiscal policies involve government expenditures and taxation policies. Not only does fiscal policy include government expenditures and tax policies, it also includes transfer payments such as Social Security payments to households and automatic stabilizers. Monetary policies involve the money supply and will follow our discussion of fiscal policy.

Nondiscretionary expenditures, such as increasing government payments to the unemployed during periods of slow economic growth, are required by law. These expenditures can be changed only by passing a new law. **Discretionary** fiscal policies result from specific decisions to take action, such as to increase expenditures for education.

Some discretionary policies work indirectly through firms and households by shifting the aggregate demand curve. For example, a decrease in taxes will stimulate aggregate demand. Other government policies have a direct effect. Increasing expenditures during a national disaster directly affects the aggregate demand in the economy.

GOVERNMENT SPENDING

Reviewing what we just covered in Chapter 14, an increase in government spending **G** will increase total output by a multiple of the increase in spending because of the multiplier. This increase in **G** will increase aggregate demand and put upward pressure on the price level. If the government wishes to dampen inflationary pressures, it can reduce government spending, for example, by cutting spending on the space program.

Changes in Taxes

Tax changes are the second major part of fiscal policy. A reduction in income taxes will increase take-home pay. Households will save some of this increase and spend some on consumer goods and services. Because the result is an increase in consumption, aggregate demand will shift upward. An increase in taxes will have the opposite effect and shift aggregated expenditures and aggregate demand downward.

Because the change in taxes comes indirectly through consumers, a $100 billion decrease in taxes will have less effect than a $100 billion increase in government spending. The reason is that the increase in **G** will enter aggregate demand directly and the final impact will be the change in **G** times the multiplier. If the MPC is 75 percent, when taxes are decreased by $100 billion, consumers will save part of the increase in income and spend 75 percent in the economy. The first time the tax reduction hits the economy, it will not be the full amount of the tax reduction but the amount of the tax reduction times the MPC. In our example with an MPC of 0.75, the tax cut of $100 billion enters the economy in the same way as an increase in **G** of $75 billion.

With a tax change, there is an additional effect that is important. Do consumers think it is a permanent or a temporary tax cut? If they think it is temporary, they will increase their consumption by much less than if they think it is permanent. A cut in taxes that is permanent is viewed as much more of an addition to their incomes than a cut in taxes they think is temporary.

Automatic Stabilizers

One of the problems with fiscal policies is that these actions take time to work themselves through the system. These lags from implementation to final result are unpredictable and a concern for policy makers.

However, there are automatic stabilizers built into the system. **Automatic stabilizers** are fiscal policy revenue and expenditure items that move in the direction opposite GDP changes and tend to dampen the swings of the economy. The tax system is an automatic stabilizer because almost all taxes, on individuals and firms, are based on income or profits. When the economy is in a downturn, incomes fall and so do tax revenues. Because households pay less in taxes, this is the equivalent of an automatic tax cut that provides some stimulus to aggregate demand during a downturn and thus moderates the severity of the downturn.

Nondiscretionary government spending also acts as an automatic stabilizer. As the economy goes into a recession and unemployment increases, more people apply for unemployment and welfare benefits. This results in an automatic increase in government spending, which increases the aggregate demand from what it would be without unemployment benefits.

Automatic stabilizers cannot stop a recession, but they can moderate a downturn. When a recession occurs, automatic stabilizers go into effect and taxes fall while government expenditures increase, moving the budget toward a deficit or a larger deficit. The opposite is true in an expansion—tax receipts increase and government expenditures fall, moving the budget toward a surplus. Many economists do not advocate a rigid balanced budget rule because this would force the government to find ways to raise taxes or cut spending in a downturn in order to balance the budget.

MONETARY POLICY

A quick review of Chapter 14 will make sure that we understand the relationships between the goods market and the money market. Once we establish these linkages, we can see how monetary policies affect the goods market and total output and how fiscal policies can affect the monetary markets. For example, we will look at how Fed changes in the discount rate can affect total output.

We will continue to link the markets together to eventually come up with a complete model of the economy that includes the goods market, the money market, and the overall price level. Figures 15.1 illustrates the linkages that integrate the two markets.

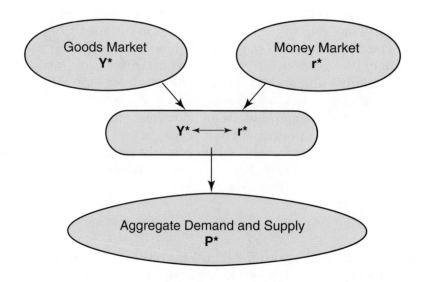

FIGURE 15.1. Integrating the goods and money markets.

This diagram shows how markets are related to aggregate demand and supply.

Integrating the Goods Market and the Money Market

Chapter 14 described the two key links between the goods market and the money market. In the first, income, which is determined in the goods market, is linked with the demand for money in the money market. The second link is between the interest rate determined in the money market and planned investment in the goods market. To review

1. Income and the demand for money: The demand for money depends on the level of income. The higher the level of aggregate income, the higher the transactions demand for money. An increase in aggregate income and output will lead to an increase in money demand.

2. The interest rate and planned investment: Planned investment spending depends on the interest rate, which is determined in the money market. Because the interest rate represents a cost of borrowing, the higher the interest rate, the lower the level of planned investment. Planned investment increases when the interest rate falls and decreases when the interest rate rises.

In the rest of the chapter we will use shorthand notation to describe these linkages between markets. The first traces how changes in the interest rate influence total output.

$$\Delta r \ \rightarrow \ \Delta I \ \rightarrow \ \Delta AD \ \rightarrow \ \Delta Y^*$$

This shorthand is read, "A change in the interest rate will lead to a change in planned investment. A different level of planned investment changes aggregate demand and the equilibrium output." Remember that the change in total output will be a multiple of the change in investment because of the multiplier.

For a specific change such as an increase in the interest rate, the shorthand looks like this:

$$\uparrow \mathbf{r} \rightarrow \downarrow \mathbf{I} \rightarrow \downarrow \mathbf{AD} \rightarrow \downarrow \mathbf{Y^*}$$

This is read, "An increase in the interest rate will reduce the level of planned investment. This reduces aggregate demand. A reduced aggregate demand reduces the level of equilibrium output."

We have looked at how changes in the money market, affect the goods market, and now we will look at how the goods market influences the money market.

Higher levels of income mean a higher level of transactions. This demand for transactions balances increases the demand for money. In terms of our shorthand,

$$\uparrow \mathbf{Y} \rightarrow \uparrow \mathbf{M^d} \rightarrow \uparrow \mathbf{r^*}$$

An increase in income increases the demand for transactions balances, which increases the demand for money. This will result in a higher equilibrium interest rate.

This works in the opposite direction with a decrease in income. A good way to remember these changes in income and the interest rate is that they move in the same direction: An increase in aggregate demand increases the interest rate, and a decrease in aggregate demand decreases the interest rate.

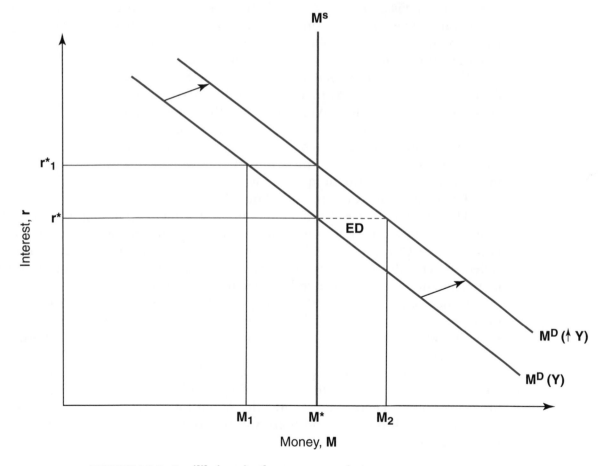

FIGURE 15.2. Equilibrium in the money market.

Money demand increases because of higher income.

In Figure 15.2, we show the increase in income and its effect on the money demand. At a higher level of income, money demand increases at all levels of interest to accommodate the need for more transactions. The immediate result is an excess demand **ED** at the old rate of interest. This excess demand for money eventually forces the interest rate up until it reaches r^*_1.

Macroeconomic Policy and the Effects on Both Markets

We have looked at one market's effects on the other. Now we can examine both markets at the same time. We want to look at the effects of expansionary and contractionary policies by the government. We will analyze them by looking at their effects on both markets simultaneously. This is a closer approximation to what happens than our earlier simplified models of one market at a time.

EXPANSIONARY POLICIES

An expansionary policy is one that seeks to increase total output and income. An **expansionary fiscal policy** either increases government spending or reduces taxes. An **expansionary monetary policy** is one that increases the money supply.

Expansionary Fiscal Policy. Both an increase in government spending and a reduction in taxes are expansionary fiscal policies. As discussed earlier, an equal reduction in taxes has a smaller effect because it an indirect influence on aggregate demand. Both of these actions have multipliers.

If the government increases spending by $50 billion, this will stimulate firms to increase output **Y**. Increasing output increases income, and this stimulates consumer spending. Without taking the interest rate into account, this process will come to an end at a higher level of output **Y**.

At the same time, the increase in income increases the demand for money and put pressure on interest rates to increase, which they will eventually do if there is no change in the money supply.

The increase in **G** will increase both **Y*** and **r***.

The increase in **r** will reduce planned investment spending and lower **Y**. Therefore, the increase in government spending will increase **Y** via the additional **G** and **C** but decrease **Y** because higher interest rates reduce **I**. This is called the crowding-out effect. **Crowding-out** occurs when increases in government spending tend to cause reductions in private investment.

If there is no change in the money supply to accommodate the increase in income and money demand, the expansionary effects of the extra government spending will be dampened by the reduction in planned investment. There will be some crowding-out.

The size of the crowding-out effect depends on several things. If the Fed completely accommodates the increased demand for money by increasing the money supply to keep interest rates the same, there will be no crowding-out. Interest rates will not rise, and there will be no decline in planned investment (see Figure 15.3).

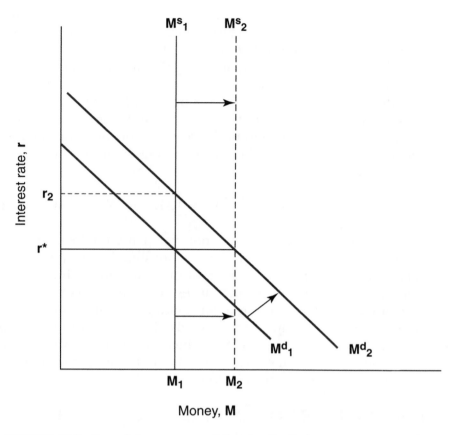

FIGURE 15.3. Complete accommodation by the Fed.

The Fed completely accommodates an increase in the demand for money, and r* stays the same.

The sensitivity of planned investment to interest rate changes is another factor that determines how much crowding-out there will be. If planned investment is relatively insensitive, the crowding-effect will be small, and if it is very sensitive to interest rate changes, the crowding-out effect will be large.

To recap in our shorthand, an expansionary fiscal policy with an increase in **G** and some crowding-out will have the following results:

$$\uparrow G \rightarrow \uparrow Y \rightarrow \uparrow M^d \rightarrow \uparrow r \rightarrow \downarrow I \rightarrow \downarrow Y$$

An increase in government spending leads to an increase in total output, which increases the demand for money and raises interest rates. At higher rates of interest, planned investment declines as does total output.

The amount of crowding-out (seen by the decline in **Y** at the very end) depends on two things:

1. If the Fed completely accommodates the increase in money demand, there will be no increase in **r** and no reduction in **Y** as a result (see Figure 15.3).

2. If planned investment is insensitive to a change in the interest rate, there will be only a small reduction in planned investment and output due to crowding-out.

Expansionary Monetary Policy. An expansionary monetary policy increases the supply of money. The monetary policies that increase the money supply are open market operations that purchase Treasury bonds in the market, lowering the reserve requirement, and lowering the discount rate.

Any Fed policy that increases the money supply starts the following chain of events. An increase in the money supply will lower interest rates. There will be more planned investment at lower rates, and aggregate demand will increase, inducing an increase in output **Y**. Because of the increase in output and income, the demand for money will increase, raising the interest rate.

In our shorthand,

$$\uparrow M^s \rightarrow \downarrow r \rightarrow \uparrow I \rightarrow \uparrow AE \rightarrow \uparrow Y \rightarrow \uparrow M^d \rightarrow \uparrow r$$

The usefulness of monetary policy depends on the magnitude of the events in the chain, especially on the relationship between the interest rate and planned investment. If firms react strongly to a fall in interest rates, that is, significantly increase their planned investment, monetary policy will have a strong expansionary effect. On the other hand, if the link is weak, there will be little effect on the economy. In other words, the power of monetary policy depends on the shape of the demand for planned investment. If the demand for planned investment is practically vertical in relation to the interest rate, there will be little change in investment as interest rates fall.

Two Recent Examples of Expansionary Fiscal Policy

What kind of evidence do we have about the effect of expansionary fiscal policies on the economy? The best examples of expansionary fiscal policy come from the 1974–1975 recession and the recession of 1980–1982. In the first case, Congress passed a large tax cut to stimulate the economy, and it appears to have been successful as consumer spending increased soon after.

Was there any evidence of crowding-out? Interest rates did not increase, probably because the Fed was expanding the money supply at the same time. It seems that the actions of the Fed were close to a situation of complete accommodation as we discussed earlier. An illustration of this is in Figure 15.3.

Because of the increase in income brought about by the decline in taxes, the demand for money increased from M^d_1 to M^d_2, which would have, without a change in the money supply, raised interest rates to r_2. But since the Fed was pursuing an expansionary monetary policy (Figure 15.3) of exactly the right increase in the money supply, the interest rate stayed at r^*. This is called **completely accommodating** the increase in the money demand. The interest rate does not change when this happens, and there is no crowding-out.

The second recessionary period was 1980–1982, and in this case Congress passed a large tax cut in 1981 to get the economy out of the recession. The tax cut led to an increase in consumer spending that helped the economy recover. Simultaneously, the Fed expanded the money supply at a rate more than necessary to accommodate the increase in output and money demand so that rates actually fell in late 1982. Here again there was no evidence of crowding-out.

One important lesson comes from this discussion of fiscal and monetary expansion policies. The economy is dynamic, so measurements of the effects of policies are difficult to untangle because several policies may be working themselves through the economy at the same time. To use the models we have set up, we have had to assume that everything else remains constant so that we can focus on particular effects. This is an unavoidable result of having to simplify to understand the very complex relationships in the economy.

CONTRACTIONARY POLICIES

Contractionary policies are designed to slow down the economy. **Contractionary policies** seek to reduce inflation and cool down the economy. The basic goals of macroeconomic policies are to produce real growth and employment. Part of this mix is inflation, which can reduce real growth. Most calls for contractionary policies are concerned with reducing inflationary pressures.

These policies are essentially the reverse of expansionary policies: The toolbox has not changed.

Contractionary fiscal policies, with a goal of reducing output and aggregate demand, are an increase in taxes and a reduction in government spending.

We can go directly to our shorthand notation:

$$\downarrow G \text{ or } \uparrow \text{taxes} \rightarrow \downarrow Y \rightarrow \downarrow M^d \rightarrow \downarrow r \rightarrow \uparrow I$$

A decrease in government expenditures or an increase in taxes decreases output and income in the economy. This decrease reduces the demand for money, lowering the interest rate and stimulating more planned investment. The increase in planned investment mutes the decline in **Y**. Again, we the question of how interest-rate-sensitive the demand for unplanned investment is and have essentially the same response as before but in a different direction.

Contractionary monetary policies, with a goal of reducing output and aggregate demand, are policies that reduce the supply of money. To refresh your memory, these are selling Treasury bonds via open market operations, increasing the reserve requirement, and increasing the discount rate.

Our shorthand for of the results of a contractionary monetary policy is

$$\downarrow M^s \rightarrow \uparrow r \rightarrow \downarrow I \rightarrow \downarrow Y \rightarrow \downarrow M^d \rightarrow \downarrow r$$

Contractionary monetary policies decrease the money supply, increase the interest rate, reduce planned investment spending, and reduce total output **Y**. A lower total output **Y** will result in a decline in the demand for money and a lower interest rate.

DETERMINANTS OF PLANNED INVESTMENT

We have given short treatment to planned investment and discussed only the relationship between the interest rate and planned investment. Of course, the situation is more complicated than that. The demand for planned investment has a negative relationship to the interest rate. The higher the interest rate, the lower the amount of planned investment in the economy firms are willing to undertake.

There are three major determinants of the demand for planned investment. They all affect the position of the demand curve, and shifts in these determinants shift the demand for planned investment.

Expectations for the future play a role in most demand curves, and the demand for planned investment is no exception. If expectations change and the outlook for the next 5 years is for a sustained period of growth, the demand for planned investment will increase and shift outward at all interest levels. Firms will gear up for an anticipated higher level of sales by purchasing the necessary capital goods now.

Current **capacity utilization** rates also affect planned investment. If firms are operating at 60 percent of capacity, they will not be as likely to invest in new capital equipment as they would at 95 percent capacity utilization.

Firms always have a choice between labor and capital expenditures in production decisions. If wage rates are stable or declining, they will **substitute** away from new capital goods and hire more labor. If wages are low or expected to be low, the demand for planned investment curve will shift inward and to the left. At every interest rate, less planned investment will be demanded.

THE FISCAL AND MONETARY POLICY MIX

The **policy mix** is the combination of fiscal and monetary policies currently in use. As we saw in the section on expansionary policies, a combined mix for expansion purposes could be either an increase in government expenditures or a reduction in taxes, with an increase in the money supply. On the other hand, a policy mix that favors private investment spending over government spending could be an expansionary monetary policy to encourage investment combined with a reduction in government spending.

There is wide and vocal disagreement about the best policy mix. These normative judgments depend heavily on views about the right size of government in the economy, the importance of public versus private investment, and the importance of government-provided social services.

MONEY AND INFLATION

As we have seen, an increase in government expenditures leads to an increase in aggregate demand and an increase in the price level. This is demand-pull inflation in the short run. If the Fed completely accommodates the increase in demand for money by increasing the money supply, then aggregate demand will not be dampened by a change in the interest rate because it will remain the same, and aggregate demand will shift even further upward and to the right. The resulting higher price level will increase the demand for money, and aggregate demand will increase even further. The result can be a sustained period of inflation. Without a continual increase in the money supply, the economy will reach its natural rate of output.

There is general agreement that demand-pull and cost-push changes in the economy lead to short-term inflation. These changes can be caused by an expansionary monetary and fiscal policy, cost shocks, and changes in expectation, as we have seen.

LONG-RUN AGGREGATE SUPPLY AND PUBLIC POLICY

If the **LRAS** is vertical as most economists feel it is, neither monetary policy nor fiscal policy changes will have any effect on the natural rate of output **Y***. Changes in monetary and fiscal policy will affect the price level or inflation only in the long run. There is also general agreement that for sustained inflation to take place, it must be continually accommodated by the Fed. In this case, sustained inflation can be viewed as a monetary phenomenon.

REVIEW QUESTIONS

Add the word or words that correctly complete each of the following statements.

1. _____ policies involve government expenditures and taxation.

2. _____ policies involve the money supply.

3. An increase in taxes will shift aggregated expenditures and aggregate demand _____.

4. _____ are fiscal policy revenue and expenditure items that move in the opposite direction of GDP changes.

5. An _____ in the interest rate will reduce the level of planned investment.

6. A decline in the level of planned investment will _____ aggregate demand.

7. An increase government spending is an _____ fiscal policy.

8. Crowding-out occurs when increases in government spending tend to cause _____ in private investment.

9. Contractionary _____ policies will reduce the supply of money.

10. A policy that favors private investment spending would be an _____ monetary policy.

Circle the letter of the item that correctly completes each of the following statements.

1. An expansionary fiscal policies is
    a. increasing government spending.
    b. increasing taxes.
    c. increasing the money supply.
    d. increasing the reserve requirement.

2. An expansionary monetary policy is
    a. increasing the reserve requirement.
    b. decreasing the reserve requirement.
    c. increasing the discount rate.
    d. selling bonds through open market operations.

3. A contractionary fiscal policy is to
    a. decrease taxes.
    b. increase the money supply.
    c. increase taxes.
    d. decrease the money supply.

4. Expansionary fiscal policy can have less impact on the economy if there is
    a. unused capacity.
    b. crowding-out.
    c. no crowding-out.
    d. also complete accommodation by the Fed.

5. Automatic stabilizers are
    a. discretionary policies to reduce the effects of recessions.
    b. nondiscretionary monetary policies.
    c. used to combat crowding-out.
    d. helpful in dampening the swings of the economy.

6. Crowding-out occurs when
    a. decreases in government spending cause private investment to decrease.
    b. increases in government spending cause reductions in private investment.
    c. increases in government spending cause increases in private investment.
    d. contractionary government policies reduce private investment.

7. Crowding-out can be completely neutralized by
    a. complete accommodation by the Fed.
    b. decreasing the money supply.
    c. increasing taxes.
    d. increasing the require reserve ratio.

8. If current capacity utilization rates are low,
    a. expansionary fiscal policy will have little effect on output.
    b. interest rate changes will have less effect on planned investment than at full capacity.
    c. interest rate changes will have more effect on planned investment than at full capacity.
    d. expansionary monetary policy will have little effect on output.

9. A combined policy mix for expansion purposes could be
    a. an increase in taxes with an increase in the money supply.
    b. a decrease in taxes with a decrease in the money supply.
    c. a decrease in taxes with an increase in the money supply.
    d. a decrease in taxes with an increase in government spending.

ANSWERS TO FILL-IN QUESTIONS

1. Fiscal
2. Monetary
3. downward
4. Automatic stabilizers
5. increase
6. reduce
7. expansionary
8. reductions
9. monetary
10. expansionary

ANSWERS TO MULTIPLE-CHOICE QUESTIONS

1. **a.** Government spending increases total expenditures and aggregate demand.
2. **b.** Lowering the reserve requirement frees up some reserves that will come into the system as loans and an increase in the money supply.
3. **c.** Increasing taxes will reduce consumption and aggregate demand.
4. **b.** Aggregate demand will first increase because of the expansionary policy and then shift to the left as increasing interest rates cool consumption and investment.
5. **d.** This is because they work in the direction opposite GDP changes.
6. **b.** Government spending can increase the demand for transactions and bid up the interest rate, reducing private investment.
7. **a.** If the Fed accommodates the anticipated rise in interest rates by increasing the money supply just enough, there will be no increase in the interest rate and no crowding-out.
8. **b.** Firms will use existing capacity and not increase investment immediately.
9. **c.** The decrease in taxes is the fiscal policy, and the increase in the money supply is the monetary policy.

PART SIX
THE GLOBAL ECONOMY

CHAPTER 16

INTERNATIONAL TRADE, COMPARATIVE ADVANTAGE, AND PROTECTIONISM

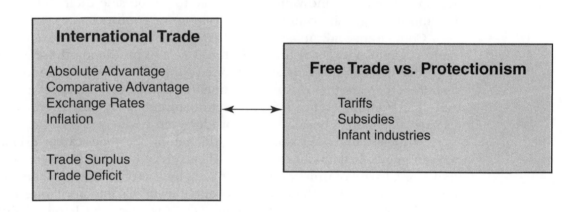

E very country in the world faces increasing globalization and dependence on trade. Because of this growth in global trade, economic factors in other countries have much more of an impact on our economies than in the past. In the case of the United States, exports grew three times faster than the rest of the economy during the 1990s, and imports grew in nominal dollars an average of 41 percent *each year* from 1990 to 2005.

TRADE SURPLUSES AND DEFICITS

One of the measures of trade is whether a country is running a trade surplus or a trade deficit. These are combined in our calculation of the net exports component of GDP. A **trade surplus** occurs when a country exports more than it imports. China in particular has been running a very large trade surplus. Relatively cheap, plentiful labor has fueled the growing export sector in China.

Recently, the United States has been importing more than exporting and is running a large trade deficit. A **trade deficit** occurs when a country imports more than it exports. A large trade deficit means that foreign competition for

U.S. goods and services is very strong. Less expensive foreign goods like steel, textiles, automobiles, and other products have forced American businesses to reduce output, lay off workers, and in some cases go into bankruptcy. Workers in these sectors are often forced to switch to other segments of the economy that are growing more rapidly.

The call from U.S. manufacturers is for protection of U.S. industries and the jobs that they provide. This call for protection comes in the form of lobbying for import taxes and import restrictions or quotas. Both of these would make fewer imports available and make them more expensive.

The major argument against protecting industries is based on the comparative advantage and the gains obtained from free trade.

COMPARATIVE ADVANTAGE

We first looked at comparative advantage in Chapter 2 when we discussed trade between two individuals. Each person was able to consume a combination of goods and services larger than the one they could produce by themselves. Remember that the individuals were able to get outside their PPFs by specializing and trading. It is no different for regions or countries.

Comparative advantage means that one country can produce a good using more cheaply in terms of the opportunity cost of producing those goods.

Absolute advantage means that one country can produce a good using fewer resources than another country. Assume that France can produce more wine per acre than Zambia. France has an absolute advantage in wine production due to its natural resources because it can produce more wine per acre than Zambia.

The **terms of trade** is the ratio at which domestic goods can be exchanged for foreign goods. If Italy can exchange 10 barrels of wine for 5 tables, the terms of trade for a barrel of wine for a table is 2. As long as it costs more than 2 barrels of wine to make a table in Italy, Italy will benefit from making more wine and trading for tables. Review the section on comparative advantage in Chapter 2 if necessary.

For trade to be mutually beneficial, both countries have to have terms of trade that cost them less by exchanging than by producing domestically. In other words, as long as the terms of trade are less than domestic opportunity costs in each country, an incentive for trade exists.

Exchange Rates

Our examples so far have focused on exchanges where the prices of goods and exchange rates were left out of the picture.

If I decide to buy a Volvo, I will probably go to a Volvo dealer, paying in dollars. The Swedish workers who made the Volvo are paid in kronor. In between, a currency exchange must take place where dollars are exchanged for kronor. The **exchange rate** is the ratio at which the two currencies are traded. In this case, dollars and kronor are traded at an exchange rate that is market-determined.

My willingness to buy a Volvo depends on the dollar price I have to pay, which in turn depends on the exchange rate. Suppose the price of a Volvo is currently $40,000, with the exchange rate of dollars for kronor at 1:1. If the exchange rate increases so that I have to pay $1.25 for each krona, the price of the Volvo will increase by 25 percent to $50,000. In this example, the dollar has depreciated or lost value against the Krona because I would have to pay more dollars today to buy a krona than I would have before the depreciation. When the dollar falls in value against other currencies, this raises the price of imports, slowing import growth and stimulating domestic production of goods.

Firms also have to make decisions about whether to buy domestically or from foreign sources. Established purchasing patterns change when the exchange rates make foreign goods more expensive or cheaper.

If the dollar depreciates in terms of the euro, you will need more dollars to make a French purchase today than yesterday. The exchange ratio is higher. The total action of all the households and firms in the economy in response to this increase in the exchange rate for euros is to reduce imports from France. On the other hand, an increase in the purchasing power of the dollar in terms of euros (a decline in the dollars for euros exchange rate) would mean that now French goods and services are cheaper than before and French imports would increase.

If you regularly purchase 10 bottles of French wine a month and the dollar appreciates, you will have money left over after your regular wine purchases. If the dollar depreciates, you will have to increase your budget for French wine in order to pay for the 10 bottles a month.

Because exchange rates determine the terms of trade, a country can import potatoes from a neighbor and export potatoes to that same neighbor the next year just because the exchange rates have changed.

Sources of Comparative Advantage

Trade can benefit both parties, as we have seen. It is comparative advantage that determines what a country specializes in and the direction of trade. But what are the sources of comparative advantage?

Comparative advantage is based on producing a product or service at lower opportunity cost than a trading partner.

Factor endowments are the quality and quantity of labor, land, and natural resources. It is factor endowments that seem to explain world trade patterns. A country is likely to have a comparative advantage in producing a product if it has ample high-quality supplies of the inputs used extensively in producing that product.

Lots of fertile land and a large number of days of sunshine has made Hungary a food exporter, just as natural deposits of oil have made Saudi Arabia an oil exporter. A small amount of arable land has made many island countries food importers. A large pool of mathematics graduates has given India a relative advantage in programming and systems work because knowledge capital is also a source of comparative advantage.

Many countries export and import the same goods. The United States, for example, exports and imports automobiles. This is an example of the wide difference in preferences that consumers have. Some buyers prefer a Volvo because of its reputation for safety; others want more fuel efficiency and prefer a Honda. Some have referred to these characteristics of safety and fuel efficiency as "acquired comparative advantage" to set them apart from natural sources of comparative advantage. Whether the comparative advantage is from natural sources or acquired, it is the basis of trade. There is also nothing inconsistent with comparative advantage in observing a country both exporting and importing the same kinds of items.

TRADE BARRIERS: TARIFFS, EXPORT SUBSIDIES, AND QUOTAS

Obstacles to trade are policies and practices that inhibit free trade and exchange among nations. The most common and pervasive obstacles are tariffs, export subsidies, and quotas. They share a common feature: They shield or protect a particular sector or industry from foreign competition.

A **tariff** is a tax on imports. For the United States as a whole, the average tariff is about 5 percent. Certain products have very high tariffs, up to 48 percent, and others have much lower tariffs. Increasing a tariff raises the price to the purchaser and results in the purchase of fewer imports and an increase in the purchase of domestically produced items.

Export subsidies are government payments to companies or industry sectors to encourage exports. They also act as a barrier to trade. If the government gives a subsidy to an industry so that it can sell its products on the world market for a lower price, it will export more of these subsidized goods.

Some export subsidies come into being only when the world price falls below a certain amount. When this happens, domestic producers receive a subsidy to keep them in business. This keeps domestic prices high but floods the world with relatively inexpensive products such as cheap subsidized grain. Foreign nonsubsidized farmers are driven out of the marketplace.

The EU countries have a tradition of providing large farm subsidies to producers of products like butter, which has to be stored and kept off the market to prop up the price.

A **quota** is a limit on the quantity of imports a country will accept.

THE TREND TOWARD ECONOMIC INTEGRATION

Two or more nations forming a free trade zone result in **economic integration**. The largest and most obvious free trade zone in the world in recent history is the European Union or Common Market.

Other agreements have been the U.S.–Canadian Free-Trade Agreement and the North American Free-Trade Agreement (NAFTA).

FREE TRADE OR PROTECTION?

One of the oldest debates in economics concerns free trade versus protection. The pros and cons in this normative arena debate center on what is best for our country.

Pro Free Trade

The basics of comparative advantage are the main arguments for free trade. Each country is able to consume combinations outside it own production possibilities, representing an increase in the standard of living. In addition, resources are directed to those industries and areas where the country has a comparative advantage. Countries that have a comparative advantage in steel production will move more resources, including labor, into the production of steel and away from other areas.

To sum up, resources in both trading countries will be more efficiently used, and their people will enjoy a higher standard of living.

Tariffs, quotas, and export subsidies interfere with this free flow of trade and reduce the gains from trade.

How does a tariff harm the gains from trade? Start with the domestic economy (on the left in Figure 16.1) in the aluminum market. The equilibrium price of the aluminum in the domestic market is $10. If there is an abundant supply of aluminum in the world marketplace and you can buy as much as you want for $4, then $4 is the world price in the global market. If imports are permitted, no buyer will be willing to pay more than $4. Domestic consumers enjoy the benefits of this low price, and total consumption of aluminum will be 1,000 tons, with 800 tons imported and 200 produced domestically.

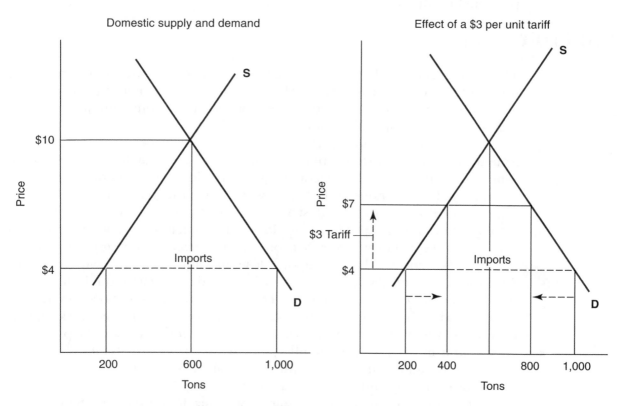

FIGURE 16.1. Effects of a tariff on the domestic aluminum market.

Higher prices and less consumption.

Suppose a tariff of $3 per unit is imposed on aluminum imports. This is illustrated on the right side of Figure 16.1. The domestic price rises by the amount of the tariff—from a free trade price of $4 per unit to a price of $7 per unit. At this price, more domestic output will be produced, doubling output from the free trade level of 200 tons to 400 tons. Some producers will be encouraged to enter the market now that there is a higher price.

Imports are reduced from 800 tons to 400 tons, and in addition, the government now has about a $1,200 revenue from the tariff ($3 × 400 tons imported).

Resources will be allocated toward the aluminum industry, where we do not have a comparative advantage, and away from other industries. Producers who buy aluminum to use as an input will be harmed and will reduce their production and hire less labor. Some buyers will leave the market because of the higher prices, as may some aluminum importers. Prices of aluminum will rise, and overall aluminum consumption will decline from 1,000 tons to 800 tons. The results of the tariff mean there is a loss of efficiency—consumers have to pay a higher price and some producers who could not make a profit at $4 per ton are now drawn into producing aluminum. On a global scale, these newly attracted producers are less efficient than their global counterparts.

Why should the United States use domestic resources to produce aluminum when foreign producers can produce it a much lower cost? Barriers to trade—in our example, a tariff—prevent the full gains from specialization, cause relatively inefficient production to take place, and force consumers to pay more for the protected products.

Pro Protection

The main arguments for trade protection are based on saving jobs, protecting ourselves from other countries' unfair practices, and protecting the national security. Other arguments are that cheap labor makes competition unfair and that we need to protect infant industries.

Protection saves jobs. Advocates say that foreign competition steals American jobs. When we do not "buy American" and buy foreign cars, some American cars go unsold, leading to layoffs in the automobile industry. Unemployed autoworkers and others harmed by an increase in imports face a difficult job prospects in the industry and will have to look in other industries for employment. Industry-specific unemployment, obsolete skills, and in some cases bankruptcy are significant costs that come about because of foreign competition.

One extreme is to ban all imports, lose the gains from trade, and pay more for these goods and services that can be imported, protecting jobs in industries that operate more efficiently abroad. The other extreme is to move toward free trade, knowing that the transition costs are very large for displaced workers, and provide relocation and training programs to minimize adjustment problems. Most countries occupy some middle point between these extremes. There are some controls and restrictions on international trade, and there are some programs for retraining and readjustment to different jobs.

Protection is needed because some countries do not play fair. Some countries engage in **predatory pricing** by setting the price below cost in order to gain market share and monopolize a market. It is illegal to do this if you are an American company, and we should not let others do it here.

Foreign labor is so cheap that it is unfair competition. How can we compete with countries that pay their labor less than one-fifth of what we pay and often do not provide medical insurance or benefits? One answer is that wages reflect productivity, and there is much more capital per worker as well as higher educational and training levels in the United States.

Protection is needed **to protect our national security**. In case of war, our national security will depend on a reliable supply of goods and services. The only way we can guarantee the availability of this supply in wartime is to produce these goods domestically. We have to protect our own resources and manufacturing capabilities in these industries.

Steel, oil, and even scissor and shear manufacturers have made the argument that their output is vital to national defense. Every industry that asks for protection makes some kind of argument that it is in the nation's interest to protect it.

Protection helps **infant industries**. A young industry needs protection to grow up in a harsh world. Global competitors make it very hard to start an industry, and a new one might develop into an industry with a comparative advantage after it grows up.

Protection has two main problems. Once an industry is protected, it is very hard to remove this protection. For years, the New England shoe industry enjoyed protection against imported shoes. Some economists argue that removing protection for the New England shoe industry took too long. It was clear that the EU, especially Italy, had significant comparative advantages in shoe manufacturing. The cost of not removing protection for the New England industry sooner was that it postponed the growth and transformation of the region, which now enjoys a vibrant economy based on high-tech and financial services.

The second problem with protection is that it may backfire. A tariff-protected industry may find it to its advantage to relocate its facilities overseas. Because of a high tariff on laptop screens, IBM and Apple eventually relocated their production overseas as the best option for them. By relocating, they chose to have a very high-quality, low-cost screen rather that pay a tariff to end up with a very high-quality high-cost screen.

GLOBALIZATION

Part of the increasing globalization is that it is now easier to relocate overseas and to form multinational corporations. More and more companies are moving some of their manufacturing facilities overseas to take advantage of much lower production costs. As it becomes easier to relocate operations overseas, tariffs and quotas will be less able to restrict the gains from trade. In other words, a decline in the cost of locating facilities in other countries will make it more profitable for companies to do so.

Global outsourcing to find the cheapest prices has also been a growing trend. Dell outsources much of its production to overseas firms in many different countries.

Globalization has not changed the fundamental arguments for free trade based on comparative advantage. They are an increased standard of living, higher employment, and a more efficient allocation of resources. However, globalization has forced us to incorporate multinational ownership and location of production—an acquired comparative advantage not based on natural resource endowments.

The Importance of Exchange Rates

Increasing globalization has been one of the most important changes in the last 100 years. We turn our attention to the nature of equilibrium in an open economy and how exchange rates are determined.

The increase in international trade has made currency exchange and exchange rates more important. Even though you pay dollars for your new Mercedes, its German producers eventually receive euros for the transaction.

The direction of trade depends in part on the **exchange rate**, which is the price of one currency in terms of another. An exchange rate of \$1.32/euro is an example. A book, priced at 10 euros, costs \$13.20. This is the **nominal exchange rate**, the rate at which one currency trades for another.

The **real exchange rate** is the rate of exchange of one country's goods for another country's goods. This is expressed in the units of the goods being traded, for example, 1 ton of steel for 5 tons of aluminum. The real exchange rate is a key determinant of net exports. An increase in the real exchange rate means that U.S. goods have become more expensive relative to goods from other countries. This change encourages global consumers to buy fewer U.S. goods and more goods from other countries. Because of the increase in the real exchange rate, U.S. exports will fall and imports will rise, lowering net exports and GDP.

The opposite effect occurs when the real exchange rate falls. The United States will export more because US goods have become cheaper and import less so that net exports will increase and GDP along with it.

Changes in exchange rates are determined by demand and supply, by the interaction of buyers and sellers. If there is an excess demand for dollars, the price of dollars will increase. For example, suppose that the current exchange rate is \$2/yen, or \$1 = 0.5 yen. If there is an excess demand for dollars relative to yen, what will happen? The price of dollars will increase, and the exchange rate will fall, for example, to \$1/yen. At \$2/yen, each dollar was worth 0.5 yen and now is worth 1 yen. It costs more yen to buy a dollar because the dollar has risen in value.

Chile and Argentina share a long border and a good climate for growing potatoes. The direction of potato importation between the two neighboring countries depends on the exchange rate. If the exchange rate is favorable to Chile, they will import Argentine potatoes. If the exchange rate is favorable to Argentina the next year, they will import Chilean potatoes.

Foreign exchange refers to all currencies other than the domestic one. In the case of the United States, foreign exchange refers to all non-U.S. currencies. The demand for foreign exchange comes from anyone who wants to purchase an item made in a foreign country. The supply of foreign currency comes from the sale of goods and services to foreign countries.

Floating or flexible exchange rates are those that are determined by market supply and demand. In this kind of environment, which has existed in the exchange rate markets for the last 30 years, exchange rates fluctuate freely. We will look at an illustration of the foreign exchange market using euros and dollars.

The Foreign Exchange Market for Dollars and Euros

Euros and dollars are exchanged every day by governments, travelers, exporters, importers, financial institutions, currency speculators, and anyone who wants to buy or sell something abroad or buy something in the United States.

THE DEMAND FOR EUROS

The demand for euros comes from holders of dollars who want to purchase euros. On the other side of the market, the suppliers of euros are holders of euros who want to sell them for dollars. The goods and services that people want to purchase include financial assets such as stocks, bonds, and mutual funds.

Figure 16.2 shows the demand for euros. The price axis is the number of dollars per euro. As the price of a euro falls, more euros are demanded.

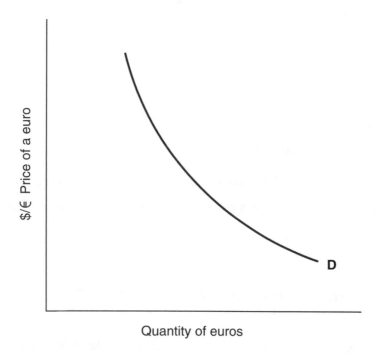

FIGURE 16.2. The demand for euros in the U.S. foreign exchange market.

As the price of euros falls, buyers purchase more European goods and demand more euros.

SUPPLY OF EUROS

In Figure 16.3 the supply of euros operates like any supply curve in a particular marketplace. The higher the price of a euro, the more euros will be offered for sale. What is going on in the background is this. The higher the price of a euro in dollars, the more dollars can be bought with a euro. Because the euro becomes stronger relative to the dollar as the price of euros goes up, there will be a stronger demand to purchase U.S. exports. More euros will be available on the market.

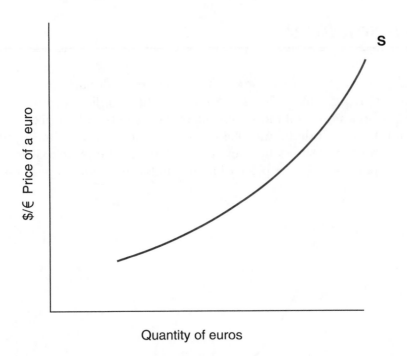

FIGURE 16.3. The supply for euros in the U.S. foreign exchange market.

As the price of euros rises, sellers can get more dollars for their euros and will supply more.

EQUILIBRIUM IN THE EURO/DOLLAR MARKET

Because the euro/dollar exchange rate is a flexible, market-determined exchange rate, it works like any other market-determined price (the price of one currency in terms of the other, or the exchange rate). An excess demand for euros works its way to a new equilibrium exchange rate by bidding up the price of a euro until a new equilibrium is reached at a higher exchange rate with more euros sold. Because the exchange rate is dollar/euro, this means that the euro has appreciated in value because of the excess demand. More dollars are offered per euro. The dollar has depreciated against the euro.

Appreciation of the dollar occurs when the dollar can buy more of another country's currency. When the dollar appreciates, it is strengthening against the other currency. Appreciation depends on a particular exchange rate, and there are as many dollar exchange rates as there are currencies. **Depreciation** of the dollar means the dollar can buy less of another country's currency. Of course, if the dollar appreciates against the yen, the yen depreciates against the dollar, and vice versa.

What are the determinants of exchange rates? That is, what can shift the demand and supply of euros in our example? The two most prominent determinants are the inflation level and the interest rate.

INFLATION

The price level is an important determinant of the real exchange rate. What happens if the US price level increases relative to the EU price level? Higher inflation in the United States make imports relatively less expensive, and U.S. consumers will increase their purchases of European imports. In Figure 16.4, this will increase the demand for euros from U.S. purchasers from D_1 to D_2, and the market will be at 2. Europeans will find U.S. goods getting more expensive because of inflation, and they will reduce their demand for U.S. exports. The supply of euros will shift to the left, from S_1, eventually ending up at 3 on S_2. The result is an increase in the price of euros from $1.00 to $1.81. The dollar has depreciated relative to the euro, and the euro has appreciated.

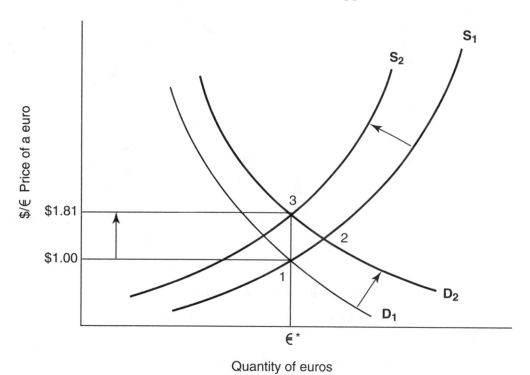

FIGURE 16.4. Equilibrium in the euro market changes in response to an increase in U.S. inflation.

U.S. inflation depreciates the dollar.

An increase in inflation in the United States will depreciate the dollar relative to the euro, and the nominal exchange rate will rise.

THE INTEREST RATE AND THE EXCHANGE RATE

An increase in the U.S. interest rate will stimulate other countries to invest in U.S. stocks, bonds, and other financial instruments. To purchase these goods, Europeans will need dollars and will have to exchange euros for them. This will increase the supply of euros outward from S_1 to S_2, which we show in Figure 16.5.

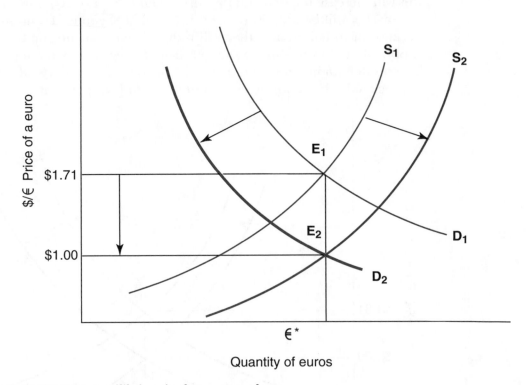

FIGURE 16.5. Equilibrium in the euro market.

Changes in response to a rise in the U.S. interest rate.

U.S. consumers will be less interested in purchasing European financial instruments now that the interest rate has risen in the United States. They will decrease their demand for euros, shifting the demand downward from D_1 to D_2. The result will be a stronger dollar exchanging at $1 per euro and a weaker euro.

THE GLOBAL ECONOMY

In the last 35 years, the U.S. economy has become more global, as have most economies. This has made fiscal and monetary policies more difficult and less predictable because each economy is much more dependent on what happens in other countries than before.

All countries are concerned with economic growth, the subject of the next chapter. We will see that international trade is a vital part of the growth plans for many developing countries.

REVIEW QUESTIONS

Add the word or words that correctly complete each of the following statements.

1. When a country exports more than it imports, there is a trade _____.

2. A large trade _____ means that foreign competition for U.S. goods and services is very strong.

3. The _____ is the ratio at which domestic goods can be exchanged for foreign goods.

4. The _____ rate is the ratio at which two currencies are traded. In this case, dollars and kronor are traded at an exchange rate that is market-determined.

5. If the dollar _____ in terms of the euro, you will need more dollars to make a French purchase today than yesterday.

6. A _____ is a limit on the quantity of imports a country will accept.

7. The EU is one of the biggest and most obvious _____ zones.

8. A _____ forces consumers to pay more for protected products.

9. The direction of trade depends in part on the _____ rate, which is the price of one currency in terms of another.

10. An _____ in the real exchange rate means that U.S. goods have become more expensive relative to goods from other countries.

Circle the letter of the item that correctly completes each of the following statements.

1. Higher inflation in the United States will make
   a. our exports cheaper.
   b. the dollar lose value.
   c. the dollar gain in value.
   d. increase our exports.

2. A trade deficit occurs
   a. whenever a tariff is imposed on an import.
   b. when a government subsidizes exports.
   c. when a country exports more than it imports.
   d. when a country imports more than it exports.

3. What seems to explain the world trade patterns is the
   a. foreign exchange markets.
   b. quality and quantity of labor, land, and natural resources.
   c. terms of trade.
   d. relative rates of inflation.

4. Who is harmed by an import tariff?
   a. Consumers of the good
   b. No one
   c. Local producers of the good
   d. The government

5. An increase in the U.S. real exchange rate
   a. encourages global consumers to buy more U.S. goods.
   b. encourages U.S. consumers to buy fewer imports.
   c. encourages global consumers to buy less from other countries.
   d. encourages global consumers to buy fewer U.S. goods.

6. U.S. exports will be relatively less expensive with
   a. a stronger dollar.
   b. a decrease in inflation.
   c. a weaker dollar.
   d. an increase in the long-run supply.

7. The terms of trade is
   a. the same as net exports.
   b. the ratio at which domestic goods can be exchanged for foreign goods.
   c. the ratio of the two currencies involved.
   d. the currency exchange rate.

8. Which of the following is an example of a quota?
   a. A maximum of 1 million tons of German steel can be imported each year.
   b. A $100 tax must be paid on each ton of imported German steel.
   c. A minimum of 1 million tons of German steel is permitted to be imported each year.
   d. For each ton of steel exported, the producer will receive $100.

ANSWERS TO FILL-IN QUESTIONS

1. surplus
2. deficit
3. terms of trade
4. exchange
5. depreciates
6. quota
7. free trade
8. tariff
9. exchange
10. increase

ANSWERS TO MULTIPLE-CHOICE QUESTIONS

1. **b.** Higher inflation lowers the real purchasing power of the dollar, so a nominal dollar will be worth less in exchange.

2. **d.** This is the definition

3. **b.** These factor endowments tend to dominate trade patterns; Saudi Arabia won't import oil.

4. **a.** Consumers will pay higher prices for these goods and services.

5. **d.** Global consumers will be encouraged to buy imports from other countries because the cost of U.S. imports has risen.

6. **c.** A weaker dollar means other currencies are stronger and will buy more exports.

7. **b.** Trade depends on the real exchange ratios.

8. **a.** A quota is a limit on the amount of imports.

CHAPTER 17

ECONOMIC GROWTH

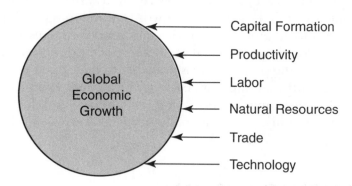

A All economies face the basic resource allocation choices and trade-offs for scarce resources, regardless of the amount or quality of these resources. This was one of the basic economic principles we discussed in the first chapter.

All the issues and tools we use apply to every country in the world. The goals of macroecomics are still to explain how inflation, unemployment, and growth occur. Modern industrialized economies have well-developed financial markets and central banking systems, established legal structures, and experience in policy management and rely heavily on market economics to allocate resources. They have well-established infrastructures and a skilled workforce and are no longer agriculture-based economies.

The U.S. economy has gone through several phases to reach what some have characterized as a knowledge or information society. Many developing nations are on the left-hand side of this continuum, which is named for the economic sector where most people work:

Agriculture → manufacturing → services → knowledge

As an illustration, compare the U.S. and Brazilian labor force percentages in each of the sectors shown in Table 17.1. The U.S. figures are for 2005, and the Brazilian percentages for 2003. Knowledge workers are included in services.

TABLE 7.1 SHARES OF THE LABOR FORCE EMPLOYMENT

Country	Agriculture and Forestry (%)	Manufacturing (%)	Services (%)
United States	1	29	79
Brazil	49	22	29

Brazil is certainly more developed than many countries yet has almost half of its population working in agriculture and forestry, whereas in the United States this number is about 1 percent.

Many developing nations struggle to become modern. Some have very high infant mortality rates, some are subject to devastating famines, and some are caught in the vicious cycle of poverty. Many are still economies where most of the people work in agriculture. Growth in developing nations is clearly more complex. Some developing countries face food shortages and very rapid population growth. Some face hyperinflation and poorly developed judicial systems.

Often the policy choices available to developed economies will not work in many countries. Lowering taxes may be a good policy to stimulate the U.S. economy, but developing nations that do not have an effective tax collection system and a smoothly functioning financial market will find tax reductions of little help.

THE DEVELOPING NATIONS: POPULATION AND POVERTY

About three-fourths of the world's population lives in the developing countries. **GDP/capita** gives us some idea of the standard of living or well-being of countries. The range is from about $70,000 per year to $600 per year.

The developed nations consume about 75 percent of the world's output, yet comprise only about 25 percent of its population. About 50 percent of the world's population lives in five countries (China, India, Russia, Indonesia, and Brazil). These five countries represent only 8 percent of the world's GDP. Global political instability will increase if these inequities increase, and many look to economic growth for the solution. Many international organizations share this hope, and there are some bright spots.

Many East Asian countries have invested heavily in their people, have put policy fundamentals in place, and have not discriminated against their rural sectors. According to the World Bank, the results have been dramatic: large private capital inflows, rapid growth, and substantial poverty reduction.

Population Growth

Rapid population growth is an important issue for the developing countries, where populations are growing at three times the rate of industrialized countries. Some of the countries are growing at rates of 4 percent per year compared to the industrialized country growth rate of 0.5 percent. These are historically high rates of population growth.

High population growth means that there are large numbers of dependent children per adult, and this makes it very difficult to generate savings. Efforts at improving human capital may be limited by the sheer numbers of additional people requiring training, education, or adequate nutrition.

Some programs aim at providing women of childbearing age with better job prospects in an effort to lower birth rates. Many other countries have put into effect economic incentives to have fewer children, in addition to family planning education and clinics.

The extreme case of population control is found in China, which has had a mandatory one child per family rule since 1979. The policy is complete with fines, pressures to abort pregnancies, and even forced sterilization measures. There are some exceptions, notably in rural areas, but the policy reduced population growth by about 300 million people from 1979 to 1999.

However, what sound policy fundamentals are there for dealing with these immense problems?

The developing countries have high illiteracy and high infant mortality rates (up to 10 times that of the United States). Some studies find that 40 percent of the populations in developing countries do not earn enough to obtain adequate nutrition. Many rely on the region's food staple—rice, wheat, or corn. The United Nations (UN) development goals for the millennium give a broad view of the major issues:

- Eradicate extreme poverty and hunger.
- Achieve universal primary education.
- Promote gender equality and empower women.
- Reduce child mortality.
- Improve maternal health.
- Combat HIV/AIDS and malaria.
- Ensure environmental sustainability.
- Develop a global partnership for development.

The major characteristic of the developing nations is poverty. Many farmers earn barely enough to keep their families alive and cannot exchange their products for other goods. In many cases, even the flight to urban areas has not allowed them to avoid poverty.

ECONOMIC DEVELOPMENT: SOURCES AND STRATEGIES

Development economics as a special area of study grew up in the aftermath of World War II. Increased attention to and concern for the developing nations sought answers to questions such as "What makes some countries rich and others poor?" became the basic question in development economics. Other questions raised were What are the barriers to growth? and What needs to be in place before an economy can grow and advance?

Often cited limits to growth are too little capital formation, a shortage of human capital and entrepreneurial skills, and a lack of social overhead capital. We will examine each of these in turn.

Sources of Economic Development and Growth

What factors increase the capacity to grow? Review Chapter 9 on long-run growth. The key ingredients are capital formation, human capital—in quantity, and quality—natural resources, and technology.

CAPITAL FORMATION

Almost all of the developing nations have very low capital-to-labor ratios. They have abundant labor but not much capital. This small stock of capital in the form of factories, machinery for manufacture, and farming equipment keeps labor productivity at very low levels. This also means that increases in the capital/labor ratio may have dramatic effects in increasing output, the "catch-up" effect as some have called it.

Why is capital in such short supply? Why is there a capital shortage? Some suggest that there is no way out. The **vicious circle of poverty** argument suggests that poverty is self-perpetuating because not enough income is earned to save and invest enough to accumulate capital. When investment levels are very low, the economy does not grow, and incomes are kept low. However, many nations have started out in poverty and grown out of it.

The vicious circle argument is incomplete because there is always a surplus above consumption and it is what happens to this surplus that is important. The surplus may be used for conspicuous consumption by the rich or siphoned off by corrupt officials or drained off to other countries.

In addition, low investment may have more to do with the high risk of saving and investing in developing countries. This may be more important than the level of savings. Many of the rich invest their savings in the United States or Europe rather than hold them in what is often perceived as a risky environment. **Capital flight** takes place when human capital and savings leave the developing countries in search of a higher, more stable return. Some local government policies, including price controls, import restrictions, and the possible expropriation, can reduce local investment.

At one time, Colombia wanted to encourage investment in its steel mill and tried to persuade Colombians to invest in it. It did not work because Japanese steel was of higher quality than the steel from the government-owned steel mill. The government then required citizens who paid taxes to buy shares of the steel company at a fixed price with their tax refunds. The price per share was much higher than what the shares sold for on the free market, so Colombians taxpayers were forced to subsidize the Colombian steel mill.

A second reason that the vicious circle argument is incomplete is the possibility of foreign investment. Investment need not be internal. It may take the form of private or international investment in the developing countries. Many countries are actively pursuing these external sources of investment.

For whatever reason, less capital formation means slower growth. However, this is not the only way to grow an economy.

HUMAN CAPITAL

The supply of labor is usually not a constraint to growth; it is usually the quality and productivity of this labor that slows growth. It is the health, knowledge, and skill of the labor force. Notice how many of the UN Millennium goals above refer to health and education.

Human capital can be developed in many ways. At a very basic level, programs designed to improve nutrition and health can improve human capital. Basic literacy training can produce high returns. Improvements that are more familiar are formal education and on-the-job training. Educational expenditure has become a large component of government spending in the developing countries.

Many students from developing countries travel abroad to complete their education. If they remain in the developed countries, they represent a **brain drain** for the developing countries. If they return, they face much lower salaries. Entrepreneurs, as well as skilled professionals, are also in short supply in the developing countries. The ability to manage and initiate economic activity is a key ingredient for economic growth.

SOCIAL OVERHEAD CAPITAL

Social overhead capital refers to the basic infrastructure such as roads, bridges, power generation, dams, and irrigation systems among the largest.

Government provision of social overhead capital is an important feature of most developing country budgets. In the case of major projects, the funding and technology may come from international organizations that provide the loans and technological expertise to build a major dam or irrigation system.

Many argue that there is also a political role that developing country governments need to play to ensure the political foundations necessary for development. On the list are efforts to ensure political stability, the ability to protect against seizure of assets, and a legal system that guarantees basic property rights and contracts.

Strategies for Economic Development

Developing countries have many strategy options. They are not either/or choices but have to be decided within the framework of trade-offs. Countries cannot escape these choices because there is a scarcity of resources to devote to the problem. These choices involve the best mix of agriculture and industry development policies, export and import substitution strategies, and how the whole effort is managed, whether by central planning or by the free market.

AGRICULTURE OR INDUSTRY?

Many of the developing countries have agricultural economies. Most of the labor is farm labor and most of the output is agricultural or mineral. Many countries have tried to imitate the history of Western economic development by engaging in a strong industrialization push.

This approach has several advantages. Factories and plants contribute to the growth of an economy by adding to the capital stock. Second, this is the second step in the process of transformation to a modern economy. Greater output from the manufacturing sector is sign of becoming a modern economy. Historically, as per-capita income increases, the share of agriculture in GDP declines and the share of output from the manufacturing and services sectors increases.

Some of the major tools used to develop the manufacturing sector are encouraging foreign and domestic firms to build plants and train workers, providing tax relief and subsidized land purchase, outright grants for manufacturing companies to lower their start-up costs, and guarantees of nonexpropriation, to reduce the investment risk.

Where industrialization has been the major policy at the expense of agriculture, the results have proved disappointing. Most governments now have mixed policies, some for industrialization and some for agricultural development.

One advantage of agricultural development is that most of the population is already in agriculture. Developing this sector should yield benefits to a large, usually the poorest, part of the population. There are educational, management, and small-scale efforts that do not need the massive mechanization of agriculture apparent in the developed economies.

Some of the major tools are improving local fertilizer and seeds, teaching basic agricultural management, and agricultural extension services that offer field support and advice directly to farmers. Many state colleges and universities in the United States had large, significant university-sponsored agricultural extension services. To this day, the University of California provides extension services to wine, almond, and other growers to help them improve the yield and quality of their outputs. The advisory service includes management assistance and specialized research that has helped California become the nation's leader in agricultural exports.

In the developing countries, these extension services are often combined with major infrastructure investments such as irrigation systems and flood control projects.

Fixed Prices for Agricultural Output

Many countries refuse to let the market determine agricultural prices. Farm subsidies in the United States and in Europe have encouraged such high levels of food production that the result is a surplus, which often has to be stored to keep up the market price.

Some developing countries have established government **produce marketing boards**, which buy directly from farmers at relatively low prices and resell to wealthier urban dwellers at government-controlled prices. The trouble with these policies is that they give farmers the wrong signal. If they can get only a very low price for their produce, they may discontinue producing that crop and switch to another one or they may sell their produce on the black market in the cities.

Other countries have established marketing boards and other associations directed toward getting the highest price for their producers who often also receive subsidies from the government.

Increasing Agricultural Output

Many developing countries use a variety of programs and sources to increase the yield per acre. The basic programs improve inputs, human capital, and technology, as we discussed earlier. These agricultural programs improve seed stock, fertilizers, farm machinery, irrigation systems, and farmer knowledge. Other programs focus on getting better land for farmers as a way to increase output.

EXPORT PROMOTION

Trade policy is part of a growth strategy, and governments in developing countries have to make some fundamental decisions. The two main vehicles for promoting trade to enhance local growth are export promotion and import substitution.

Export promotion is a policy that actively encourages exports. Remember our earlier example of Japan, which relied heavily on promoting automobile and machinery exports as a central part of its modernization strategy. The Japanese strategy focused on industrial exports.

Many have followed Japan's example, especially Hong Kong, Singapore, Taiwan, and Korea. They are now growing faster than Japan and are among the fastest-growing economies in the world.

A significant part of some export promotion strategies is to keep the local currency cheap relative to others. This places exported goods at an attractive and very competitive price in global markets. Many believe that Japan kept the yen low in the 1970s and benefited from being able to export relatively inexpensive automobiles to the United States. Many have accused China of keeping the value of its currency low to fuel its export sector growth by keeping the yuan fixed in terms of the dollar.

Another device is to subsidize export industries via favorable tax treatment or some other method. Tax-free zones, less stringent regulations, and other methods have been used to encourage development of the export sector. These same tools have been used in the United States by many states to attract clean industries such as financial services.

IMPORT SUBSTITUTION

To reduce their reliance on imports, many developing countries and some developed countries as well have adopted a policy of import substitution. **Import substitution** is a policy that encourages local industries to manufacture goods to replace imports. In the past this policy was called an "infant industries" policy. New industries that are just forming are weak and need special care and treatment to survive. For example, if radios were an important import, then import substitution policies would favor the development of a local radio manufacturing industry.

Some of the policy tools used are tariffs and quotas to block imports, subsidizing imports of needed machinery and equipment, and giving special treatment to foreign manufacturers who want to set up local plants.

One of the major problems with protecting growing industries by providing special treatment is that they will be shielded from the international marketplace. Suppose you want to grow the capacity to produce automobiles domestically. You could put a 200 percent tariff on automobile imports and invite an automobile manufacturer to set up plants inside the country. If the protected industry is very capital-intensive, as the automobile industry is, then relatively few new employment opportunities will result from this strategy. If other sectors are taxed to pay for this import substitution plan, they will be at more of a disadvantage than before. Even if the strategy works in the short term, the main problem is how to remove the protection so that the infant industry can survive on its own without continual subsidy.

CONTROLLING GROWTH: CENTRAL PLANNING VERSUS THE MARKET

A major choice that developing countries face concerns the right mix of central control and market control. At one extreme central control an include deciding what is produced, where, how, and at what price. Because of the magnitude of the effort needed to modernize, the former Soviet Union relied on a very strong centrally planned economy to become an industrialized nation. Today the Chinese government still exerts a very strong influence on the economy, although there are some signs that it is slowly allowing market forces to operatein certain areas.

The costs of rapid industrial growth in the former Soviet Union and recently in China have included violation of human rights and environmental damage. In China, the latter is seen in contaminated water and increased health problems. Estimates are that 70 percent of China's lakes and rivers are polluted.

The right mix of central planning and market control in determining growth priorities and the fastest growing sectors is part of a contining debate. It also brings us back to where we started. Every person and every country faces trade-offs between outcomes. Because there is scarcity, hard decisions have to be made to allocate the available resources.

REVIEW QUESTIONS

Add the word or words that correctly complete each of the following statements.

1. The _____ argument suggests that poverty is self-perpetuating because not enough income is earned to accumulate capital.

2. Many growth policies appropriate for developed countries like the United States will not work in other areas because of a lack of legal or financial _____.

3. _____ occurs when capital and savings leave developing countries in search of a higher and more stable return.

4. Basic literacy training is an example of an effort to improve _____ capital.

5. _____ capital is basic infrastructure such as roads, bridges, power generation, dams, and irrigation systems.

6. Some developing countries have established government _____, which buy directly from the farmers at relatively low prices and resell to wealthier urban dwellers at government-controlled prices.

7. Many developing countries focus on the _____ sector because most of the people work there.

8. Encouraging foreign and domestic firms to build plants is often part of an _____ program.

9. A government guarantee of nonexpropriation is meant to _____ the risk of investment.

10. _____ substitution is a policy to encourage local industries to manufacture their own products.

Circle the letter of the item that correctly completes each of the following statements.

1. Which of the following does *not* encourage capital flight?
   a. A weak financial system
   b. A stable government
   c. The possibility of expropriation
   d. A corrupt police force

2. Which of the following would *not* be part of a direct program designed to improve human capital?

    a. Subsidies to establish local health clinics

    b. Mandatory literacy training

    c. A tariff on automobile imports

    d. Formal education and on-the-job training.

3. Japan used an export promotion program that

    a. relied heavily on promoting automobile and machinery exports.

    b. imposed heavy tariffs to protect infant industries.

    c. was based on improving the agricultural sector.

    d. used the market system to determine priorities.

4. Which of the following is a difference between the growth policies for a developed country and for a less developed country?

    a. The key ingredients are capital formation, human capital (in quantity and quality), natural resources, and technology.

    b. There are trade-offs between current and future consumption.

    c. Resources are scarce.

    d. Poverty and dependence on agriculture are common.

ANSWERS TO FILL-IN QUESTIONS

1. vicious circle of poverty

2. infrastructure

3. Capital flight

4. human

5. Social overhead

6. produce marketing boards

7. agricultural

8. industrialization

9. reduce

10. Import

ANSWERS TO MULTIPLE-CHOICE QUESTIONS

1. b. A stable government is more predictable.

2. c. A tariff would be used to protect an infant industry.

3. a. This Japanese model has been widely used to promote growth in Asia.

4. d. Poverty and agricultural dependence are not common in well-developed economies.

Index

MOVE TO THE HEAD OF YOUR CLASS
THE EASY WAY!

Barron's presents THE EASY WAY SERIES—specially prepared by top educators, it maximizes effective learning while minimizing the time and effort it takes to raise your grades, brush up on the basics, and build your confidence. Comprehensive and full of clear review examples, **THE EASY WAY SERIES** is your best bet for better grades, quickly!

0-7641-1976-1	**Accounting the Easy Way, 4th Ed.**—$16.99, Can. $24.50
0-7641-1972-9	**Algebra the Easy Way, 4th Ed.**—$14.95, Can. $21.95
0-7641-1973-7	**American History the Easy Way, 3rd Ed.**—$16.95, Can. $24.50
0-7641-3428-0	**American Sign Language the Easy Way, 2nd Ed.**—$16.99, Can. $21.50
0-7641-1979-6	**Anatomy and Physiology the Easy Way**—$16.99, Can. $24.50
0-7641-2913-9	**Arithmetic the Easy Way, 4th Ed.**—$14.99, Can. $21.99
0-7641-1358-5	**Biology the Easy Way, 3rd Ed.**—$14.95, Can. $21.95
0-7641-1079-9	**Bookkeeping the Easy Way, 3rd Ed.**—$14.95, Can. $21.00
0-7641-0314-8	**Business Letters the Easy Way, 3rd Ed.**—$14.99, Can. $21.00
0-7641-1359-3	**Business Math the Easy Way, 3rd Ed.**—$16.99, Can. $24.50
0-7641-2920-1	**Calculus the Easy Way, 4th Ed.**—$14.99, Can. $21.99
0-7641-1978-8	**Chemistry the Easy Way, 4th Ed.**—$16.99, Can. $24.50
0-7641-0659-7	**Chinese the Easy Way**—$16.99, Can. $24.50
0-7641-2579-6	**Creative Writing the Easy Way**—$12.95, Can. $18.95
0-7641-2146-4	**Earth Science The Easy Way**—$16.99, Can. $23.99
0-7641-1981-8	**Electronics the Easy Way, 4th Ed.**—$16.99, Can. $24.50
0-7641-1975-3	**English the Easy Way, 4th Ed.**—$14.99, Can. $21.99
0-7641-3050-1	**Forensics the Wasy way**—$14.99. Can. $21.99
0-7641-3411-6	**French the Easy Way, 4th Ed.**—$14.99, Can. $18.75
0-7641-2435-8	**French Grammar the Easy Way**—$16.99, Can. $24.50
0-7641-0110-2	**Geometry the Easy Way, 3rd Ed.**—$14.95, Can. $21.00
0-8120-9145-0	**German the Easy Way, 2nd Ed.**—$14.95, Can. $21.00
0-7641-1989-3	**Grammar the Easy Way**—$14.95, Can. $21.00
0-7641-3413-2	**Italian the Easy Way, 3rd Ed.**—$14.99, Can. $21.99
0-8120-9627-4	**Japanese the Easy Way**—$18.99, Can. $24.50
0-7641-3237-7	**Macroeconomics the Easy Way**—$14.99, Can. $21.00
0-7641-2011-5	**Math the Easy Way, 4th Ed.**—$13.99, Can. $19.50
0-7641-1871-4	**Math Word Problems the Easy Way**—$16.99, Can. $21.00
0-7641-2845-0	**Microbiology the Easy Way**—$16.99, Can. $21.99
0-8120-9601-0	**Microeconomics the Easy Way**—$16.99, Can. $24.50
0-7641-2794-2	**Organic Chemistry the Easy Way**—$14.99, Can. $21.99
0-7641-0236-2	**Physics the Easy Way, 3rd Ed.**—$16.99, Can. $24.50
0-7641-2892-2	**Precalculus the Easy Way**—$14.95, Can. $21.95
0-7641-2393-9	**Psychology the Easy Way**—$14.95, Can. $21.95
0-7641-2263-0	**Spanish Grammar the Easy Way**—$14.99, Can. $21.99
0-7641-1974-5	**Spanish the Easy Way, 4th Ed.**—$14.95, Can. $21.95
0-8120-9852-8	**Speed Reading the Easy Way**—$16.99, Can. $21.95
0-7641-3410-8	**Spelling the Easy Way, 4th Ed.**—$14.99, Can. $21.99
0-8120-9392-5	**Statistics the Easy Way, 3rd Ed.**—$14.99, Can. $21.00
0-7641-1360-7	**Trigonometry the Easy Way, 3rd Ed.**—$14.95, Can. $21.00
0-8120-9765-3	**World History the Easy Way, Vol. One**—$16.99, Can. $24.50
0-8120-9766-1	**World History the Easy Way, Vol. Two**—$16.99, Can. $24.50
0-7641-1206-6	**Writing the Easy Way, 3rd Ed.**—$14.95, Can. $21.00

Barron's Educational Series, Inc.
250 Wireless Boulevard • Hauppauge, New York 11788
In Canada: Georgetown Book Warehouse • 34 Armstrong Avenue, Georgetown, Ontario L7G 4R9
www.barronseduc.com $ = U.S. Dollars   Can. $ = Canadian Dollars